Ipswich in the 18th century: a section from the prospect of the town by Samuel and Nathaniel Buck, 1741.

A History of
IPSWICH

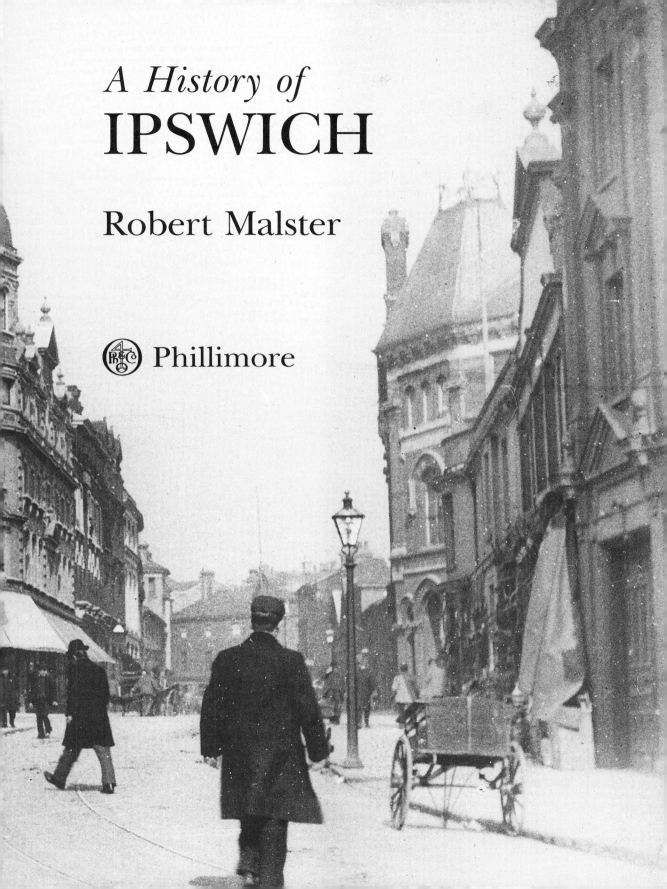

A *History of*
IPSWICH

Robert Malster

Phillimore

2000

Published by
PHILLIMORE & CO. LTD.
Shopwyke Manor Barn, Chichester, West Sussex

ISBN 1 86077 148 3

Printed and bound in Great Britain by
BOOKCRAFT LTD.
Midsomer Norton, Bath

Contents

List of Illustrations

Acknowledgements

Writing a history of this kind is a matter of teamwork. No one person can do it alone, for an author has to make use of the researches of many experts who have delved deeply into their own periods and their own subjects.

I am, for instance, grateful for permission to make use of Professor Geoffrey Martin's work on the town's wealth of early records, and it would have been impossible to tell the story of Ipswich without referring to John Webb's work on the records of Tudor Ipswich and its merchants.

Much more than that, I have been generously backed by a group of friends who have provided me with the loan of books and documents and with the results of their own research to use as I would. John Fairclough has shared with me in the basic research, has guided me past many a pitfall, and deserves to be known as the co-author of large sections of the text; his participation has been crucial in bringing the project to a conclusion.

Dr. Pat Murrell has generously made available to me the results of her researches into Stuart and Georgian Ipswich, thereby avoiding my having to repeat the work she has already done. Mrs. Jill Freestone, of the Over Stoke History Group, and Richard Smith of the Society for Sailing Barge Research have given me invaluable assistance, and so has Hugh Moffat, whose own work on Ipswich shipping will, one hopes, be published before long. Dr. John Blatchly gave me the freedom of his library and the benefit of his own deep researches, and as ever I am grateful to John Wilton for his help with the loan of illustrations. Bernard Barrell provided me with some of the raw materials of my research when he most generously gave me his copy of Pennington's map and books such as Glyde's *Illustrations of Old Ipswich*, which has provided illustrations for this new history.

Without the help and advice of David Cleveland, David Dymond, Frank Grace, Peter Northeast, Tom Plunkett, Bill and Ruth Serjeant and others too numerous to name my work would never have been completed.

I am grateful, too, for the very considerable help I have received from the staff of the Suffolk Record Office at Ipswich, who have gone to considerable trouble time and time again to provide me with the raw material of such a study as this. Sometimes they must have wondered at my presumption in attempting this task when I was so ignorant of the sources available, but they have been unfailingly kind in helping me find my way among the archives.

Members of Suffolk County Council Archaeological Service, including Keith Wade, Edward Martin, Judith Plouviez, Tom Loader and John Newman, have given time, information and valuable advice while this book has been in preparation. Without the excavations carried out by Keith Wade and his team, and earlier by Stanley West, we would know very little about the Saxon origins of the town, barely suspected by some earlier historians.

To all these I offer my sincere thanks.

Finally, to quote John Kirby's preface to *The Suffolk Traveller* of 1735, 'I know of no Mistakes … but as nothing of this nature was ever yet performed with that Accuracy, but that some small Slips might be observed by the Curious, this perhaps may be my Case.' For errors great and small the author must accept full responsibility.

The seal of Ipswich, showing a cog with a stern rudder, a reflection of the town's significance as a port and one of the earliest depictions of a vessel with a rudder rather than the steering oar on the quarter.

1   *The Ancient House in the Buttermarket, with its 17th-century pargeting commemorating
the Restoration, seen in the 1880s when it was occupied by F. Pawsey, printer, bookseller and
stationer.*

Introduction

Ipswich was granted its first charter by King John on 25 May 1200, but at that time it was already at least six centuries old. It had begun as the first post-Roman urban settlement in England, possibly set up by the ruling East Anglian dynasty as a trading port, some time in the early 600s. Its position close to the east coast of Britain, approached from the sea by a navigable estuary and opposite the mouth of the mighty Rhine, was undoubtedly responsible both for its establishment and for its subsequent importance as town and seaport.

The 800th anniversary of the granting of its first charter and the beginning of a new millennium seems an appropriate time for a reappraisal of the town's 1400-year history. To study 1400 years within so small a book it is necessary to make some difficult and painful decisions as to what should be included, what should be ignored, what should be cut out. Indeed, should we ignore the prehistory of the settlement, the period when Britons and Romans were farming and sometimes fighting in this part of East Anglia? The archaeological evidence of Roman settlement in the area is fragmentary, but there was some activity here. For example, was it the Romans who cut an artificial branch of the river that survived until the making of the first large-scale sewerage system in Victorian times? In spite of all that we have learned from archaeological investigations in the past quarter-century, we can do no more than surmise.

What disaster struck the town after the Norman Conquest? The enigmatic Domesday record suggests a catastrophic decline in population which can only be tentatively explained by reference to happenings at the same period elsewhere in East Anglia, and elsewhere in Britain.

Of more recent times much more can be discovered: Ipswich has a better account of the events surrounding the handing over of its first charter than is possessed by any other English town, in spite of the defalcation of an early town clerk who stole the town records to cover up his other crimes. One can find evidence of the successive changes in boundary as Ipswich expanded in the Middle Ages; moats, ditches and banks survive to help us unravel past history, but they have to be sought out and identified amidst housing estates and industrial development. One can, for example, still see a dry ditch marking the bounds of the Manor of Stoke, a boundary that was set down in an Anglo-Saxon document more than 1,000 years ago.

There is so much to tell, and in spite of the work of earlier historians such as G.R. Clarke and Lilian and Vincent Redstone a good deal has remained untold until now. Where was Pottaford, where was the Horsewade, and what were the limits of the various holdings described in Domesday Book? Where did Robert Ransome set up his first works when he moved to the town in 1789—and where is his grave to be seen?

Down the years Ipswich has suffered from a dismissive attitude to its history, and to the physical evidence of that history. John Glyde was indignant that the carved front of the Old Coffee House should have been destroyed 'in order that a few inches of ground should be added to the footway!' back in 1818. Yet in the 1960s Felaw's House, once home to the grammar school and a remarkable survival of a merchant's house, was demolished to make way for a car park, and in the 1990s the remains of the first Quaker Meeting House of 1700 and of the second Meeting House of 1798 were bulldozed—and with them the little graveyard in which Robert Ransome, the father of Ipswich's industrial prosperity, is buried. 'Ipswich is a progressive town, and the hand of improvement and enterprise has effaced the traces of antiquity, the signs our forefathers left of their existence and their doings, more quickly and more completely than in almost any other ancient town you may visit,' said William Hunt in 1864. 'But while we are glad at the prosperity of the old town, and like the comfort of modern dwellings and wider streets and more imposing buildings, there is among the old inhabitants a strange affection for anything that will recall the features and events of Ipswich in past days.'

That nostalgia for the past which is so often said to be a 20th-century phenomenon was creating a ready market for the mounted photographs that William Vick sold from his thriving photographic studio at Barrack Corner between about 1870 and the end of the century. Such a demand, indeed, that Vick had to make copy negatives of his most popular photographs—these were large glass plates—so that multiple contact prints could be produced. Thanks to William Vick, and to the wave of nostalgia that produced such a demand for his pictures, we in the 21st century can see some of what has been lost. Other, more recent, photographers have kept up a record of the changing town, for the destruction goes on; there is a mind-set evident among some of the town's leading citizens, now as in the past, that destruction of the old equates to progress, even though the replacement might be of very poor quality compared to what is lost.

Yet, on the credit side, much survives. Sparrowe's Ancient House has been saved from the ravages of passing traffic, Wythypoll's Christchurch Mansion (presented to the town by a member of the Cobbold family) still attracts visitors for its own sake as well as for the superb collection of Constables and Gainsboroughs on display there, and in St Peter's Street there remains a spectacular timber-framed building once owned by a member of the Bacon family, as indicated by the pigs in the mouldings of the 17th-century plaster ceilings which are its glory.

Indeed, the area of Ipswich between the town centre and the river yet contains a wealth of timbered buildings that in most historic towns would be advertised and displayed to residents and tourists alike. While the Ipswich Historic Churches Trust struggles to maintain the magnificent legacy of medieval churches that are no longer used for worship, the conversion of St Stephen's into the town's tourist information centre shows just what potential there is in these fine old buildings.

*   *   *

2   The original borough arms, which probably date from 1200, consisted only of the shield with a rampant lion in gold on a red field and three demi-ships, also in gold, on a blue field. The arms illustrated here are as confirmed by William Hervy, Clarenceux King of Arms in 1561, when he granted the supporters, two seahorses in silver, and the crest, surmounted by a demi-lion holding a ship.

At the beginning of the third millennium history is not redundant. As the Irish premier Mr. Bertie Ahern has just reminded us, if we wish to understand our present we must hold a candle to our past. Studying the history of Ipswich, as of any place, one begins to see a pattern that repeats itself century after century. Only by observing the past can we plot a good course for the future, avoiding similar disasters to those that have marred our earlier years.

The author can merely express a hope that this book will help develop the attitude of 21st-century Ipswichians to their heritage and hasten the day when Ipswich is acknowledged publicly to be an historic town. Lesser places have road-signs bidding visitors welcome to '——— Historic Town'; why not Ipswich?

This is not a definitive history; it is, however, to be hoped that more competent historians will have produced the definitive, multi-volume account of the town's many centuries of history before the 21st century reaches its end, aided, it must be said, by the work done on the town archives in celebration of the 800th anniversary of the borough charter.

Robert Malster
1 January 2000

3   A print of Ipswich from high ground in the area of Greenwich Farm, with Ransomes & Rapier's Waterside Works visible towards the left and the New Cut in the middle of the view. Oarsmen from two of the town's rowing clubs appear to be racing in the foreground. (John Wilton)

I

Romans and Britons

Evidence of early residents is to be found all around the Ipswich area, including living sites of New Stone Age farmers and burials dating from the Bronze Age, but much of the riverside area of the future town of Ipswich may have been too marshy to attract a settled population until Anglo-Saxon times.

The most spectacular archaeological find of all, made when a bank of sandy soil was being bulldozed away to provide a level site for new houses at Belstead Hills in 1968, unhappily tells us very little about the lifestyle of those inhabiting the area in the 1st century B.C. The five gold torcs that came to light might be taken to indicate that some at least of the local inhabitants were wealthy people, but although the finder called in an archaeologist from Ipswich Museum no trace of a burial or of anything else could be found. Two years later a resident of one of the new houses, digging his garden for the first time, found a sixth torc just inches below the surface, apparently in soil spread when the bank was removed.

The torcs may have been part of an Iron-Age goldsmith's stock, buried for safe keeping during an emergency at some time before the Roman conquest. On the other hand, this might be an example of the deliberate burial of groups of valuable objects, which is seen at Snettisham in Norfolk where groups of torcs were buried in small pits. Whether the owners intended to recover them at a future date or they were consigned to the earth in some ritual ceremony we cannot tell.[1] The location of the burial might be linked to the site of the holy well mentioned in the 10th-century bounds of Stoke. Outstanding examples of Iron-Age craftsmanship, the torcs can be seen in the British Museum; replicas are on display in Ipswich Museum.

Such a torc might well have been worn by the owner of an Iron-Age farm at Foxhall, just to the east of Ipswich. First discovered from aerial photography in 1977, the rectangular site was excavated in 1991, when archaeologists found in one corner traces of a large circular house, 11 metres across internally and 12 metres in external diameter, surrounded by a small stockade. Other round buildings were found in plots to the west of the main enclosure. The ditch around the site would originally have been nearly two metres deep; it enclosed an area of 2,800 square metres, a clear indication that the family living there had the power and wealth to get extensive work done. The head of the family was obviously well up the social scale. Besides their farming interests it would seem these people were craftsmen, for quantities of slag and other industrial waste from bronze and iron working were found.[2]

Much of the land in the area was clearly being farmed even before the Romans arrived. Two Iron-Age round houses and other structures were revealed in 1998 on a site overlooking the River Gipping at Lovetofts Drive on the Whitehouse Estate, towards the north-western edge of the modern town. Carried out in advance of a housing development, this excavation uncovered not only the two houses, indicated by penannular ditches 11.3 metres and 9.5 metres in diameter, but also the possible south-western corner of an enclosure and various ditches, postholes and pits. Animal bones found on the site have given archaeologists an idea of the diet of the people living there, while an unusual late Bronze-Age or early Iron-Age cylindrical loomweight provides evidence of craft activity carried on there.

These farmers and craftsmen, then, were the 'Britons' whom the Romans found when they invaded Britain in A.D.43. With sea levels high in relation to the eastern part of Britain throughout the four centuries the Romans occupied the country it is likely that part of the site of the present-day town was extremely marshy, if not actually under water at high tides. This might be why the invaders chose a site some four miles up the Gipping valley for their early forts and settlement of Combretovium, in the vicinity of Baylham Mill, Coddenham. The Roman invaders certainly established a town, presumably a port, on the promontory between the estuaries of the Orwell and Deben at Felixstowe. In the third century they added to the town one of the stone-walled forts of the 'Saxon Shore' series, later known as Walton Castle.

On the edge of the modern town centre of Ipswich there is evidence of a riverside Roman settlement between the Gipping, now represented by the Alderman Canal, and Handford Road. This site has not yet been thoroughly explored but building materials, pottery and coins indicate substantial occupation throughout the Roman period.[3] It is significant both that finds of roof tiles and hypocaust tiles suggest substantial buildings in the area and that the discovery of high-quality imported pottery indicates a settlement of fairly high status. As the section of river beside the site is almost certainly an artificial cut and is of considerable antiquity one is led to wonder if it could have been made in the Roman period; was it, perhaps, a leat for a Roman watermill on the site of Handford Mill? Roman burials in the area of Burlington Road and a single burial from the Magistrates Court site might be related to this settlement.

The alignment of the Roman road from Camulodunum (Colchester), the early predecessor of the A12, is interesting in that while it bears left near Copdock to reach the supposed site of Combretovium at Baylham and Coddenham, a branch directed almost straight ahead and continued down Crane Hill would cross the Gipping in the vicinity of the later Handford Bridge and thus reach the Handford Road settlement. Much remains to be discovered about the Ipswich area in the Roman period.

The only evidence of Romano-British activity found so far in the area of the modern town centre is a bronze flask from the site of Wolsey's College which was purchased by the British Museum in 1857 and a few coins and pieces of pottery found during excavations in 1979 and 1982 north of St Mary Quay Church, which may represent a small farm or some activity beside the possible ford from Great Whip Street.[4]

On higher ground just to the north of the site later occupied by Ipswich, at what is now known as Castle Hill in the parish of Whitton, the Romans built a large villa that was much more than a farmhouse, though it was most likely the centre of a farming operation. It is by far the largest and most richly decorated Roman building of its kind known in Suffolk, and must have dominated the surrounding area. Whether he was a Roman or a native Briton who adopted the Roman lifestyle, the owner of this villa was a man of substance; possibly he was a wealthy farmer who made a fortune out of supplying the Roman army with food, a merchant trading from the Orwell, or a provincial official.

The first excavation was carried out in the 19th century, when a patterned mosaic floor was lifted and put on display at Ipswich Museum. Other tessellated floors and painted wall plaster were uncovered in later excavations. Basil Brown, the archaeologist who was responsible for the discovery of the Sutton Hoo ship burial, worked on the Castle Hill site in 1946-50 and was able to produce a plan of part of the main block of buildings to the north of Chesterfield Drive, one of the new roads laid out as the town expanded after the Second World War. The largest building was about eighty metres long and half that in width. The block excavated by Basil Brown was clearly only part of a much larger complex of buildings.

The area is now covered by modern houses, but further investigations in 1989 revealed a cobbled yard with a barn over 18 metres long on one side and on the other side a bath-house with three or four heated rooms and three others that were not heated.[5] Not far from the villa was a cemetery with rows of inhumation graves, including six females with their skulls placed between their feet, an arrangement which has been noted in a number of late Roman cemeteries.[6] The cemetery site had links with pre-Roman traditions as finds of pottery from the Beaker period and from the Iron Age have been reported. In the 1930s Reid Moir found three 'ritual' shafts, one more than 66ft. deep, of a type recognised elsewhere in both pre-Roman and early Roman contexts.[7]

Investigations elsewhere on the periphery of the modern town have revealed that the Castle Hill villa estate was not the only agricultural operation in the area. Just under two miles from the site of the villa complex, building operations at The Albany on the outskirts of the town revealed the remains of a Roman farmstead at the head of a valley draining towards the Orwell. The living area of the farm was enclosed by a ditch some two metres deep, with a gated entrance.[8] Material from the ditch would have formed a bank which appears to have been still visible in the 19th century; J. Wodderspoon mentions an earthwork on the way to Tuddenham in his *Memorials of the Ancient Town of Ipswich*, published in 1850, and this might well have been the farm bank. The heavy clay soil of the farm must have presented problems to the farmers who worked the land throughout the Roman occupation. Some of the complex of ditches found on the site might have been divisions between animal compounds as well as performing a very necessary drainage function.

It looks as if farming continued in the area throughout the Iron Age, Roman and Saxon periods. The ditches of the field system relating to the Iron-Age farm at Foxhall, referred to above, show that this land was still being farmed during the Roman period, although the location of the farm buildings is unknown. However, in Saxon times new timber buildings were constructed just outside the Iron-Age enclosure, while the centre of the later medieval settlement was 550 metres away at Foxhall Hall and church.[9]

Similar evidence of continuity in rural activity was found on the other side of Ipswich where a farming community in the Whitehouse area (on the site now occupied by the Hewlett Packard factory) overlooked the Gipping valley about a mile north-west of the Roman villa at Castle Hill. At Whitehouse there were pits of the early Iron Age, much Roman pottery associated with ditches, and a timber building that was presumably a small farm, followed by a (Middle) Saxon settlement in a ditched enclosure 80 metres by 100 metres.[10] A settlement, possibly a farm, was revealed during the building of Violet Close on the Chantry side of the river, and another overlooked the river from the north bank downstream from the modern town at Ravenswood (formerly Ipswich Airport). It would seem not only that the countryside was being managed in the Roman period but that it had already been brought under extensive cultivation before the invasion. One section of the Roman road from Coddenham to Venta Icenorum, the regional capital at Caistor St Edmund (the modern A140 road from Ipswich to Norwich), cuts across the field pattern in a way that suggests that the fields had already been laid out before construction of the road; they might be pre-Roman.

Downriver from Ipswich at Downham Bridge[11] an area of what some have described as stone paving crossing the river bed is said to be Roman in origin. Others contend that the 'paving' is natural. Bearing in mind that sea level in the Roman period was high, a tidal ford at this point seems unlikely, and it is more likely that any road communicating with the Saxon Shore fort at Walton (Felixstowe) ran across the site of the later town and on to Combretovium, the hub of the Roman road system in the area. Evidence of a timber causeway beneath Westgate Street and Norwich Road might indicate its line, but this feature is as yet undated.[12] However, the structure at Downham Bridge might just possibly be part of a barrage constructed in Roman times. If so, it might have included some type of lock to permit the passage of ships upriver to a quay at Combretovium and a bridge across it carrying a road from Walton/Felixstowe to the Roman colony of Colchester, the most important town in the region at that time. There is still much to be discovered about the extent of Roman engineering.

II

The Saxon Town

Towns and urban lifestyles were unknown when the first Anglo-Saxon settlers set up their wooden houses on the north side of the Orwell close to the lowest crossing point of the river. The sea had probably retreated since Roman times[1] and it is likely that the river, although wider than it is now, was fordable at a point a few metres east of where Stoke Bridge was later built. Below the settlement the river broadened out into the estuary of the Orwell, a waterway which enabled sea-going ships to come inland to this point and to unload their cargoes on the sloping foreshore on the site of the new settlement.

Although hard evidence is so far lacking, it is likely that Gipeswic, as the new settlement was known, was established at the beginning of the 7th century by the Wuffingas, the ruling royal house of East Anglia whose palace was at Rendlesham and whose burial place was at Sutton Hoo, on the escarpment above the Deben. The fabulous treasure found in the ship burial at Sutton Hoo in 1939 contained items from as far away as Constantinople and provided evidence of the far-flung trading links of this Anglo-Saxon dynasty, and there is a strong suggestion that Gipeswic was intended as an entrepôt handling trade with the continent of Europe. Possibly the Wuffingas had one of their royal halls on the site now occupied by Cornhill and the town hall, though firm archaeological evidence is lacking.

The name Gipeswic, sometimes said to be derived from a personal name or nickname, is more likely to have the meaning 'the town at the corner (gip) of the estuary'. The river name Gipping is no more than a back-formation from a settlement name, and there is evidence that the river as well as the estuary was originally known as the Orwell, from a spring of that name in Rattlesden; there is still an Orwell meadow in that village.[2]

The establishment of Gipeswic came at a period that used to be known as the Dark Ages, so called by historians of the past to reflect the total lack of knowledge of those years. The work in Ipswich of Keith Wade and his team of archaeologists since 1974 in probing beneath the modern surface, usually in advance of building development in the central area of Ipswich, has cast a good deal of light on the town's earliest years, while the operations of the Sutton Hoo Research Committee under Martin Carver between 1983 and 1993 have begun to put the royal burial ground into the wider context of the kingdom of East Anglia as a whole. As Keith Wade has pointed out, much further research into rural settlement at this period is needed to reveal the history of that kingdom.

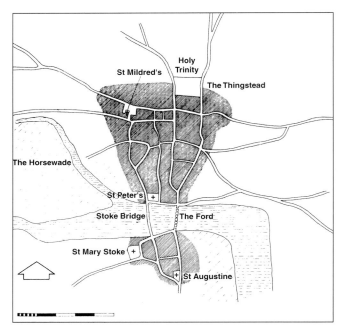

4   The Saxon town. By the 8th century Gipeswic had expanded to cover the whole area of the present-day town centre and of Stoke, to the south of the Orwell. There appear to have been no defences until a ditch and bank were constructed during the Danish occupation, which lasted from about 879 to 918, almost certainly resulting in the diversion of the main cross-town road; there seems to have been no gate at the end of what is today Carr Street, the east gate being in the vicinity of today's Orwell Place.

There was certainly Anglo-Saxon settlement in the Ipswich area before Gipeswic was established, since 6th-century cemeteries exist at Hadleigh Road, on the west bank of the Gipping close to Handford Bridge and only 2 km. from the Butter Market site, and at Boss Hall, just a little further away on the other bank.[3] The Hadleigh Road cemetery was investigated in 1906 and 1907 by the redoubtable Miss Nina Layard, who worked just ahead of a large team of labourers engaged in a land-levelling operation, instigated by Ipswich Corporation as a way of relieving unemployment, to record and rescue the contents of some 165 graves before the land surface was destroyed. These two cemeteries indicate the presence of communities in the area that co-existed with Gipeswic; the Hadleigh Road cemetery continued in use into the middle or second half of the 7th century, while that at Boss Hall seems to have been brought back into use for a single high-status burial in the late 7th or early 8th century. Gipeswic was no isolated township far from its nearest neighbours.

While the first inhabitants of Gipeswic were pagan, Christianity arrived in the East Anglian kingdom by the middle of the 7th century. According to Bede, the first East Anglian king to embrace Christianity in about 616 was Rædwald, he who was buried with his treasure in a ship at Sutton Hoo, though he hedged his bets by retaining a pagan shrine as well as building a church. Rædwald's son Earpwald was also converted to Christianity, but it was only with the accession of Sigeberht in about 630 that the Church really began its mission in East Anglia. Sigeberht, who had been converted while living in exile in Gaul, sent for help from Burgundy, and Felix arrived to set up his see at Dommoc, which some identify with Felixstowe, others with Dunwich. An alternative, some might say a rival, mission was carried on by the Irish monk Fursey at Burgh Castle.

At least three Ipswich churches are thought to date back to the middle Saxon period, though little is known of these early buildings. They were probably constructed of timber and all traces were eradicated by later rebuilding in stone,[4] though future excavation such as was carried out within St Stephen's Church during restoration might yet produce new evidence. St Mildred's on the Cornhill had a very early dedication; St Mildred, who became abbess of Minster, between Richborough and Reculver in Kent, was a daughter of Merewalh, a 7th-century ruler of south Shropshire and Herefordshire. It has been assumed that when she died, somewhere about A.D.700, King Aldwulf of East Anglia, who was her grandfather's nephew, dedicated the Gipeswic church to her.[5] St Augustine's in Stoke and St Mary Stoke are both likely to be early churches, while Norman Scarfe argues that its large landholding at the time of Domesday Book indicates that St Peter's was a minster, a religious community serving as a centre from which priests were sent to serve other churches in the area at a time when the ecclesiastical parish system was not firmly established. The existing medieval structure might well stand on the site of a foundation of the Wuffingas, who supported the mission of St Felix, first bishop of the East Angles.[6]

The 7th/8th-century settlement, almost certainly the first post-Roman urban community to be established in Britain, covered an area of some six hectares on the north bank of the Orwell, with its northern boundary in the area of Falcon Street, the Old Cattle Market and Dog's Head Street. Just to the north of the settlement was a cemetery, part of which was excavated in 1987-8 in preparation for the building of the Butter Market Shopping Centre. Right from the beginning, to judge from the pottery and other materials found by archaeologists investigating this early settlement, there were trading links with the continent. Rhenish wine was imported, along with whetstones and Neidermendig lava quernstones from the Cologne area.[7]

Like any other seaport and trading centre of later days, Gipeswic was a cosmopolitan town inhabited, during the trading season at least, by a temporary population who brought with them their own style of cooking pot and other articles of continental origin. One of the burials in the Butter Market cemetery which has been dated between A.D.640 and 670 was of a man of some substance who clearly belonged to another country. The coffin

5 *One of the people in the 7/8th-century cemetery excavated in 1987-8 was a woman wearing a necklace of glass beads. She had been buried face down. (Copyright Suffolk County Council)*

6 *A broken quernstone of Neidermendig lava found during excavations in Ipswich by members of the Suffolk Archaeological Unit. Such quernstones were imported from the Rhineland not only in Saxon times but also in later periods. (Copyright Suffolk County Council)*

7   *The surviving remains of an 'Ipswich ware' bottle from the pottery kiln found on the Buttermarket site. The earliest post-Roman wheel-thrown pottery to be made in Britain, 'Ipswich ware' was distributed over a wide area of eastern England. (Copyright Suffolk County Council)*

contained a shield, two spears, a broad heavy seax in a scabbard with elaborate copper-alloy fittings which had been hung from a belt with accoutrements of copper alloy, and two palm cups; the shield boss, the seax and the belt suite were all continental types. It is probable that the man who was buried in Gipeswic in the mid-7th century came from Frankish or Alamannic territory in the upper part of the Rhine valley.[8] Did he perhaps die while on a visit to East Anglia in the course of trading, or was there some other reason for his presence here? It might be that he was visiting the trading fair which some archaeologists postulate was held within, or close to, the settlement, a temporary international market that might have resembled the present-day Suffolk Show with its marquees and open-air displays.

From the mid-7th century a variety of wheel-thrown pottery which the archaeologists have labelled 'Ipswich ware' was being produced on a large scale, mainly in an industrial suburb in the area of what is now Carr Street. This pottery, the earliest post-Roman wheel-thrown ware to be made in Britain, was distributed widely in East Anglia and beyond, very largely by sea and inland water transport. Examples have been found in excavations not only in Norfolk and Suffolk but in coastal areas of Essex and Kent and at places along the rivers Nene and Welland.[9] Such a wide distribution of pottery made in Gipeswic points to the important position it held in the region's trade. By the 9th century the settlement had expanded to cover some 50 hectares, an enormous area for a town in the Anglo-Saxon period. It had become one of the four major trading settlements of that period— the others being Hamwic (modern Southampton), London and York—and carried on a thriving trade with the continental port of Dorestad, and probably with other ports of the Rhineland and the near continent.

The street pattern laid down as the settlement expanded in the 8th century remained the basis of the town layout until the Victorian period, and many town-centre streets continue to reflect the Anglo-Saxon arrangement. The thoroughfare represented today by Carr Street, Tavern Street, Westgate Street, St Matthew's Street and Norwich Road is almost certainly even older; it possibly originated as the Roman road running from

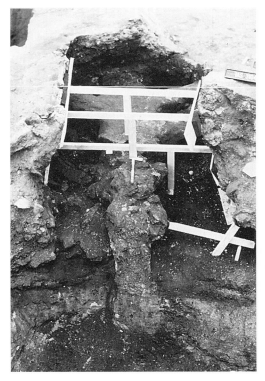

8   *Clearest evidence of the important Gipeswic pottery industry to be excavated was this Anglo-Saxon kiln found on the Buttermarket site. Some pots from the last firing were still in the kiln. (Copyright Suffolk County Council)*

9   *The Buttermarket kiln was so complete that it proved possible to remove it for future study and display. (Copyright Suffolk County Council)*

the Roman settlement at Walton and its Saxon Shore fort (Walton Castle), on the coast near present-day Felixstowe, to Combretovium (Coddenham).

When excavations were made in Tavern Street, Westgate Street and St Matthew's Street for the laying of a sewer in 1881, Dr. Taylor, curator of Ipswich Museum, saw that a corduroy road formed of logs had been used to carry an earlier road over marshy ground in the Westgate Street area. He reported that the logs were piled on each other in alternate fashion as if to bridge the marshy places. He had a piece of the wooden roadway dug out, and found that the logs were secured to each other by wooden pegs, and associated with it were a bone comb and evidence of antler working. This roadway, which Dr. Taylor seems to have considered to be Saxon, was some 1.5 metres below the level of the Victorian street.[10] A rather similar roadway of oak logs laid on a mat of furze, heather, broom and branches of alder and birch was found in Norwich Road near the *Emperor* public house a few years later.

The Roman road, if such it was, might have formed a baseline for the laying out of a roughly rectangular grid of streets during the 8th-century expansion. The alignment of the north-south highway represented today by Upper and Lower Brook Streets, which followed the line of a natural watercourse, with what is now Great Whip Street on the south side of the river suggests clearly that the original river crossing was a ford approximately 130 metres below where Stoke Bridge was built some time in the 9th-10th centuries. Memory of this crossing, which continued to be used for wheeled traffic in the Middle Ages, survived into the 19th century, for John Glyde refers to 'The Ford' in his *Illustrations of Old Ipswich,* published in 1889.

It is thought that the other north-south highway consisting today of Bridge Street, St Peter's Street, St Nicholas Street and Queen Street might have been laid out at the same time that the first bridge was built. It linked the original trading centre beside St Peter's Church with the Cornhill, which, if the inferences drawn from the early dedication of St Mildred's Church are correct, might have been a centre of royal authority; it might not be without significance that John Ogilby's map of 1674 names the whole of this route from Stoke Bridge to Cornhill 'King Street'. Evidence of Saxon royal occupation of the site might one day be found by excavation, if it has not been lost through the building of the Victorian Town Hall and the 20th-century rebuilding of what is now Debenhams store. The foundations of the rebuilt department store cut deeply into the ground that might have revealed so much had archaeological investigation been carried out at the time of the rebuilding.

The first Stoke Bridge would have been a timber structure spanning a stream that was a good deal wider than the present river at that point, for the north bank was right back on the line of College Street. Ships bringing cargoes from Dorestad and elsewhere lay on the foreshore, unloading and loading between the tides as the mudbanks were left dry, or relatively so.

Beyond the bridge lay the hamlet of Stoke, which came into existence at an early stage in the development of the Anglo-Saxon settlement. When the Danes took control of East Anglia after killing King Edmund in 869 they destroyed the monasteries, and it was some time before the Church recovered control of parts of its ancient holdings. The process was apparently initiated in our region by Bishop Theodred, who was Bishop of London,[11] and was continued by Bishop Ethelwold of Winchester, a powerful figure at the court of King Edgar. It was he who in 970 recovered for the Abbey of Ely, founded in the 7th century by St Etheldreda, daughter of King Anna, its original endowment of the 5½ hundreds of the Wicklaw in East Suffolk and the estate of Stoke. It has been suggested that the original Wicklaw might have included Ipswich itself[12] and that its court met at the Thingstead (St Margaret's Green), just as the court for the West Suffolk hundreds of St Edmund met at Thingoe in Bury St Edmunds. If that is so, the king carefully kept in his own hands the borough of Ipswich (including the parish of St Augustine on the Stoke side of the river) as it remained in royal hands until the grant of the town's charter in 1200.

The grant of Stoke to Ely in 970 defines the bounds of its 10 hides.[13] They start from a hythe or landing place on the south bank of the river, presumably downstream of the small parish of St Augustine; possibly it was the one occupied by the Harnies family, wealthy merchants, in the 14th century. The boundary continues down the river to the river Bourne (or the Belstead Brook at Bourne Bridge), and then follows that stream past Theofford, now the bridge on the road to Belstead, to the probable site of a watermill at what is now the corner of the Ellenbrook Road playing field. Where the boundary strikes off at right angles from the Belstead Brook one can find a short section of boundary ditch, possibly a thousand years old, rapidly being filled with refuse from neighbouring gardens.

The next point on the bounds is a holy well, most probably the place where the Iron-Age gold torcs were found on Holcombe Crescent, from where it runs on to Haldane's Ho, which must be the top of Crane Hill at Chantry Park. From there it runs through the low ground, called Holdessie Valley in the bounds of 1352 and now filled by the Hadleigh Road industrial estate, and so to Pottaford, which seems to have been a river crossing near Boss Hall known in the 16th century as Bordshaw Bridge. Pottaford presumably gets its name from the Saxon cemetery at Boss Hall, in which there were a number of cremations buried in earthenware pots; perhaps erosion of the river bank revealed some of these burials.

The boundary then runs along the river to Hagenefordabrycge (Handford Bridge) and on (by the stream now represented by the Alderman Canal) to Horsewade (site of a second medieval mill, downstream from the one at Handford, and after the foundation of the Franciscan Greyfriars known as Friars Bridge). From there it probably cut across the marshes to the salt water of the Orwell beside a *merscmylne* ('marsh mill' or 'mill in the fen') and downriver to Stoke Bridge.

Anglo-Saxon Gipeswic grew into a bustling, flourishing town that was at the centre of an extensive trading network. The smoking kilns south of Carr Street produced pottery that was shipped from the Orwell, but the potters were not by any means the only craftsmen at work in the town. Archaeologists have found spindle whorls used in spinning wool, fired clay loom weights used by weavers, combs made from antlers, evidence of leather working and a bronzesmith's site complete with crucible and moulds, all these finds pointing to the industrial nature of this

10 Awls, pins and thread-pickers made of bone found on the Buttermarket site provide evidence of the activities carried on by residents of the Anglo-Saxon town. (Copyright Suffolk County Council)

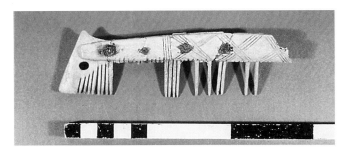

11 A bone comb provides further evidence of craft working in Gipeswic. (Copyright Suffolk County Council)

thriving community.[14] In St Stephen's Lane excavations revealed a row of buildings occupied by a variety of tradesmen all crowding along the edge of the roadway, thought to have been laid down across the earlier cemetery shortly after AD 700. The impression given is of a dense, closely packed community occupying a relatively small area, but as the settlement expanded and building spread out it became much less crowded. Later buildings in the lane stood back from the highway and were less tightly packed together.

Ipswich was an important commercial centre, and it is almost certain that some of the silver coins (series R sceattas) of the early 8th century were minted at Ipswich.[15] The first silver pennies with the names of East Anglian kings from Beonna onwards, which bear the names of moneyers Efe and Tilbert under King Beonna, *c*.758, and Lul under King Ethelbert, *c*.792, are also likely to have been minted in the town. These moneyers were doubtless men of some status, and they might be the first English residents recorded by name.[16] The first coins with the mint mark of 'Gipswic' were the silver pennies of the 'reform coinage' of Edgar, King of the English, dated 937–5 and minted by the Ipswich moneyers Leofric and Lifinge.[17] From that period the moneyers continued to strike silver pennies, the currency on which commerce operated once it had ceased to function on a barter system. A collection made by a Suffolk man and sold in 1991 contained no fewer than 72 different Ipswich coins struck between the reign of Aethelred II and that of King John.

During its long history Ipswich has suffered from alternating periods of boom and depression, often linked to fluctuations in the condition of the Orwell. From the archaeological evidence so far available it would seem that the first downturn in the town's fortunes might have occurred in the 10th century, for during that and the succeeding century there is much less evidence of craft activities. There are also fewer indications of international trade at that period. It is tempting to link this somewhat dramatic change in the nature and functions of the settlement with the arrival of the Danes, who were in control of the town from 869 to 917, but there is little to suggest that it is more than a coincidence. The Danish invasion certainly brought an end to the East Anglian kingdom as it had existed for three or more centuries, the killing of the last East Anglian king, Edmund, in 869 heralding two generations of Danish domination.

Changes in the appearance of the town came about with the introduction of a new type of house, a building with a cellar standing up to 30 metres back from the street. In place of the crowded craft workshops jostling shoulder-to-shoulder along the street front, there were from the late 9th or early 10th century fairly scattered residences set within their own plots. Buildings of this kind have also been found in the late Saxon town of Thetford.[18] Just such a property as this was acquired in Ipswich by Bishop Theodred, who was responsible for reviving Christianity in East Anglia after the withdrawal of the Danes. Referring to it in his will, which dates from the 940s, Theodred uses the word *hage* (a hedge or enclosure), which describes very well the large detached buildings in a ditched or hedged enclosure that were excavated in Thetford. Excavation evidence from the Foundation Street area suggests plots of about a quarter-acre per tenement, which if divided into the 50 hectares of settlement fits the Domesday figure of 538 burgesses in 1066.

It was during the Danish occupation that the first town defences were formed. The digging of a roughly circular ditch and bank around the town led to a distortion of the original street layout; for one thing, the ditch cut across the original line of Fore Street, which had led straight into the town before being diverted to join the present line of Lower/Upper Orwell Street, presumably entering the town by way of the East Gate.[19] Beginning at the edge of the marsh on the western side of the settlement, the ditch and bank ran around almost the whole of the populated area, finishing close to the river on the east side, with the river and marsh providing a defence to the south and south-west.

These defences were presumably set up in response to the advance of the army of Wessex early in the 10th century, but it is believed they were never used for defensive purposes; the East Anglian Danes capitulated in 918 after Edward the Elder had occupied Colchester. What is perhaps surprising in view of the troubled times in which the Wuffinga dynasty ruled is that Gipeswic apparently had no earlier defences.

The sequence of defences is obscure, but it is known that the ditch was at one stage filled in and that it was then redug some time in the 11th century. The Anglo-Saxon Chronicle tells us that in 991 the Vikings (which is just another way of describing the Danes) 'harried' Ipswich before marching south to win the epic Battle of Maldon in which Byrhtnoth and his Essex thegns were killed. Then in 1010 a Viking army under Thurkill the Tall sailed up the Orwell and landed at Ipswich, from where they marched west to the great battle at Ringmere, between Bury St Edmunds and Thetford.

Did the marauding Vikings put the residents of Gipeswic to the sword? Did they burn the town after plundering the storehouses and workshops? We simply do not know; it is uncertain exactly what the writer of the Anglo-Saxon Chronicle meant when he wrote of the town being 'harried'. Archaeologists have found burnt buildings, and they have found bodies apparently hurriedly buried close to domestic buildings, but there is no evidence to show whether the conflagration was the result of accidental overturning of a candle or of torching by the invaders, and little is known about those bodies.

What we do know is that the potteries of Gipeswic continued to function, but that by the end of the 9th century they had ceased producing 'Ipswich ware' and were instead turning out a different kind of pot, one which archaeologists have labelled 'Thetford ware' after the place in which it was first recorded. In comparison with the earlier 'Ipswich ware' the new products enjoyed a much more local distribution, though there was a limited export trade to London, shown by the discovery of Ipswich-made 'Thetford ware' pots in excavations there.[20] The potteries continued in production until the middle of the 12th century; it might be added that a later pottery survived to give its name to an area of 19th-century working-class housing.

III

The Norman and Medieval Town

A new management took over in 1066. In Ipswich the old landowners were replaced by a new landowning elite, headed in the extent of his holdings as well as in power by William the Conqueror himself.

In East Anglia the Saxons and the Anglo-Danes remained the majority of the population, but for the most part the ruling class were men who had come from Normandy with William; they were men who had ridden into battle with their duke, and they soon showed that they could be as ruthless in ruling the kingdom as they had been on the battlefield. Almost immediately after his coronation William set off on a journey that brought him into East Anglia; there is no information as to whether he came to Ipswich, but as he visited Barking in Essex and then journeyed to Norwich he might well have travelled by way of the town on the Orwell.[1]

It used to be supposed that William the Conqueror brought order to a decadent and unruly kingdom governed by weak kings and self-seeking earls, but later scholars have revised opinions and restored the balance in favour of the Saxons. Professor Sir Frank Stenton, the most eminent scholar of the period, writes of the Normans as 'the closest of all western peoples to the barbarian strain in the continental order. They had produced little in art or learning, and nothing in literature, that could be set beside the work of Englishmen.'[2] Ipswich, and East Anglia in general, was soon to suffer from William's barbarian strain.

The invasion of 1066 is often seen as a turning point, but in fact some Normans (that is, Vikings who had settled in Normandy a century or two earlier) had been resident in Britain long before the Battle of Hastings. In 1002 Aethelred II married Emma of Normandy, daughter of Duke Richard I and sister of Duke Richard II, and it was at the Norman court that Aethelred and his family found refuge after the Danes under Sweyn had occupied England in 1013. It was natural that when Aethelred's son Edward the Confessor became King of England in 1042 he should be accompanied by a number of Norman friends, among whom were Ralph the Staller (probably a Breton) and Robert fitz Wimarc, both of whom acquired lands in East Anglia.

Following the conquest William made Ralph Guader or Wader Earl of East Anglia and put him in charge of eastern England, with his headquarters in Norwich Castle. In 1075 Ralph, having just married Emma, daughter of William fitz Osbern and sister of Roger, Earl of Hereford, conspired with others to rebel against William, who at that moment was away in Normandy. The conspiracy had disastrous results for the region. Ralph and Emma escaped, but lesser men who had taken part in the rebellion were hunted down and at best had a leg amputated, presumably to ensure that they did not march against their king again.

William spent much of his time dealing with uprisings in various parts of his new kingdom. In 1069 he had to put down an uprising in the north aided by a Danish force that came into the Humber in between 200 and 300 ships, and that winter, as Orderic Vitalis tells us, 'in the fulness of his wrath he ordered the corn and cattle, with the implements of husbandry and every sort of provisions, to be collected in heaps and set on fire until the whole was consumed, and thus destroyed at once all that could serve for the support of life in the whole country lying beyond the Humber.'[3] There is some evidence that he did just the same in East Anglia following the putting down of Ralph's rebellion, either as punishment for the uprising or to denude the countryside of supplies that might be used by Danish invaders.

Twenty years after the Conquest, King William ordered that a survey be compiled of his kingdom, an account so complete of who held what and where, how much each holding was worth and to whom the tax was due, that the people likened it to the Day of Judgment. As David Dymond and Peter Northeast have pointed out, Domesday Book has to be seen not simply as a survey of Norman England but as a stocktaking of centuries of Anglo-Saxon history.[4] The most striking thing we learn from the Domesday Book about Ipswich is the sorry state of the borough. In the time of King Edward, as the scribes put it (that is, in 1066), there had been 538 burgesses, but at the time of the survey (1086) there were only 110 who paid tax, plus another 100 who were so poor they could not afford to pay anything more than a penny a head. Without any explanation, the scribe adds 'And in the Borough, there have been laid waste 328 dwellings, which paid a levy to the King's tax before 1066.' In the case of the lands of Swein of Essex, who succeeded his father Robert fitz Wimarc as Sheriff of Essex, it is specifically and rather ominously mentioned that 15 of the 41 burgesses over whom he had jurisdiction before 1066 were dead.

Something catastrophic had occurred between 1066 and 1086, just as it had in Norwich where the number of English burgesses had dropped from 1,320 to 655, and where there were 190 empty houses as well as those demolished to make way for the castle. In the case of Norwich the scribe has an explanation: 'Those fleeing and the others remaining have been utterly devastated partly because of Earl Ralph's forfeitures, partly because of fires …' Had Ipswich, too, shared in the terrible retribution for Earl Ralph's treachery? One might add that Domesday Book shows that in Dorset all the four main towns, Dorchester, Bridport, Wareham and Shaftesbury, had suffered a great loss of houses. East Anglia was not alone in this destruction, whether it was done by Danes or Normans.

Domesday Book lists 11 churches in the borough, including two dedicated to St Mary and two to St Peter. There are indications that it is not a complete list;[5] St Mildred's does not appear. Central Ipswich, including the holdings of the resident merchant burgesses, together with four carucates which had been held by Queen Edith (wife of Edward the Confessor and daughter of the troublesome Earl Godwin of Wessex) and two carucates which had been held by Earl Gyrth, was in the king's hands and was looked after by Roger Bigot, whom William had made Sheriff of both Suffolk and

Norfolk. As such Roger had not only great power in the region but also considerable land holdings. The appellation 'bigot' appears to have been applied to certain tribes living in Southern Gaul—it was also applied as a term of abuse to the Normans generally.

The other holdings were six carucates held by St Peter's Church in Ipswich under Richard FitzGilbert of Clare and three carucates held by the Abbey of St Etheldreda at Ely, giving us a total of 15 carucates. Ely's liberty in Stoke, three carucates, represents one fifth; it is interesting that if the half hundred was reckoned as 50 hides (the hundred being 100 hides) then the 10 hides referred to in the 970 bounds of Stoke would also represent one fifth under that system. We can place Ely's liberty with certainty in Stoke, but the other holdings are less certain. The following, however, is the most likely arrangement. If the two carucates that had been held by Earl Gyrth were traditionally regarded as the earl's holding, then it is likely to have been restored in due course to become the Wicks Ufford of the later Ufford earls, identified on later maps as starting north-west of Bishops Hill in the direction of Back Hamlet. The 1764 edition of Kirby's *Suffolk Traveller* places Westerfield Church in Wicks Ufford, so that may be its western limit. The area between Bishops Hill and the river is later known as Bishop's Wick, presumably centred on the large moated site of the bishop's residence in Holywells Park overlooking the river, and was certainly held by the Bishops of Norwich from at least the time of Richard I until the reign of Henry VIII. It is possible that the tradition identifying this as Queen Edith's four carucates is correct.

It seems that the borough bounds did not in 1086 extend as far as they did in the later Middle Ages, because the settlement listed in Domesday Book as Grenewic is almost certainly that later known as Greenwich Farm. It is entered in Carlford Hundred, as is Alnesbourne, so it seems that at some later date Alnesbourne was transferred to Colneis Hundred and Greenwich to Ipswich borough, extending the borough bounds to John's Ness. The limits of Bishop's Wick had previously been near, and possibly marked by, Cliff Lane or the straight footpath running almost parallel to Cliff Lane up the edge of Holywells Park; this footpath appears to be a good candidate for an early boundary, if it is not a result of later park planning.

This leaves the holding of St Peter's Church unplaced, though the composition of medieval coroners' juries offers a clue. In addition to 12 burgesses the jury had four representatives from each of four 'hamlets', Stoke, Brookes, Wicks Ufford and Wicks Episcopi (Bishop's Wick). If these are the Domesday holdings then only Brookes is left unaccounted for, and it can be identified as the origin of the later Brooks Hall estate attached to a moated house on Norwich Road just beyond the Anglesea Road junction. In support of placing the St Peter's manor on this side of Ipswich we might note that the Domesday entry (25.52) states that part of the manor was disputed with the king's manor of Bramford, and this is most likely to refer to property somewhere in the region of Boss Hall, where there is still an outlying section of Bramford parish on the 19th-century tithe map. St Peter's also held 91 acres in Thurleston in Claydon Hundred (Domesday 25.62), which could have adjoined part of Brookes. (The figures in brackets relate to the entries in *Domesday Book: Suffolk* published by Phillimore, 1986.)

It is clear that in Domesday both Thurleston and Whitton were in Claydon Hundred, so the borough bounds on this side might not have extended far beyond the later Castle Hill Farm (in the Chesterfield Drive area, and site of the large Roman villa). Confirmation of this identification comes from the information[6] that King Edward [the Confessor] gave Brokes to Aluric de Clare[7] and that Robert de Badele later held it of the Earl of Clare by one knight's fee.[8] Copinger[9] tells us that in the time of Henry III Geoffrey de Badele was the lord of the manor of Badley under the Honour of Clare for a knight's fee[10] and that Close Rolls (1 Edw. I, 9) has an order to the Escheater not to intermeddle with 4½ knights' fees in Badley and Brokes unless Geoffrey held them of the King in chief, as the King learns from the Exchequer Rolls that he held them of Gilbert de Clare, Earl of Gloucester, of the Honour of Clare. It is also notable that the Cartulary of the Priory of SS Peter and Paul[11] includes a number of references to properties in Brookes or Brokes and to Geoffrey de Badele.

This accounts for the four holdings outside the town centre listed in Domesday, although it seems impossible to identify the precise boundaries between them, and suggests that the borough was less extensive than in the later Middle Ages. However, even in Domesday the borough did have links with some holdings in Claydon Hundred, as among the king's burgesses in Ipswich (1.122e) Godric held the church of St Botolf in Thurleston in Claydon Hundred with one acre, and in addition to the 91 acres belonging to St Peter's Church Richard FitzGilbert of Clare also had 18 free men with 64 acres in Thurleston (25.60). Also in Thurleston Aelfric, a burgess of Ipswich, held 12 acres along with St Julian's Church in the borough of Ipswich (74.8 & 9). Such complications suggest it might have been difficult to maintain strict boundaries, and they prefigure later extensions of the borough bounds.

It is worth noting that at some date at or after the founding of Holy Trinity Priory in the early 12th century a large block of land north of the town centre became the property of the priory, and this included at least all land between Westerfield Road and Tuddenham Road. In Domesday Book Holy Trinity Church had 26 acres, which is not a particularly large holding, so one has to wonder whether additional land was taken from the original St Peter's holding; both were Augustinian houses and seem to have enjoyed equal status, perhaps because there had been some agreement to divide the church lands and the town centre parishes between them. It might be relevant that both seem to have had a share of Handford Mill, recorded for Holy Trinity (Inspeximus of King John, 1204) as given with land in Brokes by Robert son of Geoffrey and Geoffrey his son, who is likely to be the same as Galfridus (Latin for Geoffrey) son of Robert de Badele who features in the Cartulary of SS Peter & Paul as giving that priory a share in Handford Mill and in lands in Brokes.[12]

Beyond Stoke Bridge, the hamlet of Stoke belonged to Ely Abbey, to which it had been given in 970. The Domesday Book entry gives no clue to any destruction or depopulation there, so it might be that Stoke escaped, or suffered less severely, whatever calamity had struck the main part of the town on the north side of the river.

H.C. Darby estimates that the population of Ipswich in 1086 must have been about 1,600, or maybe more, as against some 5,000 in Norwich.[13] There is, however, considerable argument about the multiplier that should be employed to obtain the population figures, and Darby himself points to the problems faced by anyone trying to make sense of Domesday Book: 'All we can say, with certainty, is that Ipswich, with its burgesses and its many churches, and its mint, must have been a substantial settlement in 1086 despite the misfortune that had fallen upon it since the conquest.'

The fee which the burgesses had to pay to the king was increased to £60 a year, no small sum in the 11th century. The moneyers who struck coins in the Ipswich mint had their payment increased from the £4 that they had paid before the Conquest to five times that sum. Perhaps it is not surprising, in view of the state of the town, that neither the burgesses nor the moneyers were able to pay all that was demanded of them.

There were further troubles in store for the people of Ipswich, for the Bigot family proved just as unruly as any of the barons. The Conqueror implanted a system in England that established his authority over his tenants-in-chief and ensured that for the most part their ambitions were held in check, but when Henry I, the Conqueror's youngest son, died in Normandy in 1135 civil war ensued between his daughter and heir Matilda and his nephew Stephen. During 18 years of almost continuous warfare many of the barons built their own castles without royal sanction, one of them apparently being erected at Ipswich by Hugh Bigod, son of Roger Bigot (the 't' became changed into a 'd' over the years); Roger had died in 1107. The Anglo-Saxon Chronicle tells how the barons 'filled the whole land with these castles. They sorely burdened the unhappy people of the country with forced labour on the castles. And when the castles were made they filled them with devils and wicked men.'

No doubt that applied to Ipswich men as much as to others, but so little is known of the story of Ipswich Castle that we have no details of its erection; there is a possibility that it could originally have been a royal castle, taken over by Hugh Bigod or by his father when he held Ipswich for the king. Whether it was built by Bigod or merely occupied by him, Ipswich castle was besieged by Stephen's army in 1153 and was captured. We can only surmise what effect the siege might have had on the town and its inhabitants, many of whom probably fled from their homes at the approach of the royal army. After losing Ipswich, Hugh Bigod built a new castle in 1154 in the former Roman fort at Walton, but had to surrender it in 1157 to Henry II, whose royal garrison withstood a four-day attack in 1173 when Bigod rose in rebellion with the Earl of Leicester. The rebels were soundly beaten at Fornham, close to Bury St Edmunds; Hugh's son Roger Bigod fought on the king's side, and later claimed to have carried St Edmund's standard in the battle.[14]

It has been claimed that the castle at Ipswich was torn down in 1176 on the orders of Henry II, along with that at Framlingham, but more likely it was destroyed almost immediately after being captured by Stephen's army. Unlike Framlingham, Ipswich Castle, whenever it was demolished, was never brought back into existence. So completely did the king's engineers dismantle the castle, almost certainly a wooden construction apart from the earthworks,[15] that today even its site is a matter of conjecture. John Kirby says in 1735 that the castle was 'so entirely demolished, that not the least Rubbish of it is to be found'. Some have claimed that it must have stood at Castle Hill, in the parish of Whitton, though the 'castle' referred to in that case is certainly the Roman villa remains and not a Norman fortification; Norman Scarfe suggests it must have been outside the town beside what is now the Henley Road.[16] Neither of these suggested sites seems to fulfil the main requirements of a fortification, that it should control the river crossing and the main entrance to the town, and that it should establish the owner's authority over the urban population. There is, however, a position within the town boundaries that satisfies all these criteria, and there is topographical evidence that this site on the western side of the town was once occupied by a castle. Let us examine that evidence.

The Saxon settlement was laid out on a grid pattern, with the streets aligned approximately north-south and east-west, and this pattern remained largely unchanged until Victorian times. There is one street, Elm Street, that does not fit into this pattern, however. It runs southward from the vicinity of the Cornhill but curves round to the west and runs past St Mary Elms Church, then bears north-west, crossing the town rampart close to where the Police Station now stands, and links rather awkwardly with Handford Road, or Handford Bridge Way as it used to be known. What could have been responsible for this diversion of the Saxon street running from near the Cornhill to Handford Bridge if it were not the earthworks of a small motte and bailey castle?[17] Further evidence for the existence of a castle in this area comes in the form of a name, the Mount, used until the mid-20th century for the area west of St Mary Elms Church; could this be a folk-memory of the remains of a Norman motte, the flattened remnants of a castle mound? Situated just to the west of the Cornhill, such a castle would have dominated the town and would have controlled the main entrance from Bury St Edmunds and Norwich at the Westgate or Barrgate. The main entrance to the bailey would have

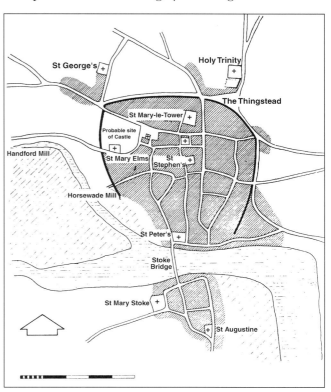

12   The early medieval town. By 1086 there were at least a dozen churches, several of them such as Holy Trinity and St George's outside the ramparts serving early suburbs. The Normans built a castle, almost certainly on the site bordered to the north by Westgate Street and to the south by a diverted Elm Street, but it had only a short existence and had been destroyed by the end of the 12th century.

been by Little King Street (now King Street); it is a coincidence that looking down King Street today one sees a Victorian arch which one can almost imagine as the castle gate.

As has been said, part of the purpose of a Norman castle was to hold the local population in subjugation, but gradually the burgesses began to gain some degree of local autonomy, even if the town courts were presided over by the king's reeve, the steward who looked after local affairs on the king's behalf. It would seem that Henry I, the Conqueror's third son, made changes in the organisation of the town courts, and Richard I, the second of the Plantagenet kings, gave certain privileges to the town. Quite what those privileges amounted to is obscure, but the changes made imply that there was already some form of local government within the town which was distinct from that of the Sheriff of the county.[18]

In spite of all the upheavals of the 12th century Ipswich seems to have remained a successful trading centre, with a mint which continued to turn out silver pennies until the reign of John. At the time of Henry II there were three moneyers working in the town, Nicolas, Robert and Turstain. Even their trade was affected by the troubles of the time, it would seem, for the last products of the mint display what can only be described as a highly stylised portrait of King John and are no more than a continuation of the coins of Henry II.

The Charter

It is perhaps one of those ironies of history that the mint ceased to funtion at just about the time that Ipswich gained a degree of independence from the Crown. In 1200 King John gave to the town a charter conferring on it the status and privileges of a free borough; the document was sealed on 25 May 1200 at Roche d'Orival in Normandy.[19]

> JOHN, by the Grace of God King of England, Lord of Ireland, Duke of Normandy, Aquitain, and Earl of Anjou ... Know Ye, that We have granted, and by this Our present Charter have confirmed, to the Burgesses of Ipswich, Our Borough of Ipswich, with all its Appurtenances and Liberties, and all its free Customs, to be holden of Us, and Our Heirs, to them and their Heirs, hereditarily; paying by the Year, the right and accustomed Farm, by the Hand of the Provost of Ipswich; and One hundred Shillings sterling, over and above what they used to pay at the said Term.[20]

Having established the price to be paid, the charter went on to enumerate the privileges the king granted to the burgesses. It gave them the right to choose their own officers, permitted them to associate in a gild merchant for carrying on trade in the town, and to hold their own courts in the borough. It also confirmed to the burgesses the free customs of the town, which implies a body of usages and obligations that had grown up over the years and were now to guide them in their new independent status. 'Heres much by confirming and little by granting,' comments Nathaniell Bacon, the 17th-century Recorder and Town Clerk who made a useful digest of the town's records; he took the view that the charter did little more than authorise what had been happening for some time past.[21] The great difference was that while before the burgesses might,

13   King John, who gave Ipswich its first charter in 1200. (John Wilton)

just possibly, have been electing the king's officials operating in the town they would henceforth be appointing not the king's but their own officers.

Already by the beginning of the 13th century, upwards of 40 English towns had corporate status, a large proportion of these having been granted a charter in the second half of the 12th century. Ipswich was, however, one of the first towns to be given the privilege of having two bailiffs elected by the inhabitants assembled in common council, and it was also among the first to be allowed a merchants' gild. Ipswich is fortunate indeed in having preserved an account of the way in which the charter was received and the manner in which the newly-independent body of townsmen set about organising the government of their town. Although the original document describing the reception of the charter and the election of the first bailiffs and coroners has long been lost, the text of it survives in a number of later copies.[22] On the Sunday next after the feast of the Nativity of St John the Baptist, 29 June, the townspeople gathered in the churchyard of St Mary-le-Tower (St Mary's, the church with the tower, as distinct from those other ecclesiastical buildings without such an appendage at that time). There they elected John Fitz-Norman and William de Belines to be the first bailiffs; they followed up by electing the same two men together with Philip de Porta and Roger Lew as the coroners to act within the borough. They also made the decision to elect 12 'capital portmen … as there are in other free boroughs of England'.

A panel of electors, four from each parish, was chosen for the next meeting on 2 July, when the 12 portmen were elected. We even know the names of this dozen, the body on which the future local government of the town was to be based: there were the two bailiffs and the coroners, and the other portmen were Peter Everard, William Gostalk, Amise Boll, John St George, John le Mayster, Sayer Fitz-Thurstan, Robert Parys and Andrew Peper.[23] The dozen portmen having been sworn in, it was the turn of the townsmen to take an oath of obedience to the bailiffs, coroners and portmen and to swear to uphold the honour, liberties and free customs of the town. It being impossible to administer the oath individually, a Bible was held aloft and the assembled populace all stretched their right hands towards it as they repeated the oath. It should have been a most moving occasion.

14   Last surviving traces of the rampart were still to be seen in the 1930s in Tower Ramparts, where these 19th-century houses were perched on top of the bank. Only the name remains today.

That was just the beginning. On 13 July the officers gathered to formulate the ordinances by which the town was to be governed, and these were read to the assembled townspeople and approved by them on 10 September. At that meeting the bailiffs were re-elected and new coroners chosen for the coming year. A month later at a further meeting in the churchyard an alderman of the Merchants' Gild was elected; it was agreed that he should be granted a monopoly of sales of stone in the town in return for his work. The capital portmen were given Oldenholm meadow on which to pasture their horses as recompense for their exertions; this meadow was later known as Portman Marsh.

At the meeting on 12 October it was ordained that the laws and free customs of the town should be copied on to a roll to be called *le Domesday*, and also that the statutes of the gild merchant should be copied on to another roll. These were to be the written rules and regulations for the ordering of the new organisation; *le Domesday* was to be kept by the bailiffs and the second roll by the alderman of the gild merchant for the guidance of these officers in their duties.

An early Town Clerk proved a broken reed. John le Blake was facing prosecution when he fled from the town and from justice in September 1272, taking with him out of the hutch or chest in which they were kept *le Domesday* and other town records; neither he nor the records was ever seen again, so far as we know. Possibly the reason Black John stole away the records was to remove the evidence of his crimes, but one of the rolls that he left behind provides testimony of his misdeeds, its final membrane bearing a note of his defalcation.[24]

Not surprisingly the loss of the rule-book caused dismay and not a little confusion, yet it was nearly 20 years before anything positive was done to make good the loss. That might well have been because in 1284-5 Edward I seized the town into his own hand on account of 'certain transgressions and offences to us donne by the Burgesses'; an official was appointed by the king to run the town courts and collect the £60 a year fee-farm on his behalf, though if Bacon is to be believed the bailiffs continued to operate under his supervision. However, in 1290 Edward I was engaged on one of his expeditions into Scotland and called on Ipswich to supply ships to carry troops to the north. The Ipswich seamen seem to have given such excellent service that the king was persuaded to restore the town's privileges.

15 *Another view of houses in Tower Ramparts built on top of the earthen bank. When this photograph was taken in the 1920s the rampart was obvious, but it was later flattened to provide space for a car park and then a bus station.*

16 *Steps leading up to the front door underline the fact that these houses in Old Foundry Road, or St Margaret's Ditches as the street was known earlier, are also built on top of the rampart.*

Having got back their self-government, the leading men of Ipswich decided it was time they remedied the loss of *le Domesday* and the other records purloined by Black John. As Nathaniell Bacon put it, 'The ancient laws and customs of this town being brought to an uncertainty by the loss of the Doomsday book forementioned … to the great dishonour of this town', it was ordered that the customs and constitution should be 'again brought into writing' by 24 of the better-advised men of the town. Among those 24 were men like Bailiffs Vivian fitzSilvester and John Clement, Thomas le Maister, and John and Richard Lew, whose families had

17   The West Gate in an engraving published in 1772, ten years before the structure was demolished. The date of its construction is not recorded, but in 1448 it was converted into a gaol by one of the bailiffs, John de Caldwell; it served in this capacity for many years. The one-handed clock was set above the gate about 1629, its maintenance being paid for by St Matthew's parish.

long taken a part in town affairs, and others such as Thomas Stacy, John and Philip Harneis, Thomas le Rent, John de Whatfield and Arnold le Peleter who were representative of the wealthy mercantile community that would increasingly dominate town government in the years to come.[25]

These men proceeded to compile a new *Domesday* roll; when finished it was sealed with the common seal of the town, which it is believed was made very soon after the granting of the charter in 1200. As befits a seaport, the seal bears a somewhat stylised medieval vessel, a cog, the kind of craft in which Ipswich merchants were sending wool to the continent and fetching Gascon wine from Bordeaux. It is of particular interest as being one of the earliest depictions of a ship with a rudder hung on pintles on the sternpost rather than the earlier steering oar on the quarter. The theft of the original *Domesday* and the other records by the defaulting common clerk startled the town's leading citizens and, as Prof. Geoffrey Martin puts it, 'directed the attention of the burgesses to their remaining records'.[26] It is likely that the delinquency of the common clerk was responsible not so much for the loss of the early records as for the survival of the town's later medieval archives. The *Domesday* was again copied in the very early 14th century, and it might well have been the memory of what had happened in 1272

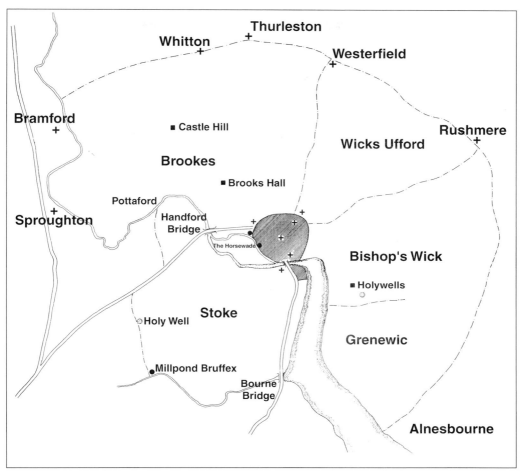

18   The Domesday holdings. The medieval hamlets of Ipswich reflect the division of holdings outside the town centre as described in Domesday Book. On this map can be seen Grenewic or Greenwich, the Bishop's Wick (probably the pre-Conquest Queen Edith's holding), the Earl's Wick or Wicks Ufford, and Brooks, with the suburb of Stoke, held by Ely Abbey, across the river.

that persuaded the burgesses to duplicate their customs in what would prove to be a more durable form. This copy became known as the *Little Domesday*.

There is evidence from the record of town officers in the 13th century of the way in which the growing town was attracting men from the surrounding countryside and from further afield, men who became influential and sometimes powerful in local affairs. From within Suffolk and north Essex came Robert de Orford, Gilbert de Burgh, John de Langham, John de Preston and John Horkslee (Great and Little Horkesley, north of Colchester), and from Norfolk came Edward de Castleacre and Thurstan de Clay. From Flanders, perhaps, came John de Irpe, whose name might have been a corruption of de Ypres; a William de Ipre was in 1345 granted property adjacent to the

19 The excavation of a cellared building of the 11th or 12th century in St Stephen's Lane. (Copyright Suffolk County Council)

20 These carbonised bread rolls were found in an 11th- or 12th-century building on the Buttermarket site that had been burnt down. Whether this was evidence of Danish 'harrying', William's revenge for the Ralph Wader rebellion, or the result of an accidental fire is not known. (Copyright Suffolk County Council)

town rampart next to 'le Shirehouse'. One is puzzled by the appellation of Thomas de Petra, otherwise known as Thomas del Stoon, who was several times bailiff; Petra is latin for stone, but which Stone did he come from? There are places of this name in Buckinghamshire, Gloucestershire, Kent, Staffordshire and Worcestershire.

Some of the leading citizens such as Vivian fitzSilvester, who was bailiff 10 times between 1270 and 1290, were clearly willing to play their part in town affairs to the full and to serve as bailiff and coroner on a number of occasions. Others, however, seem to have had more than the public interest in mind when they took office, and one suspects that some of the 13th and 14th-century local politicians were, like the dictators of a later age, concerned primarily with wielding power and improving their private fortunes. One notices particularly Thomas Stacy, who became bailiff in 1295 and held that position with various partner-bailiffs until 1300, and was again in power from 1303 to 1305 and 1307 to 1313. He was also bailiff in 1314, 1316 and 1318-20, a total of 16 years in office. From 1296 to 1298, from 1303 to 1305, from 1307 to 1312 and from 1318 to 1320 his partner was one Thomas le Rent, who was also bailiff in 1313 with Richard Lew. An extraordinary record, unparalleled in the history of Ipswich and highly suggestive of what would today be referred to as a local mafia.

Thanks to the researches in both national and local records of Stephen Alsford we have a fairly clear picture of the career of Thomas le Rent, or de la Rent as he is called by Bacon.[27] Thomas and his father John first appear in the records in 1281, and John le Rente is listed in the lay subsidy of 1283 among the more prominent townsmen who lent the king 100 marks, but John, unlike his son, seems to have taken no part in local affairs. There are indications that both were boatowners, possibly taking part in the local herring fishery. In 1305 Thomas had a ship in which he brought a cargo from St Valery. The character that emerges from Stephen Alsford's account is not a pleasant one, for Thomas le Rent was one of those people who made a career of insolvency and when sued for debt made use of legal trickery to delay repayment. He was adept at avoiding his own appearance in court for as long as possible, and appears to have prospered at others' expense.

Thomas built up a web of contacts with other members of the Ipswich business community. His neighbour and a business partner was the Thomas del Stoon already mentioned, while his son John married Nichola, daughter of John de Whatfield, who according to the 1327 subsidy roll, listing those liable to the king's tax, was then the wealthiest of Ipswich burgesses. Thomas's daughter Isabelle married Richard, the son of another neighbour, Gilbert Roberd. Thomas, John de Whatfield, Gilbert Roberd and Thomas Stacy were participants in a partnership which took a ten-year lease from the town of Horswade mill in 1312. It is not difficult to see how such a network of business and family ties could prove of mutual benefit to members of a clique of this kind. Nor is it possible to avoid the suspicion of manipulation when one finds not only that other members of the clique occupy the post of bailiff in those few years that Stacy and le Rent were out of office but that other offices such as that of coroner were also in the hands of the same circle of associates. According to the archives no burgesses were admitted between 1308 and 1321, which seems extremely odd; one can only surmise that burgesses were being admitted privately by the bailiffs, not in open court, and that their names were never recorded.

After a quarter-century of misrule it was natural that an opposition should appear, perhaps as a result of a disputed election. In 1320 Thomas le Rent and his sons John and Richard, Thomas Stacy and four of his sons, Thomas le Rent's son-in-law Richard Roberd, and 11 others had to seek royal letters of protection, and two of their group, John Irp and Alexander Margaret, were summoned to answer unspecified crimes against the community. On 12 December that same year a set of ordinances was issued prohibiting certain prevalent market offences and seeking to remedy abuses of power by the bailiffs, who were accused of extorting fees to which they were not entitled, of misusing the town seal and of imposing inordinate taxation; they were also alleged to have put money raised by the taxes to personal use. The bailiffs were also accused of creating new burgesses without common consent, and, most telling of all, it was alleged that the bailiffs were being maintained in power by a group of burgesses who held private elections.

To put matters right it was ordered that 'from hence forthe the Bayliffs of this town shall allwaies be elected upon ye day of the Nativity of the Virgine Mary' at a public meeting. Additionally the community was empowered to depose bailiffs during their term of office in case of misbehaviour. To prevent further misuse of the common seal

21   The site of the North Gate. It is said that the remains of the gate are incorporated into the cellars of the Halberd Inn, *which stands on the corner of Northgate Street and Tower Ramparts.*

and to avoid embezzlement of the town's money it was agreed to appoint clavigers who should hold the keys of the town chest in which the seal and the treasury were placed, and chamberlains who should supervise the borough finances and generally monitor the behaviour of the bailiffs.

Stacy and le Rent resisted the reforms, but the latter was hampered at this crucial time by a case in which he was impleaded for debt; employing his usual tactics, he stayed away from court for more than six months, his absence by no means helping his cause. In spite of their efforts to attract royal support Stacy and le Rent were deposed in 1321. There was worse to come for le Rent. He had been in the customs service for 16 years, and in 1321 was prosecuted for misdeeds while collector of customs and heavily fined. He died deeply in debt in 1323.

It would be satisfying to believe that there was an end to such abuses as this manipulative clique had been guilty of, but Stephen Alsford remarks that none profited more from the transfer of power than the reformers' leaders, John de Preston, John de Halteby and Geoffrey Costyn, to the extent that old abuses found new life in them. Preston held the offices of chamberlain, coroner and bailiff in succession in the years 1322-5, was again bailiff in 1336, and then was bailiff for four years from 1341 to 1345 and coroner from 1344 right through to 1356-7, sometimes holding both offices in tandem. He also represented the town in Parliament 10 times. Halteby was never bailiff, but he was nevertheless extremely active in local affairs, making himself generally unpopular. His murder in 1344 was greeted with popular approval; in 1338 Costyn, too, met a violent end, slain in a quarrel by Roger the son of John Bande as they walked home from a tavern one Sunday night.

Three years after obtaining the charter the town reconstructed the town rampart and ditch on the line of the Danish-period ditch, and in 1299 a grant of murage was obtained from the Crown entitling the town authorities to raise money for the further repair of the defences. So it was that in 1302 it is recorded that 'a parcell of the Town Ditches [was] granted to Robert Joyliffe, at the yearly rent of sixpence for ever, unless it comes to pass that the town shall be enclosed with a stone wall'. In 1352 a licence was indeed obtained to strengthen the town with a stone wall, but while excavation evidence suggests a foundation trench might have been dug for this wall it was never built, though town gates were certainly erected at points where important roads entered the circuit of the ramparts, the last of them surviving until the 18th century. It is true that there are references in the town archives to 'walls', but an order of 1604 makes it clear that the word is being used to describe the earthen bank and not a stone wall.

The Medieval Port and its Trade

Very little is known about the waterfront area of Ipswich in the Middle Ages, although recent archaeological work has shed some light on the port of that period. When the Anglo-Saxons were laying down the street pattern of the new town the road that is now College Street, Quay Street and Salthouse Street would have run alongside the river bank, much as the Shotley road does at Wherstead Strand. One can compare The Strand in London, which received its name from the time when it was alongside the Thames. In medieval times, however, the river was pushed back by the construction of successive timber quays enabling ships to be brought alongside at high water; possibly material was also laid down to form a safe berth for a vessel to lie on as the tide ebbed.[28] In the absence of reliable archaeological evidence we cannot suggest the actual shoreline at different dates, but it is to be expected that the medieval quays would have been some feet inland of the present quay, constructed as part of the Wet Dock project of the 1830s. We do know that the shoreline was broken up by a number of inlets; until the carrying out of the dock project there was one more or less where Foundry Lane now runs. Some at least of these inlets could have been used for unloading small craft into warehouses running back from the river.

There is a possibility that some of these inlets might have been the sites of early shipyards, for shipbuilding was being carried on in the town from a very early period. When in 1294 Edward I ordered that 26 towns on the east and south coasts should share in providing a score of galleys for the French war, Ipswich was one of the towns chosen to build a galley and the barge which was to be its tender. The Corporation records include the accounts for this shipbuilding operation, rendered to the Exchequer by John de Causton and John Lew, the bailiffs, in 1295; this is the earliest record of shipbuilding on the Orwell. The total cost of building the galley was £195 4s. 11½d. and of the barge £23 7s. ½d. A detailed account includes items for 'timber bought from various sources for building the galley £19 9s. 6d. and in felling the said timber and transporting it by land and water from various places with ropes bought for dragging the said timber £6 14s. 9d.; and for 1,097 planks, 32 pieces of timber to be sawn into planks and various items for the said galley with carriage of the same £29 4s. 6d.; and for 9,300 of iron[29] bought for the said galley with the wages of smiths working the said iron £24 4s. ½d.; and for 13,000 nails bought for the said galley 52. 6d.'[30] Needless to say, an attempt to add up the costs of the individual items does not produce the answer given at the foot of the account.

This was clearly a sizeable vessel with a mast and sail that together cost £8 7s. 4d.; once the timber and all the other materials had been assembled the building of the vessel occupied some five months. The barge was a much smaller vessel requiring only 30 oars compared with the 100 bought for the galley, but it was still much more than a mere ship's boat. On completion the galley was taken down the Orwell and out of Harwich harbour for its sea trials. Unfortunately the trials were interrupted by a storm in which the vessel was quite badly damaged; it was, say the accounts, 'torn apart and broken by the fury of the sea'. An additional £5 6s. 6d. had to be expended on repairs which occupied seven men for eight days. It has been suggested that the damage was the result of bad workmanship by the shipwrights employed, but this cannot be so as the Exchequer accepted the cost of repair as well as the costs of building; there is ample evidence in medieval records that where bad workmanship had to be made good the Exchequer made certain that it was done at the expense of those responsible and not at the king's.

In some of the towns chosen for the building of the royal galleys there were problems in enrolling a skilled workforce and it was found necessary to bring together teams from different parts of the country and even abroad; at Southampton a master builder of Bayonne was fetched from Portsmouth to supervise the design of the galley.[31] There is no mention in the Ipswich accounts of any such difficulties, nor is there any mention of having to rent the land on which the vessels were laid down and of enclosing the building site with an enclosure of hurdles and thorns, as at Southampton. One is led to consider the possibility that at the end of the 13th century Ipswich was a shipbuilding centre capable of taking a contract such as this in its stride.

The galleys were the only purpose-built warships in an age when it was normal for the monarch to take over merchant ships in time of hostilities either as transports to carry the army to the scene of conflict or for conversion to fighting ships. Ipswich was called upon on many occasions to supply ships for royal service in both capacities, and when English kings were endeavouring to uphold their continental claims the town was a supply base for the armies in France.

The position of Harwich at the entrance to the Orwell and the Stour was certain to lead to problems for the traders of Ipswich, particularly as the Essex town was in the hands of that powerful magnate Roger Bigod, Earl of Norfolk and Earl Marshal. In 1274 there were complaints that Roger Bigod had been interfering seriously with the trade of Ipswich; he not only held Harwich but was also in charge of Orford. 'That the Earl Marshall, late deceased, made purpresture upon the water of the King in the Port of Orwell, which is a port of the king and common to all persons for buying and selling, extending from the sea as far as the town of Ipswich. And neither the said Earl nor his men of Oreford allow the merchants, who wish, to put in at the town of Ipswich with their merchandise, but against their will he compels them by force to put in at Herewiz, which is a town of the said Earl's, taking their sails, anchors, and steering gear and drawing their ships to dry land, taking their merchandise at will, and they pay what pleases them for the said merchandise, whereby the town of Ipswich is much depreciated.'[32]

IV

The Later Medieval Port and Town

The port of Orwell, not a town but the anchorage in the river below Ipswich, was a vital base used by the infant navy as well as by merchant vessels trading with the continent throughout the Middle Ages, and it was a stretch of tidal water that Ipswich was determined to control. Whenever the king wished to gather a fleet on the east coast it was to Orwell that ships were directed from ports between London and the Humber; when in 1336 Flanders took offensive action against English mercantile interests and it became necessary to organise two convoys to protect ships trading to and from Gascony, one of them was ordered to make rendezvous at Orwell.

Queen Isabella, the estranged wife of Edward II, and her lover Roger Mortimer landed on the Suffolk coast on 24 September 1326 with an army of at least 1,500 men, of whom about half were mercenaries from Hainault, and began the campaign that resulted in her son Edward of Windsor being crowned as Edward III. The intention had been to land in the Orwell, but the landfall was made further north; preparations had been made to defend the Orwell with 12 ships from Ipswich and Harwich. The new king was no stranger to this part of Suffolk, which gained an enhanced importance with the beginning of the Hundred Years War. In 1338 and 1339 Edward III spent a considerable time at Walton Manor assembling his fleet in the rivers Deben and Orwell for the attack on France. Walton Manor was a handy base from which to plan and carry out such an operation, for on one side was the Orwell anchorage and on the other the port of Goseford, centred on the 'Goose-ford' across the King's Fleet, a creek off the Deben, which provided a link between Walton Castle and Falkenham and Kirton.

It was while Edward was at Walton that he mistakenly granted jurisdiction over the haven to the town of Harwich, provoking an immediate appeal by the burgesses of Ipswich, who pointed out to him that 'the whole Haven of Erewell in the arme of the sea there to the said Towne of Ipswich dothe belong, and from all times passed hathe belonged'.[1] If not the beginning, it was the continuation of a rivalry between the two towns that soured relations between them for centuries. In an attempt to convince the king of his error, the burgesses of Ipswich averred that because of the interference of the Harwich men they were prevented from raising the fee farm, the sum of money that they paid to the Crown each year. Edward consulted his advisers. From Walton on 11 July 1338 notification was issued

> that the king has revoked his late grant to the bailiffs and men of Herewicz of a murage
> for four years at the said town and the port of Orewell as pertaining to the town, at the
> prosecution of the burgesses of Ipswich setting forth that the whole port of Orewell
> ought to belong, and has belonged in the past, to the town, and that none but their

bailiffs and ministers ought to make distraints or attachments or levy toll or other custom there.[2]

After celebrating Pentecost at Ipswich, Edward sailed from the haven of Orwell for Flanders with 260 ships on Thursday, 22 June 1340. Two days later he gained a notable victory over the French fleet at Battle of Sluys, near the mouth of the Wester Schelde.

Nearer home the disputes between Ipswich and Harwich rumbled on. In 1379 Ipswich petitioned Richard II that they might have the haven to Poll Head, a point to seaward of Landguard Point 'wch they have time out of memory belonging to them', officially and clearly assigned to the town. The 13-year-old king gave directions for an inquiry to be held, and at an inquest held at Shotley on 3 November 1379 a dozen witnesses declared under oath that the port of Ipswich extended downriver to the Poll Head, 'and soe hathe donne time out of minde, and remaineth soe …'[3]

The town of Ipswich had gained jurisdiction over this muddy river initially as the result of King John's charter. Succeeding monarchs confirmed the charter and extended the privileges enjoyed by the citizens, Henry VIII more particularly stressing the maritime nature of the town by specifically confirming the Corporation's jurisdiction over the Orwell. He granted the Corporation admiralty jurisdiction: 'That the Bailives of the said Town, for the Time Being, shall be Our Admirals, and the Admirals of Our Heirs, for and within the whole Town, Precincts, Suburbs, Water, and Course of Water.'[4]

22   *The later medieval and Tudor town. The main feature of the later medieval Ipswich is the number and size of the religious houses and the appearance of further extra-mural parish churches such as St Helen's, St Clement's and St Matthew's. In spite of the growth of new suburbs the ditch and rampart were reconstructed in 1203, soon after the granting of the town's charter; the purpose might have been as much to regulate trade as to form a military defence.*

Death and Rebellion

In the middle of the 14th century the Black Death killed so many people that there was a serious shortage of labourers throughout the country, leading to government attempts to control wages through the Statute of Labourers. Opposition to this measure as well as the imposition of poll taxes, together with a desire to break the hold of manorial lords over their villein tenants, created the Peasants' Revolt of 1381.

The leaders of the revolt were men of some substance. In Ipswich the rebellion was proclaimed by Thomas Sampson, a well-to-do yeoman of Harkstead and Kersey, who was supported by Richard Tollemache of Bentley and John

Battisford, the parson of Bucklesham. The rebels ransacked the houses of John Cobat, a burgess and the town's representative in Parliament in 1377, who had collected the first instalment of the poll tax, and John Gerard, another burgess and MP in 1377, who was a wealthy parishioner of St Lawrence's. They murdered William Fraunceys, who might have been an official of St Etheldreda's liberty, and attacked the archdeacon's house, although the archdeacon was the non-resident Cardinal of St Angelo. They also robbed the rectory of John, the parson of St Stephen's, because he supported the hated chief justice, Sir John Cavendish, who himself met his death in West Suffolk. The Earl of Suffolk, who was soon involved in putting down the revolt, had his house at Hollesley attacked; the court rolls of his manors, including Wicks Ufford in Ipswich, were burned, the burning of court rolls being a widely used method of resisting manorial control.

Such insurrections had little lasting effect on the trade of Ipswich, which continued to flow to and from the town quays. These lay downstream of Stoke Bridge; they were not one continuous quay as today but a series of mainly private quays hidden behind and between buildings, some of which came right to the water's edge. With the exception of the Common Quay, on which was built the 16th-century timber-framed Custom House, all these quays were the private property of various merchants and businessmen. The size of ships that could reach these quays was limited by the depth of the Orwell and by the windings of the channel, though at a period when vessels sailing to foreign parts as well as coastwise were very small this proved no serious handicap to trade.

At a time when English armies were fighting in France in support of the claims of Henry VI to be King of France as well as of England and the Maid of Orleans was leading French resistance, maritime trade was subject to interruption by more than bad weather. There was, for instance, the experience of Matys Mathuesson and John Cotoroke from Brabant, whose ship called the *Cogship* was freighted by Rumbald Herryesson, an Ipswich burgess, with cheese and other victuals for transport from the port of Orwell to the port of Calais, then in English hands. On the way they and their ship were captured by three ships from Dieppe and Harfleur; for five hours they sailed towards the ports of Picardy, and then a Sandwich ship appeared on the scene, 'when in a manner set forth in the now much defaced certificate the deponents regained possession of their ship the *Cogship* and her freight' and sailed into Sandwich.[5] If only we had the stirring story set down in that much-defaced document!

Among the Corporation records is a document under the king's privy seal in which the bailiffs and townspeople of Ipswich agree to take sureties from the owner, master or purser of every English ship in port to ensure that the ship's crew 'keep the peace towards all the King's subjects and allies, and all others having the king's safe-conduct; And to do their endeavour to arrest every robber or spoiler … as soon as a knowledge of the spoil or robbery shall come to them …'. The word piracy is not used, but there is little doubt what was in the minds of those who drew up that document.[6] Such 'spoil or robbery' was by no means confined to the high seas, for in 1399 an inquiry was held into the alleged seizure of a vessel belonging to William Fuller, of Nacton, together with a priest, Dominus Johannes Brygge, in Harwich Harbour. The assailants, 'having boarded it by force of arms removed from it the said priest, with a boy and other things, viz a fardel packed with fourteen pieces of cloth worth thirty marks' and took from the priest two purses containing money.[7]

The 15th century was a time of discontent and strife. The struggle between the houses of York and Lancaster, each with a rose as its badge, brought in its wake a breakdown of law and order, while the continuing wars on the continent brought little or no success for the English. It was all too easy for the ordinary people to link the parlous state of affairs abroad with the breakdown of government at home, and to blame prominent personalities for both, however unjust this might in fact have been. One who suffered great unpopularity was William de la Pole, 1st Duke of Suffolk, who had in 1445 stood proxy for Henry VI at the king's marriage with Margaret of Anjou. It was from Ipswich that de la Pole sailed in 1450 after Henry VI had banished him not only from England but from all his dominions for five years.[8] The duke had spent six weeks at Wingfield or elsewhere in Suffolk while arrangements were made for ships to be made ready to carry him and his servants overseas; towards the end of April he moved to Ipswich, where on 30 April he took the sacrament and, watched by some of the leading county gentry, swore on the sacrament that he was innocent of treason.[9] Later that same day he and his retinue left Ipswich in two ships and a pinnace.

When the little fleet reached the Straits of Dover it was intercepted by an English vessel, the *Nicholas of the Tower*, whose master sent a boat across with orders that Suffolk must come and speak to the captain. The duke must have known the game was up as soon as he stepped aboard and was greeted by the master with the words 'Welcome, traitor!' He had a 'safe conduct' from the king, but it proved of no use to him; the seamen on the *Nicholas of the Tower* simply tore it up. Next day he was transferred to a small boat and executed by one of the seamen, who hacked his head off on the gunwale with a rusty sword.[10]

Was it by chance that the *Nicholas of the Tower*, a Bristol ship that seems to have been engaged in privateering and semi-piratical activities in the Channel, came on de la Pole's little fleet, and was the murder of the duke simply the act of a disgruntled ship's crew whose hatred for the 'traitor' was such that they scorned the king's 'safe conduct'? Or was the interception planned by some of the Duke of Suffolk's enemies and carried out on their orders? We shall probably never know, but it could be relevant that in February 1453 a number of the followers of the Duke of York and John Howard, Duke of Norfolk, were indicted before a grand jury of the county of Suffolk accused of plotting to raise a rebellion, conspiring to put the Duke of York on the throne, and planning the murder of the Duke of Suffolk.[11] The conspiracy was alleged to have taken place at Bury, where the conspirators would be in a position to keep a close watch on de la Pole's movements. The information the conspirators gathered could have enabled the *Nicholas of the Tower* to be in just the right place, at just the right time.

The Trade of the Port

Over the years there was controversy over whether or not ownership of a quay gave a man the right to import goods without paying the normal customs duties. An order was made in 1539 that 'all strangers comming by water to the Common Kay shall unlade theire Merchandise uppon the Common Kay, paying the Tolls and Customes of the Towne and King, according to the Table in ye Kay house. And noe person shall unlaide at any other Kay unless the Toll and Custome shall first be payde'.[12] The 'Kay house' was the Custom House already referred to. The first mention of a crane on the Common Quay seems to be in 1477, when the town spent money on a new crane.[13] Orders were given in 1618 for the erection of 'a new crane and cranehouse',[14] which certainly suggests that the crane erected in 1727 when John Sparrowe and John Cornelius were bailiffs was by no means the first; that survived until the construction of the Wet Dock.

The career of Richard Felaw, eight times bailiff and twice the town's representative in Parliament, illustrates the extent to which Ipswich was involved in 15th-century maritime and naval affairs. The Patent Rolls reveal his activities on behalf of the Crown during the reign of Edward IV, who came to the throne in 1461 after defeating the Lancastrian forces at Mortimer's Cross and Towton. Felaw and three other men were in 1461 appointed to provide wheat, malt, mutton, fish, salt and other things required for victualling the king's ships, and in June of that year he was among the commissioners raising a fleet for use by the king against his French and Scottish enemies; they had to provide six ships with 700 men-at-arms and archers. Three years later Felaw was one of the men appointed to assist the Duke of Norfolk in an inquiry into Lancastrian activities in East Anglia.

At a time when England was divided by the struggle between the houses of York and Lancaster there can be no doubt of where Felaw's sympathies lay; he was a Yorkist. He acted as local agent for Sir John Howard, of Stoke-by-Nayland, who served as vice-admiral for Norfolk and Suffolk and was involved in 'furnishing forth ships for the wars' following the outbreak of war with France in 1468. Sir John became Duke of Norfolk and Earl Marshal of England in 1483, and died with Richard III on Bosworth field. It is possible that Felaw took care of Sir John's son Thomas when he attended the grammar school at Ipswich, that same school to which Felaw left his house in St Edmund Pountney Lane (now Foundation Street) on his death in 1482-3. The Howard accounts for 1462-9, which were published in 1841, throw considerable light on Felaw's work with Sir John, who in 1463 visited 'Richard Felawys howse' and in 1466 'did recken with Herman berebrewer of Yipswyche' at Felaw's home. The accounts also describe Felaw's lading of the *Mary Talbot* of Lynn, carried out on Sir John's instructions; among other things he supplied corn, hides, tallow, iron, salt and that staple Ipswich product, beer.

While a Member of Parliament in 1449, Felaw served on a commission of inquiry into the evasion of customs duties, and about 1458 he became Comptroller of Customs and Subsidies for the port, his task being to keep an account of the customs duties paid by vessels entering and leaving the Orwell. Not surprisingly, efforts were made from time to time to avoid the tolls and customs. In 1438 the bailiffs heard a case at the

Wardmote court concerning a cargo of wool and woolskins landed by a vessel from the Low Countries at the quay of John Cadon of Ipswich. The cargo was put into a warehouse belonging to Thomas Cadon, but some time later 'on the night of Saturday next after the feast of St Mark the Evangelist' (26 April) William Horald and Thomas Ingram took the cargo from the warehouse and loaded it into Ingram's boat. In spite of the intervention of one of the serjeants-at-mace the two men, with John Cadon's consent, spirited the boat and its cargo away to Woolverstone, 'with intent to defraud the king of customs pertaining to him'.[15]

Even when the customs were paid the king did not always receive the money. In 1401 Thomas Godeston, John Arnald and John Bernard, the collectors and controller of customs at Ipswich, were charged with frauds upon the customs.[16] Geoffrey Martin has described the elaborate organisation that existed by the beginning of Henry IV's reign (1399-1413) for the collection of the king's customs. At the centre of this organisation was the Exchequer at Westminster, where a permanent staff supervised the work and audited the accounts of an army of part-time officials in the principal ports. In each of the chief ports were two collectors who kept a joint account, and a controller, who kept a separate account, of each ship, the name of its master and the date of sailing, together with the amounts of cargo shipped and the sums paid for customs and subsidies. The controller's task was to verify the accounts of the two collectors, but to ensure honesty—or at least to detect fraud—there was a somewhat elaborate system of checking the documents.

So far as the wool trade was concerned, all shipments of wool from England had to be handled at a single mart, the staple. This arrangement ensured that the king could control the trade, not only for purposes of collecting revenue but also to enable him to use the trade as a means of bargaining with the Flemings. Martin has a list of 45 sailings between December 1399 and September 1402 between the port of Orwell and Calais, where the staple then was. It will be remembered that Geoffrey Chaucer's merchant was anxious that the sea 'were kept for anything Betwixte Middelburgh and Orwelle'. Ships sometimes loaded at the downriver moorings, perhaps because they could not move from the quays on neap tides when fully laden. An account of the expenses incurred in handling the king's wool in 1337-8, when the government attempted to manage the entire trade for its own profit, details the money spent in carrying the wool by small boat from Ipswich downriver 'to the port of Orwell'.

Martin's research on the customs documents suggests that in favourable conditions vessels could sail the 70-odd nautical miles (82 statute miles) from the Orwell to Calais in as little as 24 hours, as when the *Goodeyere* and the *Trinite* cleared customs at Ipswich on 10 December 1399 and apparently arrived at Calais on the 12th. On the other hand, the *Cokjohn*, *le Peter*, the *Godeffrend*, the *Seintmariship* and another vessel that cleared customs on 31 January 1400 all took between a week and ten days to make the passage; they were probably overtaken by bad weather and foul winds and spent much of that time swinging at their anchors in the Colne or in some other sheltered anchorage.

Churches and Religion in the Middle Ages

The parish churches of medieval Ipswich stood firmly at the centre of the local communities; not only was attendance at services obligatory for parishioners but when times were bad handouts to the poorer members of the community were doled out from the churches and so were not available to those who failed to turn up for services. Much local administration was carried out on a parochial basis, and it was important to know in which parish a person lived, hence the ceremony of perambulating the bounds so that everyone knew just where the parish boundaries were.

The Archdeacon of Suffolk was the local representative of the Bishop of Norwich. In 1471 William Pykenham became Archdeacon of Suffolk and the following year became also Dean and Rector of Hadleigh, where he built the brick Deanery tower. In Ipswich he added a substantial gatehouse at the entrance to his house in Northgate Street. That house was rented from Holy Trinity Priory at 2s.6d. in a 13th-century rental of the priory, and the town records include the grant by the town in 1487 at a yearly rent of two pence to Master William Pakenham, Archdeacon of Suffolk, of a piece of the common soil in Ipswich adjoining the tenement of the said archdeacon.[17] Perhaps this was the land fronting the street on which he built the gatehouse that still stands; one carved spandrel appears to show a pike and a boar, a pun on his name (pike and ham). The bishop himself had a residence in his hamlet of Wicks Bishop, the site of which is almost certainly marked by the large moated enclosure in Holywells Park, close to the Holy Well and to Bishops Hill. He lived there when his duties brought him into Suffolk. The first official record of the hamlet of Wicks Bishop, in the Latin form Wicks Episcopi, being held by the Bishop of Norwich is a grant by Richard I (1189–99), but this might be merely a confirmation or restoration of an older ownership of this wick. It remained in the ownership of the bishops of Norwich until they were deprived of it by Henry VIII.

The church of St Mary-le-Tower enjoyed a certain pre-eminence as the civic church attended by the town officials; that it enjoyed this position from an early period is shown by the meetings held in 1200 in the churchyard and in the church to receive the charter and to put its provisions

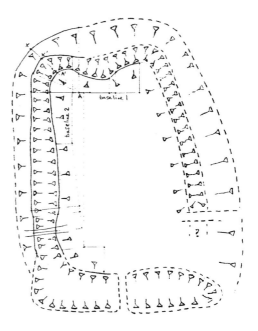

23   *A plan of the moat in Holywells Park which is though to be the site of the palace of the Bishop of Norwich. Inside the ditch the platform measures approximately 54m by 106m and the width of the moat varies between 16m and 23m. The depth of the moat is at least 3m. (Jennifer Scott)*

24   *The civic church of St Mary-le-Tower as it was before the 19th-century rebuilding by R.M. Phipson. The medieval tower was surmounted by a spire until it blew down in a gale on 18 February 1661, crashing through the nave roof and doing considerable damage. The spire was not replaced until the Victorian 'restoration'.*

25   *The interior of the medieval church of St Mary-le-Tower, seen in a 19th-century lithograph. The pulpit, made about 1700 by cabinet maker Edward Hubbard, with its massive tester is on the south side of the nave with the 17th-century bailiffs' seat opposite surmounted by 'a lofty square canopy, supported on four twisted pillars'. When the Corporation attended church the two maces were 'supported in a reclining position, upon each of the two front pillars'. When the church was rebuilt between 1850 and 1870 the tester was bought by the Diocesan Registrar, who turned it upside down and used it as a hall table. (John Fairclough)*

into effect. St Mary-le-Tower is presumably a medieval rebuilding of the St Mary's listed in Domesday Book as having 26 acres, the other St Mary's with 12 acres probably being St Mary Elms. Also appearing in Domesday Book are Holy Trinity, also with 26 acres, which was most likely where Christchurch Mansion now stands; St Augustine (11 acres) on the south side of the river, perhaps with its parish downstream of Stoke Bridge and surrounded to the west and south by the neighbouring parish of St Mary Stoke; St Michael, whose site is unknown; St Laurence (12 acres); St Stephen (1 acre); St Peter (6 carucates, that is 720 'acres'), presumably the St Peter's by Stoke Bridge; another St Peter (1 acre), whose site is unknown; St George (1 acre) in St George's or Globe Street; St Julian (20 acres), whose site is unknown; and a church in St Etheldreda's holding in Stoke (with 40 acres), presumably St Mary Stoke. Outside the town and beyond the boundary of the half-hundred at the time of Domesday is St Botolph in Thurleston (1 acre).

This list is apparently incomplete as it does not include St Mildred, which is almost certainly pre-Conquest. One of the three churches whose sites are not known might have been the church of Osterbolt which stood roughly between Fore Street and Shire Hall Yard. It survived into the 14th century, but is now lost without trace. Another early church missing from Domesday is All Saints, which John Kirby suggests might have stood on the triangular site at the junction of what are now Handford Road and London Road, close to Handford Bridge.[18] By 1383 All Saints had been linked to St Matthew's. John Wodderspoon refers to 'a chapel to

26   St Margaret's Church in 1865, before the upper stages of the tower were raised and given the distinctive double window openings and flushwork decoration. The parapet of the nave clerestory bears visual evidence of the families who paid for the 15th-century clerestory and hammerbeam roof.

the honour of All Saints, a small curacy in the town ruined and unproductive in 1535 according to the Liber Regis, but still annexed to St Matthew'.[19]

A group of carved stones incorporated into the fabric of St Nicholas' Church in the 14th or 15th century might have come from All Saints. These stones, which include the semi-circular tympanum in Barnack stone from the head of a Romanesque door, have been dated to about 1120.[20] The tympanum bears a carving of a boar with an inscribed Latin dedication of the church to All Saints, 'In dedicatione eclesie omnium sanctorum', and on the other side is a consecration cross; it presumably came from the entrance to All Saints' Church. A panel of Caen stone is carved with a winged figure of St Michael fighting a dragon, together with an inscription in Old English, 'Her sanctus Michael feht wid dane draca'. St Michael is sometimes shown separating saints and sinners at the final judgement, as in the painted 'Doom' at Wenhaston, so he might be appropriate in a church dedicated to all the saints; alternatively this stone might have come from the disused church of St Michael.[21]

The existing parish churches date very largely from the Middle Ages, although St Mary Elms incorporates a Norman arch which might have come from the earlier church of St Saviour. Evidence of the Domesday churches might lie beneath the present buildings, but there is little to be seen above ground or in the fabric of the existing churches.

One of the town's finest churches is St Margaret's, built on the medieval town's northern outskirts in the 13th century as the growing population spilled outside the line of the ramparts. Two hundred years later a magnificent double hammerbeam roof was added. In the carved woodwork of the roof, and in the stonework of the clerestory parapet outside, appears the merchant's mark of one of the town's prominent tradesmen, together with a series of initials which together provide clues to the benefactors who paid for the work in the 1490s. The initials are IH (or JH), KH and WH. John Hall, woodyer (dyer), was three times bailiff, as was his son William in his turn. John died in 1503 and his wife Katherine in 1506. The work was undoubtedly carried out in their lifetime, ensuring that John and Katherine were accorded burial in the most privileged place in the church, 'in front of the crucifix', as requested in John Hall's will.

27   The mark of Henry Tilemaker carved in a roof brace of St Margaret's Church. It is formed by the first and last letters of his name. (Dr. J. Blatchly)

28   The mark of John Hall, the dyer, also to be found in the roof of St Margaret's. This most appropriate mark consists of a dyer's posser, a form of 'dolly' for agitating the cloth in the vat, and a pair of tongs for handling the cloth. (Dr. J. Blatchly)

The Halls were not the only people involved. In the carving of one of the bays appear the initials H and I T/R, who must be Henry and Isabel Tilemaker, a middle-class couple who lived in the parish. Henry's will is dated 1445 and Isabel's was made in 1460. They were both buried in the churchyard, and their gifts to the high altar of the church were respectively 'half a thousand tiles called Brekkys' and ten shillings, a considerable sum in the 15th century. The tiles would have been useful at the time new work was in hand on the upper part of the church. Henry Tilemaker mentions in his will 'my tenement in the parish between the tenement of John Bryd the elder, thatcher, on the west and a lane called Warrockeslane', later known as Cox Lane. The initials of John Bryd or Byrd also appear in the roof, so it seems that he also helped with the cost of building it.[22]

Two priories of Augustinian canons were established in Ipswich during the 12th century, Holy Trinity or Christchurch outside the North Gate and SS Peter and Paul beside Stoke Bridge. These canons, who lived according to a monastic rule but also provided priests for most of the town's parish churches, gained considerable properties in the town and elsewhere through wealthy patrons in addition to the properties

29 The seal of the Priory of Holy Trinity, drawn and etched by Walter Hagreen for Wodderspoon's Memorials of Ipswich. *(John Wilton)*

recorded in Domesday Book as belonging to the churches attached to them. It seems most likely that both priories were founded at the instigation of, or at least with the support of, King Henry I (1100–35). A charter of this king of about 1133 was addressed to the Bishop of Norwich and the joint sheriffs of Suffolk regarding 'the canons of the King's alms at Ipswich' who are to plead any judicial claims only before the Bishop of Norwich and the sheriffs.[23] A charter by King Stephen (1135–54) says they are to plead only before the Bishop of Norwich and the king's demesne justice ('mea justicia dominica') because they are the king's canons and claim to hold their property from him.[24] H.A. Cronne points out that this charter of Stephen is addressed in an unusual, if not unique, form to the Bishop of Norwich and his archdeacons and to Hugh Bigod, presumably as sheriff, and his officials, thus including the representatives of both ecclesiastical and secular justice.[25] This marks the canons out as special, perhaps because Holy Trinity church itself and the other churches they held in Ipswich early in the 13th century had been part of the king's holding in Domesday Book.

Whatever doubts there might be about their origins, there can be no doubt about the impact of the various religious houses on the town. The visual impact alone must have been substantial, particularly after the establishment of the Blackfriars with its massive church; they were also a significant element in the economy of the town through their ownership of property and the number of clerics and employees involved in their affairs. The site of the church and monastic buildings of Holy Trinity is now occupied by Christchurch Mansion. The existing timber-framed building at the west end of Soane Street is said to have been the guest house of the priory; the priory arms can be seen carved on the cornerpost.

Some of Holy Trinity's earliest benefactors were priests who gave their churches, with their endowments, and themselves became canons of the priory, and other donors included Earl Hugh Bigod. It seems that the priory founded St Margaret's to serve its parishioners, and by 1291 it held the town churches of St Lawrence, St Margaret, St

*30   This timber-framed building on St Margaret's Plain is thought to have been the guesthouse of the Holy Trinity
Priory. The badge of the priory is carved on the cornerpost.*

Mary-le-Tower and St Mary Elms as well as the property of the disused churches of St
Michael and St Saviour together with others outside the town, St John's at Caldwell,
Rushmere, Foxhall, Tuddenham and Bentley. Further afield it held a large share in the
church of All Saints at Mendham, which was recorded as a minster church in the will
of Bishop Theodred in 952, and the church of St Mary at Preston, near Lavenham,
which had been given by Thomas de Mendham with other property in Preston. Having
been granted the church of St Mary, Bentley, by Hervey de Dodneis, Holy Trinity was
probably mother house to Dodnash Priory, founded about 1188 by Wimer the chaplain
after he had resigned as sheriff of Norfolk and Suffolk, having been the royal official
accounting for the construction of Orford Castle. Wimer himself was probably a member
of the Dodneis (Dodnash) family.[26]

The Priory of Holy Trinity was rebuilt by the Bishop of Norwich, John of Oxford,
after a fire in 1194, for seven canons under a prior, the complement being enlarged at
one time to 20 as endowments were increased. According to one source King Richard I
then transferred the patronage to the bishop.[27] The fire might well have destroyed the
priory church, since part of a broken Tournai marble font found in a ditch during the
construction of William Pretty's works on Tower Ramparts could well have come from
there; the splitting of the marble is such as would result from extreme heat. A complete
Tournai font, imported from Belgium in the 12th century, survives in St Peter's Church,
so it seems that each priory had one of these prestige items.

At some time between 1158 and 1162 Henry II granted the Priory of Holy Trinity a three days' fair at the feast of the Holy Cross (14 September), which grant was confirmed by King John in 1204, together with all the lands and rents formerly belonging to the churches of St Michael and St Saviour in Ipswich.[28] In 1331 Edward III confirmed this grant with amendment to 'a yearly fair on the feast of the Exaltation of the Cross and two days following within and without the town of Ipswich on the soil of that town'.[29] Two 13th-century records of property in Ipswich rented out by Holy Trinity Priory[30] show that it owned 12 shops, three taverns, 62 houses and more than 70 other properties as well as a share in Handford Mill.

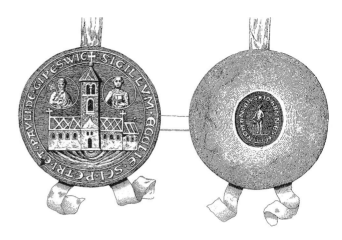

31   The seal of the Priory of SS Peter and Paul, with St Peter shouldering the key of Heaven and St Paul holding a book. Could it be that the church with its central tower is a depiction of the Saxon St Peter's Church? (John Wilton)

The other Augustinian priory, that of SS Peter and Paul, received endowments from the ancestors of Thomas Lacy and his wife Alice. It was based on St Peter's Church beside Stoke Bridge, which held a large estate at the time of Domesday. St Peter's is comparable with St John's Church at Clare in West Suffolk, as both had large endowments given before the Conquest by the same family, Withgar and his father, and both may have been minsters served by a group of priests. Both churches became part of the Honour of Clare, held by the fitzGilberts, so we might expect that the fitzGilbert family, otherwise known as the de Clares, would as tenants in chief and head of the Honour be involved in the foundation of St Peter's Priory. At Clare itself Gilbert de Clare in 1090 turned the collegiate minster church into a Benedictine priory, which was moved in 1124 to Stoke-by-Clare.

The importance of St Peter's may explain the statement in Domesday Book (25.60) that Richard fitzGilbert had established his claim to the church against Bishop Erfast, who held the East Anglian see, then based at Thetford, as the bishop would be keen to have direct control of a major minster church in Ipswich.[31] According to Dugdale's *Monasticon* the Priory of SS Peter and Paul held the town churches of St Edmund à Pountney, St Austin, St Mildred, St Nicholas, St Clement, St Mary-at-Quay and St Peter, along with Thurleston and four other out-of-town churches.

In 1296-7 Edward I stayed at the priory, where he celebrated the marriage of his daughter Elizabeth to the Count of Holland in the priory church on 8 January. It was a period of great rejoicing in the town, with the king dispensing alms most generously to the town's poor people.[32] Though it was the Priory of SS Peter and Paul that was at the centre of all the festivities, the king also visited Holy Trinity Priory, to which he presented a chalice that had belonged to the abbot of Glastonbury. There was a great coming and going of London jewellers with jewels for the royal bride and for other courtiers, though one man seems to have had a wasted journey. Wodderspoon quotes from the Wardrobe accounts regarding jewels provided for the king's daughter Margaret, Duchess of Brabant:

> To a certain jeweller of London, coming by order of the treasurer from London to Ipswich with certain jewels provided for the Duchess of Brabant, which jewels did not please the said Duchess. For his expenses going, tarrying, and returning, and for the hire of one hackney for carrying the same jewels, in the beginning of the month of January, 4s. 5d.

The royal expenses on this occasion also included 40 shillings to replace the two stones lost when the king threw his daughter Margaret's coronet into the fire at Ipswich. One wonders what made him so angry that he did this; could it have been her rejection of the jewellery brought from London?

Both priors were involved in the affairs of the town and became burgesses. On the back of the earliest roll remaining in the borough records we read how in 1255 William, the Prior of Holy Trinity, was admitted to the franchise of the borough. He swore to do to the town as his predecessor was wont to do 'and agreed to give to the community towards the expenses of the new charter of the aforesaid lord King already petitioned for one mark and to the feast of the guild one coomb of wheat and one quarter of malt and will pay lot and scot [taxes] as a resident burgess'. William, the Prior of St Peter, likewise promised to do like his predecessor to the town, giving ten shillings towards the expenses and a coomb of wheat and six capons to the feast of the guild, and to pay scot and lot as a resident burgess.[33] They had several preaching crosses in and around the town, including one on the town boundary of 1352 which is said to have belonged to the Prior of St Peter's and which must have stood somewhere on what is now the Chantry housing estate.

The priors of Holy Trinity and St Peter called a meeting in St Margaret's Church in 1325 for the Corpus Christi or merchants' guild to organise procedures for the annual procession through the town on Corpus Christi day.[34] Those taking part were to process in alternate years

32 The seal of the Blackfriars, also drawn by Walter Hagreen for Wodderspoon's book. (John Wilton)

33   Joshua Kirby's print of the former Blackfriars as it appeared in 1748, when it housed Christ's Hospital, the Grammar School and the Bridewell. The building with Gothic windows on the left is the former refectory; it has been assumed incorrectly by some writers to be the church. Larger than any other in the town, the friars' church stood to the left of the group of buildings seen here and was demolished soon after the Dissolution.

from St Peter and from Holy Trinity to the other and back. They also made guild regulations for foot washing on Maundy Thursday in St Mary-le-Tower Church, for funerals of members, for the tabernacle of the guild to be kept in St Mary-le-Tower Church under the charge of the two aldermen of the guild, and for an annual feast. Further regulations were made in the reign of Henry VII and, although the suppression of the monasteries presumably put an end to the religious procession, the guild feast was still being held in the reign of Elizabeth. The Priory of SS Peter and Paul was dissolved in May 1528 for the creation of Wolsey's college, but Holy Trinity survived and its prior took part in the celebrations at the opening of the college. It was, however, suppressed in 1536.

A feature of late medieval religious activity was the preaching of the friars, who devoted themselves to a life of poverty and self-sacrifice and active well-doing. Three of the orders of preaching friars set up houses in Ipswich in the 13th century, with large churches in which to preach, the emphasis being on spreading the gospel as taught by the Vatican and combating unorthodox heresies. There was also accommodation for friars who preached here and throughout the region, and for their students.

The Blackfriars (Dominicans) were established in Foundation Street when in 1263 King Henry III purchased a property in Ipswich, formerly the house of Hugh de Langeston, for them. In 1265 the king purchased more property for them, and so did the provincial of the order in 1269. The stone house given in 1263, or parts of it, survived until the destruction of the Blackfriars in the mid-19th century; a Norman arch can be seen in pictures of the demolition. In 1275 a royal commissioner was appointed to enquire whether it would harm the interests of the king and the town if the Friars built an external chamber extending from their dormitory to the dyke (rampart) of the town. This almost certainly refers to the 'external chamber' found during excavations, which was built as a toilet block with first floor access by a bridge from the dormitory. The need for the bridge is explained by the terms of the grant of a further piece of land in 1349 on condition that the friars keep up the walls opposite their plot and also the two great gates, one in the north and the other in the south of their court, and through these great gates the men of the town should have access to the defences in time of danger or whenever necessary; this would require a clear passage through the friars' property immediately behind the rampart.

Their church, dedicated to St Mary, was 177ft. long, of which the nave was 98ft. by 50ft., aisled and divided by columns into six bays. It was demolished, probably soon after the suppression in 1538 and certainly before Joshua Kirby made his plan and prospect of the Blackfriars buildings in 1748; this has led to much confusion as many authors have assumed that the refectory, which is the most conspicuous building in the prospect, was the church. In fact the church of the Blackfriars was much larger than any of the surviving churches in Ipswich.[35]

The Whitefriars (Carmelites) were founded in 1278-9 behind the Buttermarket and the site was extended in the 14th century to cover most of the area between the Buttermarket and Falcon Street, extending from Queen Street to St Stephen's Lane.[36] In 1297 they were given permission to close a street known as Erodes Lane and build across it. This lane probably followed the line recreated as Market Lane after the demolition of the friary, but now closed by the Buttermarket Centre. It is said that King Henry VI and all his suite were entertained here in 1452 and that provincial chapters of the Carmelite order were often held here.[37] We know that completion of a rebuilding of the church was marked by its consecration in 1477. Excavation in 1987 by the Suffolk Archaeological Unit revealed much of the church, the cloister and the chapter house.[38] After the dissolution one building was retained as the County Gaol until demolished about 1698.

The Greyfriars (Franciscans) were established close to St Nicholas' Church before 1298, on a riverside site where some of their buildings are still shown on Ogilby's map of 1674. It was this friary that gave its name to Friars Bridge, the approach to the marshes west of the town, earlier known as the Horsewade.

Besides the priories and the friaries there were several institutions for those suffering from leprosy and other ailments which made it necessary for the sufferers to be cared for in some isolation. The leper hospital of St Mary Magdalene, first mentioned in 1199, was in 1469 granted the profits of a fair on the feast of St James the Apostle; it was in the 14th century united with the hospital of St James. The joint mastership of the hospitals was in the gift of the Bishop of Norwich and was usually linked with St Helen's Church in its extra-mural suburb.

Then there was St Leonard's hospital in the parish of St Peter, apparently on the south side of the river as it was said to be near the old church of St Augustine, while in Lower Brook Street was another lazarhouse, that of St Edmund, presumably linked with the chapel of St Edmund Pountney. This chapel was dedicated to Edmund Rich,

Archbishop of Canterbury from 1234, who had taught philosophy at Oxford. Born at Abingdon *c.*1174 and buried at Pontigny in France in 1240, he was canonised in 1247. The associated cemetery was excavated by the Suffolk Archaeological Unit in 1975, when 106 burials were investigated.[39]

There seem also to have been other smaller hospitals, some at least of them staffed by groups of religious women. It could be one of these that stood in St Matthew's parish in 1338, according to a note in Bacon's *Annalls*.[40]

Burgesses and Foreigners

The medieval town of Ipswich was a cosmopolitan place, for all that the town authorities sought to limit trade to those who were burgesses or freemen and to those outsiders who paid their foreign fine. To be a foreigner a man did not need to have crossed the sea; a foreigner was merely one who had not acquired his freedom either by service, that is by having completed his apprenticeship with a burgess, by purchase or in some other way. In 1464 it was enacted that no man should be made a free burgess for less than 40 shillings.[41] To be a burgess was to be enfranchised; it was the burgesses who elected the town officers and officials, and who in later days at least cast their votes for the town's representatives in Parliament. A burgess had many privileges, the most important of which was the right to trade within the town without paying for doing so, but he also had duties, the most basic of which was to be 'lottant and scottant'; he had to pay his way whenever the town authorities needed cash for the purposes of the town government. Those who refused to pay scot and lot, or who delayed too long in making payment, ran the risk of being disfranchised, of becoming foreigners in their own town.

A non-resident might become a burgess and enjoy trading rights within the town on payment of a fine or fee, such a one being known as a forinsec burgess. It was found that non-residents were glad to have the privileges of a burgess but were less keen on the duties, and in 1274 the town authorities decreed that forinsec burgesses should not be able to pass on the freedom to their sons, and only those who paid scot and lot should be toll free within the town.[42]

Few youngsters received any kind of education, but in Ipswich there were distinct advantages in a boy or girl being at least numerate, for it was the custom of the town that a person had come of age when he or she could count and weigh and measure cloth. In 1342 a deed made by Robert de Walsham and his wife Isabell and Hellen, the daughter of John Lew, was enrolled, and Hellen was 'proved by othe to be 15 yeres old, and allowed by numbring and measuring'; the following year Walter, the 19-year-old son of John de Dunstall, qualified to enroll a deed 'by numbring 20s., and measuring 12 elns of clothe'.[43]

From time to time prominent people were made burgesses either in gratitude for their efforts on behalf of the town or in hope of favours to come. In 1200 Roger Bigod was admitted a burgess in recognition of his assistance in obtaining the charter from King John.

The coroners' roll of the reign of Edward III, when John Irp and William de Causton jointly held the office almost continuously from 1329 to 1343, serves to illustrate how attractive Ipswich must have been to people from foreign parts. They inquired into the death of Hugh de Coventry in a tavern brawl, into the death of William Arras (was he a Frenchman, as his name implies?) from a knifewound to the heart inflicted on him by John le Carter of Tuddenham, and into the death of a Welshman ('a foreigner from the parts of Wales'), Dany Ryrad, who was murdered by John Cole of Torksey in Lincolnshire.[44] Not that it was only such 'foreigners' whose deaths concerned the coroners, for in 1338 they held an inquest respecting the death of Alureda, widow of William Malyn of Ipswich, from a sword-wound inflicted on her by that same Roger Bande of Ipswich who had been responsible for the killing of Geoffrey Costyn. They also investigated less violent deaths like that of Symon de Calde Welle, surely a local man, who fell dead while chopping firewood in Matilda dil Ty's house.

Notwithstanding the apparently accidental deaths of John the son of William Owyth, who drowned in the Orwell while swimming with some fellow-mariners, and of William Sored, who being full of wine fell into the water by mischance and drowned, one has the feeling that medieval Ipswich was a violent and unruly as well as cosmopolitan town. The graphic description given by Dr. Calvin Wells of the attack on a man whose skeleton was unearthed in Cox Lane some 40 years ago is an example. After examining the evidence of injuries still visible on the bones, Dr. Wells deduced that the man was riding a horse when attacked by a number of armed men, one of whom slashed at his thigh with a sword, cutting through the muscle so that he could no longer retain his grip on the horse. Other injuries were inflicted as he fell from the horse, the final, fatal wound cleaving the top of his skull as he lay helpless on the ground with his assailant standing over him.[45]

It is perhaps hardly surprising that in 1447 it was ordered that anyone living in the town or the liberty who failed to come to the aid of anyone being assaulted should be disfranchised. At that period the whole of England was suffering from violent men and the threat of violence, for the Yorkists and the Lancastrians were at one another's throats and there were plenty who were glad of the excuse for lawless behaviour. In 1452 an order went out that every shopkeeper should keep a good staff handy in case of trouble, while other inhabitants 'of greater ability' should have 'Jacks, Sallets, Bowes, arrowes, swords, Targetts, Poleaxes, and other weapons of warre ready at an hower, to defende themselves and withstand the enemies of the king and kingdom as they ought'. That was by no means the last time the Great Court issued instructions to the townspeople to arm themselves and be ready to defend 'the good and honour of the Towne'.

Popular depictions of medieval towns show pigs roaming the streets and cockerels crowing from the top of muckheaps, and this does seem true enough of 14th-century Ipswich. Wandering hogs appear to have been a perennial problem, and in 1464 it was agreed that if an inhabitant found another man's hog in his garden he should be at liberty to sell it, half of the money being his and the other half the town's.[46] A few years later the fine for allowing one's hog to wander was set at 4d. (a penny a foot), with forfeiture being the penalty for a third offence or for failing to pay the fine. The wandering of hogs continued to prove a nuisance, and by 1543 the fine to be imposed on the owner of any pig found by the Crier in the streets and lanes had risen to 16d. 'And if the swine shall not be redeemed within four days after proclamac'on made, then shall the same be sold to the use of the Town, and the Crier shall have 2d. for every foote.'[47] It might have been thought that as the town grew the problem would have been solved, but it is clear that the weavers and other urban tradesmen were as keen to higgle up a pig as any of their country cousins. Eventually the bailiffs were given the power to appoint hoggards and a pound for straying animals was constructed in what were known as Warwicks Pits.

Every cock is entitled to his own dunghill on which to crow, but the town authorities found it necessary to rule that 'Noe person shall lay any horsdung in any place within this Borough and liberties thereof, nor any manner of muck or filthe uppon the Dikes, or nigh to the same.'[48] Street sweepings might, nevertheless, be dumped in the aforesaid Warwicks Pits, which were in the area known descriptively as the Cold Dunghills. Medieval Ipswich was without doubt a town that offended the nostrils.

Trades and Industries

Ipswich lay at the centre of a largely agricultural region, for which it served both as a market town and to some extent as an outlet to wider markets such as London. That it was a busy place, with all kinds of trades represented among the burgesses, is not to be doubted, but real evidence of the activities of the townspeople is hard to find earlier than the 16th century. Nevertheless, items can be found in the town records that reflect the occupations of individuals in the medieval period.

An important trade was that of blacksmith, who was required not only to shoe the horses on which both private travel and transport so much depended but also to make hinges and locks for the doors of houses, iron brackets for supporting the shelves upon which shopkeepers stored their wares, and a variety of other ironwork. In 1470 Geoffery Osberne and his heirs were granted a plot in St Clement's Street, now known as Fore Street, on which to build a 'travus'—that is, the building in which horses were shod.[49] Smiths would certainly not be the only craftsmen operating in medieval Ipswich; in 1433 when it was decided to sail the bounds of the town by water it was ordered 'that every craft of the Towne shall find botes'.[50]

Although Suffolk was largely a farming area there was one trade that was helping to make the county one of the most populous and the most prosperous regions in the country. The manufacture of woollen cloth was most prominent in the Babergh hundred, in the south-west of the county, but Ipswich also played its part in this thriving business, with a proportion of its population engaged in various operations connected with the trade. The subsidy roll for 1282 indicates that there were then four dyers and two weavers at work in the town, and it is likely that this is not the full tally of men engaged in the trade; many a man had more than one string to his bow. The cargoes that left Ipswich for 'the partys of the see' were almost certainly not all 'of Cogeshale, Maldon,

34   The section of the Gipping which fed water to Handford Mill, seen in a mid-19th-century photograph probably taken by Richard Dykes Alexander. An artificial cut, it carried barges up to the mill as well as providing water to power the mill's machinery. (John Wilton)

Colchestre, Sudbury, and of other clothes that ben bought in the cuntre and comyn into the town …'.[51]

The miller was an important man in any medieval community, and Ipswich had several, although it is only in the 15th century that we are able to put a name to any of them. Quernstones of Neidermendig lava imported from the Rhineland were used by the inhabitants of Saxon Gippeswyk to grind corn into flour, but as the population grew and trade became more specialised watermills were set up to harness the power of the river to produce supplies of flour for the local community. The miller became a figure of some power and much envy, for he enjoyed something of a monopoly in trade.

That there was at least one mill on the Gipping and possibly another on a tributary stream in Saxon times is indicated by the document of 970 recording the bounds of Stoke, which mentions a 'marsh-mill' in the vicinity of the Horsewade, a place where horses could ford the river later known as Friars Bridge.[52] As it is inconceivable that this mill was employed in marsh drainage at so early a date we are left to assume that this Anglo-Saxon document is referring to a mill-in-the-marsh, in what must have been a somewhat inconvenient position so far as access was concerned. It seems highly likely that this is the Horsewade mill referred to frequently in documents from the 13th century onwards until the seventeenth. Horsewade Mill made use of the same stream that had already passed the wheel of Hagenford or Handford Mill, which was served by a channel leaving the main river some way above Handford Bridge. This channel was an artificial one formed at some unknown period to bring water to the mill, which was built conveniently on firm ground on the northern side of the Gipping valley where the high ground rose out of the marsh. The new channel or leat was dug along the edge of the natural terrace some 10ft. above the flood plain; after passing over the wheel of Handford Mill the stream ran along the edge of the marsh to Horsewade Mill and on to rejoin the main river just above Stoke Bridge. It is probable that this lower part of the river course was natural, having originated as the course of a stream flowing down from springs on the edge of the high ground to the north in the vicinity of what is now Warrington Road.

To direct the flow along the artificial channel the river, still flowing down the middle of the valley as it must have done for centuries, was dammed at what later became known as Horseshoe Weir, immediately below the point at which the new channel left the old river. When the Stowmarket Navigation was constructed in the 18th century the upper section of the artificial channel was used as part of the navigation, a lock providing a link with the main river below Horseshoe Weir. The antiquity of the freshwater channel of the

35   *The tidemill on the town side of Stoke Bridge apparently took the place of an earlier mill on the Stoke side of the river.*

Gipping, referred to on early maps as the Great River to distinguish it from the older channel always known as The Salt Water, seems to be indicated by the fact that it formed the boundary of Stoke at the time it was held by Ely Abbey.

Both the priories of Holy Trinity and SS Peter and Paul had an interest in Horsewade Mill and Handford Mill, which are named separately and distinctly in the cartulary of the latter priory.[53] With the dissolution these two mills passed into the town's hands.

However obscure the early history of Horsewade Mill, we do know that it was burnt down in 1336; wooden mills, whether powered by wind or water, proved very vulnerable to fire. The miller, John Haltebe, expressed his willingness to rebuild the mill at his own expense and was granted by the town authorities a lease of the mill for eight years, together with Odenholme Meadow, for which he paid a nominal rent of one red rose at midsummer.[54] Was this the same John Halteby who involved himself in the town's affairs and made himself so unpopular that his murder in 1344 was greeted with common approval? It certainly appears that the mill was in other hands within a very few years of his agreeing to rebuild it. Horsewade Mill disappeared at some time in the mid-17th century, but Ogilby's map of 1674 shows a broadening of the river above Friars Bridge that might well represent the millpond. Handford Mill, on the other hand, continued in use into the 19th century, when it was crushing seed for oil production.

There is documentary evidence for a watermill standing on the Stoke side of the river just above Stoke Bridge which had apparently gone by the mid-16th century; a terrier of the lands of the manor of Stoke *c.*1560 refers to 'one piece of land next le haven where the mill lately stood'.[55] Perhaps this was a predecessor of the double mill, with two wheels and two sets of machinery, that stood on the Ipswich side of Stoke Bridge, frequently referred to in the town records as the new mills. The earliest reference to them seems to be in the middle of the 14th century when Gilbert de Boulge, William Gunnyld, Henry Walle and John Arnold were granted land to build two watermills; the agreement made with the town was that after this quartet of entrepreneurs had recouped their costs from the income the mills were to become town property.[56]

Richard II seized the mills because the handover of land had been carried out without royal licence, and because the building of the mills was likewise carried out without royal licence. When Henry IV usurped the throne in 1399 he restored the mills to the town, which had already acquired them before their seizure by the king. Thereafter there appear almost annual references in the town records to the leasing of the new mills. In the 15th century the mills belonged to the manor of Stoke, for a rent was paid to the Prior of Ely by the town in respect of them.[57] A dispute arose between the town and the Prior of Ely in the 1490s over Stoke Mills, but it seems to have been settled amicably, it no doubt being relevant to the settlement that the Prior of Ely was in 1492 made a free burgess and admitted also to the fraternity of the Guild.[58]

The mills by Stoke Bridge received into the millpond water that had already been used by Handford Mill and, until its demise, by Horsewade Mill, but at least in their later history Stoke Mills harnessed also the water of the tides. Tidal water was admitted to the millpond through sluices on the flood, was penned up there and, as the tide ebbed, was let past the twin wheels to power the mills. It is uncertain whether these were always tidemills or, if they were not, at what stage this method of working was adopted. The economic importance of these mills can hardly be over-estimated, since they not only ground for local consumption but almost certainly exported some of their flour to London and elsewhere. From time to time the Great Court issued injunctions to the inhabitants to have their grain ground only at the town mills and not to take it to other mills in the countryside. Those who did take their corn elsewhere were to forfeit half a bushel of corn for every bushel they had ground, it was ordered in 1473.[59] Ten years later it was decreed that any burgess who took his corn other than to the town mills should suffer disfranchisement.[60]

At the same time that they thus supported the local millers the town authorities sought to ensure that those men did not take advantage of their monopoly position by charging too much. As early as 1295 it was ordered that millers taking more than their just toll should be put in the pillory, those committing a third offence being forbidden to continue with the milling trade.[61] When in 1572 John Faircliff obtained a 20-year lease of Stoke Mills he was forbidden to trade in the corn market for fear he should misuse his position. His obligations were clearly set down: he was to repair the mill, the floodgates and the banks of the millpond twice a year, the work being overseen by the headboroughs; every three months he was to open his floodgates so that the water from his millpond should scour the shipping channel; and every year he should take '60 Tonne of Earth and Mainour' (manure) out of the millpond.[62]

V

The Tudor Town

The defeat and death of Richard III at the Battle of Bosworth in 1485 and the subsequent accession of Henry VII marked the end both of the Wars of the Roses and of the Middle Ages. Ipswich had taken the Yorkist side, but happily for the town the worst of the strife that resulted from the power struggle between the two factions passed Ipswich by.

While facing repeated uprisings in the early years of his reign, Henry VII strove to curb the private lawlessness that had characterised the 15th century and by marrying Elizabeth of York, daughter of Edward IV, united the houses of York and Lancaster. His treaty of Étaples, signed in 1492, brought a profitable peace with France and, together with the subsequent stabilisation of trade with the Low Countries, benefited Ipswich and the resident merchants.[1]

The town was approaching one of its most prosperous periods and, except when it was disrupted by interruptions of foreign trade, the woollen industry was developing towards its peak. Edward IV had forbidden the import of foreign cloth and the export of unfulled cloth, and Henry VII not only confirmed the latter prohibition but did all he could in other ways to encourage the cloth trade.[2] The industry was largely in the hands of the clothiers, men who bought the wool either straight from the sheep's back or from middlemen who provided a very necessary link between the many small flock-owners and the producers of cloth; most of the wool used in Suffolk came from outside the county.[3]

While much of the cloth produced in the country towns of Suffolk went to Blackwell Hall in London there was a market in Ipswich through which passed not only cloth woven in the town but that made in adjacent areas of Suffolk and Essex. The town authorities decreed in 1448 that all fullers and clothiers should sell their cloth each market day at the Moot Hall, and not elsewhere. Wool merchants and mercers were likewise to hold their market at the Wool House.[4] A very similar order was issued in 1559, when people bringing cloths into the town for sale were to bring them to the Cloth Hall next to the Moot Hall.[5] In 1575 the bailiffs were empowered to appoint a hallinger to take charge of the Cloth Hall,[6] and then in 1598 it was ordered that 'all maner of wollen clothe and clothes long and shorte cottons bayes kersies frises and rugges which shalbe brought to this towne to be sold in grosse or to be transported into the partes beyond the Seas by waye of merchandise shalbe first brought to the Clothe Hall of this towne and there discharged before the sale or transportinge thereof uppon peyne' of forfeiture.[7]

Some of the clothiers, but by no means all, became men of great wealth and entered the land-owning class. Many prospered in a more moderate way, and others possessed only a minimum of capital and found difficulty in keeping themselves in business, if we are to believe their protestations of poverty when petitioning the government against the activities of the wool-brokers in 1585.[8]

Before the wool could go to the weaver it had to be carded, to clean and separate the fibres, and spun into yarn. This work was largely done in their homes by women and children, as is revealed by another petition drawn up in 1575 by the Suffolk clothiers:

36   Ipswich contained a wealth of timber-framed houses like this one in Lower Orwell Street, seen in a woodcut from a drawing by John Smart which appears in G.R. Clarke's The History & Description of the Town and Borough of Ipswich, *published in 1830. The house, with unglazed windows on the ground floor, was still standing at that time. (John Wilton)*

The custom of our country is to carry our wool out to carding and spinning and put it to divers and sundry spinners who have in their houses divers and sundry children and servants that do card and spin the same wool. Some of them card upon new cards and some upon old cards and some spin hard yarn and some soft ... by reason whereof our cloth falleth out in some places broad and some narrow contrary to our mind and greatly to our disprofit.[9]

Clearly the clothiers had difficulty in regulating the work of these women and children, in spite of legislation passed in 1512 which threatened any worker guilty of fraud with punishment by pillory and ducking-stool.

Poor people in Ipswich gained a precarious living by preparing yarn, while after the foundation of Christ's Hospital in 1569 the children resident there were employed at carding and spinning wool. Unlike the weavers, to whom the yarn was taken after being collected by the clothiers' agents, the spinners never had any kind of trade organisation and so were liable to be put upon by the clothiers, who not only paid low wages but sometimes imposed payment in kind and exacted arbitrary fines for work that they considered inferior.

Weaving was for the most part carried on in the weaver's home. Although the more prosperous weaver might aspire to become a clothier, many weavers found themselves in the 16th century being reduced to the situation of mere wage-earners, fully dependent on the clothiers. The Ipswich weavers and those of other Suffolk towns complained in a petition of 1539 that the master weavers were being rendered destitute by the employment of weavers and other operatives by the clothiers on their premises: 'For the rich men the clothiers be concluded and agreed among themselves to hold and pay one price for weaving, which price is too little to sustain households upon, working night and day, holyday and weekday, and many weavers are therefore reduced to the position of servants.'[10]

Fulling, the operation of cleansing and beating the cloth to raise the nap, and dyeing were both carried on in Ipswich. 'The fulling mill' had been granted to Alexander Fornham in 1434,[11] and there are also references to 'wodehouses'; woad (*Isatis tinctoria*) is a cruciferous plant used for producing the blue dye used for colouring the Suffolk cloth.

After fulling, woollen cloth was stretched on tainters, large frames bearing tenterhooks which held the cloth under tension. These can be seen on the marshes west of Stoke Bridge in Speed's prospect of the town in 1610; in 1570 Henry Ashley and George Wilds were given permission to set up tainters on Warwicks Pits,[12] and some

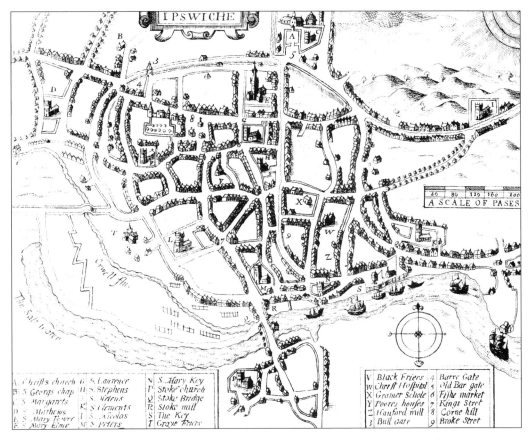

37 *The early 17th-century town, as depicted by John Speed, with the central area surrounded by an earthen rampart. Tenter frames for stretching cloth can be seen set up on the marshes above Stoke Bridge, the crane on the Common Quay looks very much like a post windmill without its sails, and there are 13 churches, including St George's chapel. There are errors in the key: Y is in fact Handford Mill and Z the Poores Houses, and V, the Blackfriars, is out of place. Seckford House is conspicuous to the west of Cornhill, and Christchurch is notable for the structure just north of St Margaret's Church which might be a survival from the days of Holy Trinity Priory. (John Wilton)*

38   Carved corner-posts were a feature of many Ipswich buildings, such as this house at the corner of Oak Lane and Northgate Street. Some of them were removed to the Ipswich Museum when the houses were demolished in the 19th and 20th centuries.

years later the headboroughs were considering whether tainters should be set up at the Cold Dunghills.[13] An elaborate code regulating the manufacture of cloth, enacted in 1551, required that no cloth should be stretched more than one yard in length or an eighth of a yard in breadth, but it would seem that the stretching of cloth beyond the legal limit was common enough. The code also stipulated that no person should use 'any wrinch, rope or ring, or any other engine for the purpose of such unlawful stretching', but such 'engines' were commonly employed in Suffolk. Indeed, the Privy Council found it expedient at times to grant a dispensation for the stretching of a certain number of cloths for the Eastern market; it was pointed out that if Suffolk clothiers did not stretch their cloth 'the Dutch (as they often have done) would buy our unstrained cloth … strain it six or seven yards per piece more in length, and make it look a little better to the eye, and after that carry it abroad to Turkey … and there beat us out of trade with our own weapons'.[14]

The woollen trade in Ipswich, and in Suffolk generally, was highly dependent on export business, and whenever foreign policy required or resulted in an interruption of communication with Flanders those involved in the trade found themselves in serious difficulties. Unrest among the weaving fraternity was the inevitable consequence of the resultant laying off of weavers and other cloth workers when the clothiers were unable to dispose of their goods. Thus in 1528 a rumour that English merchants had been detained in Flanders caused a flutter among the Suffolk clothiers that had to be dealt with by the Duke of Norfolk, who wrote to tell Wolsey of the steps he had taken to persuade the clothiers to retain their men in work. It was a trying year, for two months later the duke received complaints from the clothiers that the London merchants were not buying Suffolk cloth, and if a way were not found of selling their goods they would have to lay their workpeople off.

The duke suggested to Cardinal Wolsey on this occasion that he should put pressure on the London merchants. The story is told of how Wolsey sent for the merchants and addressed them thus:

> Sirs, the King is informed that you use not yourselves like merchants, but like graziers and artificers, for when the clothiers do daily bring cloths to your market for your ease

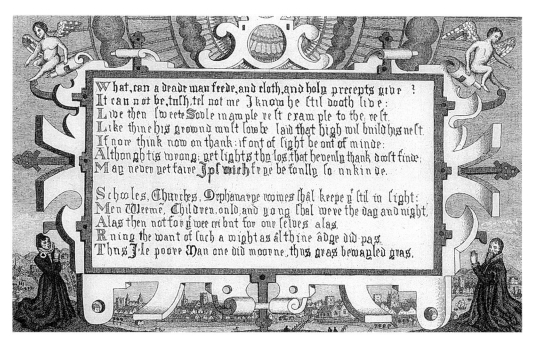

39 *A view of late 16th-century Ipswich forms part of William Smart's memorial in St Mary-le-Tower Church. This etching by Walter Hagreen appears in Wodderspoon's* Memorials of Ipswich, *published in 1850. (John Wilton)*

to their gret cost and there be ready to sell them, you of your wilfulness will not buy them, as you have been accustomed to do. What manner of men be you? said the Cardinal. I tell you the King straitly commandeth you to buy their cloths, as before time you have been accustomed to do, upon pain of his high displeasure.[15]

Towards the end of the 16th century the sacking of Antwerp by the Duke of Parma and war with Spain caused a decline in Ipswich trade with the Netherlands and brought hardship to the woollen producers. Before the decline, in 1572-3, Ipswich exported 2,886 short cloths, mainly to Spain, the Low Countries and the Baltic port of Danzig, with small quantities going to Scotland and France. The other major export from Ipswich at this period was beer, of which 154 tons (or tuns?) went abroad, mainly to the Low Countries, in the same period.[16]

When in the Armada year Ipswich was expected to make its contribution to the prosecution of the war with Spain the town justices pleaded poverty on account of

the decayed state of this poor corner, growing chiefly if we be rightly informed by restraint made by a Statute prohibiting that no Suffolk cloth should be transported and not here dressed before they were embarked, thereby changing the accustomed gainful trade … with such cloths as were best saleable in Spain and now through long want of vent into those parts we find the stocks and wealth of the inhabitants greatly decayed.[17]

40   This roof, which was sold in the 19th century and put on a church in Wiltshire, was possibly made for the hall of the Cloth Company. As can be seen in this print, the decoration of the brackets includes shears such as were used in the cloth trade. (John Fairclough)

It might be thought merely an excuse to avoid unwelcome expense were there not other evidence of the town's problems at this time. On the first day of April 1591 an order was made that clothiers and clothmakers living in Ipswich should put out at least half of their carding, spinning, weaving, shearing or dressing within the town, and only with the prior knowledge and permission of the bailiffs could they put work outside the liberties. It was specifically stated that the order had been made to lessen the distress of the poorer people of the town and to find more employment for them.[18]

At the end of the same month regulations were made for a fraternity or company of clothiers, clothworkers, weavers, shearmen and dyers which would control the cloth trade within the town and supervise the binding of apprentices and employment of servants.[19] The Cloth Company's book containing the regulations was later, after some words had been amended, sealed with the borough seal.[20] It was a move to counter the increasing activities in the cloth trade of foreigners, that is, men who were not burgesses. Some years later, in 1598, another order was made with the same intention, that no artificer or craftsman should take as apprentice a child who had been born or bred outside the town unless he had permission from the bailiffs and, just to make sure, five other portmen.[21]

Perhaps it was the Cloth Company that occupied premises in Pleasant Row, off Star Lane, from which the timber roof went in the 19th century to Cholderton church in Wiltshire.[22] This roof, advertised for sale in the *Ipswich Journal* as 'A superb antique ornamental Gothic roof, 80ft. long and 19ft. wide within the walls … well deserving the attention of Antiquaries …', has carved on it the shears which were the emblem of the clothworkers.

Sailcloth Weaving

It would have been natural enough if a seaport such as Ipswich had been producing sailcloth for many centuries, but in fact the weaving of this material from hemp was not introduced to the town until around 1570. Up to that time the best canvas was imported from France, though it must have been difficult to obtain when relations between England and that country were strained.

A 21-year licence was granted in 1574 to John Collins of Ipswich, his brother Richard and those who had been apprenticed to them to make medrinacks, poldavies and other sailcloth.[23] (Poldavis took its name from the Breton town of Poldavide, in

Douarnenez Bay, in which it was formerly made; the origin of medrinacks is unknown.) Just how the Collins brothers had learnt the trade is not revealed, but the licence states clearly that

> The Crown is informed by Edward, earl of Lincoln, high admiral, and other officers of the navy, that John Collins has at great travail and expense attained the art of making the said cloths, has furnished himself with looms and has already instructed several apprentices, so that shortly the Queen's subjects may be served with the native commodity.

Authority was given for John Collins to search all pieces of sailcloth and to seal with a stamp engraved with the rose and crown, made for him at the Royal Mint, all those pieces that were adjudged satisfactory, charging the maker a penny for every piece sealed.

It is interesting that Collins' case had been taken up by Thomas Seckford, Master of Requests, who had a house in Ipswich and interests also in Woodbridge, the two towns to which the manufacture of sailcloth was by the licence to be restricted:

> Since, as the Crown is informed, the towns of Ippeswiche and Woodbridge, co. Suffolk, are the fittest places for making sail-cloth (yarn and other necessaries being there most plentiful, because the inhabitants are by experience found the best dressers and spinners of hemp and the soil brings forth such hemp as is not commonly found elsewhere), the grantees are forbidden to exercise the said art outside Ippeswiche and Woodbridge and three miles round, unless the Crown hereafter assign some of them to another town.[24]

There is a suggestion that the early Ipswich sailcloth was of a somewhat inferior quality, but nevertheless the weaving of canvas became well established in the town, and during the 17th century there are numerous references to Suffolk canvas in the navy records.

One wonders if by any chance Henry Piper, poldavis weaver, whose belongings were appraised by Robert Howe, John Walters and Thomas Laster after his death in 1615, was one of the apprentices taught by John Collins. With his nine looms in two workshops, his stock of poldavis worth £13 4s. and debts both good and desperate (unlikely to be paid) of £4 10s., Piper was quite a substantial tradesman, probably with several apprentices and employees.[25] Altogether his worldly goods were appraised at more than £66, a substantial amount. Though we cannot tell where Piper lived, his residence was a house of some pretensions with about a dozen rooms and a gatehouse giving admission from the street into the yard, in which he kept two pigs and some poultry. Ipswich tradesmen of the early 17th century obviously believed in being self-sufficient.

Thomas Wolsey

Probably the grandest man of all to acknowledge Ipswich as his birthplace, Thomas Wolsey, cardinal legate, Archbishop of York and Lord Chancellor to Henry VIII, was supremely self-sufficient in an entirely different manner. For the 14 years that he served as Henry's chief minister Wolsey was, next to the king, the most powerful man in

England.[26] He was the son of Robert and Joan Wolsey, of St Nicholas parish. His birthplace was almost certainly a house in St Nicholas Street, long since demolished, at the corner of a passage leading through into the churchyard.[27]

Robert Wolsey, or Wulcy as the name was sometimes spelt, was by repute a butcher. There is evidence of this being his trade in the borough court rolls; on one occasion he appeared and was, 'in company with another Stowmarket butcher, one John Wood, fined for selling bad meat at the Ipswich market and for not exhibiting the skins of beasts which they had slain'. On a later occasion he was before the court accused of brewing ale and selling it in illegal measures; providing horse provender for excessive gain; failing to maintain the gutter in front of his house; allowing his pigs to wander at large; and defiling the highway with filth from his

41 Cardinal Wolsey, seen in an engraving after the well-known portrait by Hans Holbein. Through the window is a view of Cardinal College, Oxford. (John Wilton)

stables instead of removing it to the public pits.[28] All these were the kind of minor offences that fill the membranes of the court rolls. This particular reference is interesting in that it indicates that while Thomas Wolsey's father might have been a butcher he also had other strings to his bow; perhaps he is best described as a successful businessman.

The Wolseys were related to the Dandy or Daundy family, one of the town's leading families, several generations providing bailiffs and other town officers. Edmund Daundy, who was twice elected to represent the town in Parliament, in 1514 endowed a chantry in St Lawrence's Church for a priest to say mass for the souls of Robert Wolsey and his wife Joan, as well as for the good estate of their son Thomas and members of the Daundy family.

Thomas Wolsey would have been about nine when Richard Felaw left his house in Foundation Street to the grammar school, and there is every likelihood that he attended the school. George Cavendish, who was the cardinal's secretary and his earliest biographer, does not specifically mention the grammar school but begins his account of his master's life:

> Truth it is, Cardinal Wolsey, sometime Archbishop of York, was an honest poor man's son, born in Ipswich within the county of Suffolk, and being but a child was very apt to learning; by means whereof his parents, or his good friends and masters, conveyed him to the University of Oxford … He was made a Bachelor of Arts at 15 years of age, which was a rare thing and seldom seen.[29]

Thomas's 'good friends and masters' might well have been the Daundy family. What is more, it could have been John Squyer, Master of the grammar school, who influenced him in his choice of Magdalen College, Oxford, to which he went at the age of eleven.

A brilliant pupil, Thomas attained the degree of Master of Arts and went on to become a Fellow of his college. He was ordained priest in 1498 and was presented by Thomas Grey, Marquis of Dorset, to the living of a Somerset parish, but he was not destined to remain a parish parson for long. In 1501 he became chaplain to the Archbishop of Canterbury, Henry Deane, while retaining the living of Limington, Somerset, for a further eight years; presumably he put in a curate to look after the parish for him. The Archbishop died in 1503, and Wolsey's last duty as his chaplain was to arrange his funeral, preceded by a solemn journey from Lambeth Palace by water to Faversham and then overland to Canterbury. He next entered the service of the elderly and ailing Sir Richard Nanfan, Lord Deputy of the port of Calais, who when he returned to England in 1505, 'intending to live more at quiet', recommended Wolsey to the king. The son of an Ipswich tradesman thus became chaplain to Henry VII, for whom he was soon travelling on some delicate diplomatic missions.

Though the story told by Cavendish of the extraordinary speed with which Wolsey accomplished an errand to Flanders is taken by modern scholars with the proverbial pinch of salt, Wolsey was certainly a man of more than ordinary ability and efficiency, and he commended himself to his royal master by his thoroughness and dispatch.[30]

On the death of Henry VII Wolsey remained at court in the service of the teenaged Henry VIII. His rise to power was remarkably rapid; first he was made Bishop of Tournai, then Bishop of Lincoln, and within a relatively short time he was appointed Archbishop of York; within 20 months of his first appointment to a bishopric he was elected to the College of Cardinals. In 1515 Wolsey was appointed chancellor, having, so it is said, pestered his predecessor into resignation by constantly interfering with his jurisdiction in the name of the king. For the next 14 years he was not only chancellor but in effect Henry's chief minister, his boundless energy extending his interests into all departments of government.

Wolsey's ambition knew no bounds, and as his power grew he used it for his own aggrandisement. He has been much criticised for his magnificence and for the princely style in which he lived, but it has to be pointed out that magnificence was a political weapon and one Wolsey was ever ready to wield on behalf of his king. Before leaving Calais in 1527 to negotiate an Anglo-French alliance he briefed the members of his household: they were to treat him with the respect due to the king, since he was the king's appointed representative. When he was waited on at dinner with more servile ritual than the king of France, Francis I, he was perhaps making a public statement of Henry's supremacy.[31]

His enemies, who were many, accused Wolsey of greed and pride, and his actions did little to give the lie to such criticisms; if these were his besetting sins, it is only right to point out that greed and pride were the occupational diseases of international statesmen. When the cardinal was condemned for allowing his grandeur to diminish his diplomatic effectiveness one might consider the evidence of the papal nuncio in France, who in giving a pen-portrait of Wolsey at Amiens in 1527 said that 'although in all his outward acts he shows excessive pomp and great ostentation, nevertheless, in speaking, in behaviour and in negotiation, he reveals an intellect capable of every greatness, proper to any undertaking or affair, because he is a dexterous and gracious man, full of glorious and noble intentions'.[32]

One of his most noble intentions was to found a college at Oxford and feeder schools in 15 of the 17 English dioceses, the first and perhaps the chief of which he planned for his birthplace. Many bishops had endowed educational establishments in the past ranging from grammar schools to university colleges, but Wolsey set himself to surpass them all; his colleges at Oxford and Ipswich were to make all others look inferior in every way. Erection of the buildings of Cardinal College at Oxford began in January 1525. Work there was still proceeding when in the summer of 1528 building materials began to be stockpiled on the site at Ipswich, formerly that of the Priory of SS Peter and Paul which had been dissolved to provide both the land and the money for the new project. Flints were being brought from the cliffs at Harwich and Caen stone from Normandy. Early in 1529 the master masons involved, Richard Lee and a man named Barbour, both of them East Anglians, showed the plans of the college to Wolsey, who took a close personal interest in the project, 'to know his pleasure therein'. In the middle of that same year it was reported that 'My Lord's college at Ipswich is going on prosperously, and much of it above ground, which is very curious work'. In the context of the time we have to understand 'curious' to mean richly decorated.[33] Wolsey not only took a keen interest in the planning of the buildings of his new establishment but prepared the grammar textbook to be used there.

Towards the end of his life Henry VII had built the Savoy Hospital in London and had made up his mind to build another hospital at Bath, and to accomplish this he had appropriated the revenues of monastic institutions which were falling into decay. It was an example that Wolsey followed with enthusiasm when establishing his educational foundations at Oxford and Ipswich; the endowments of his Ipswich college included not only the property of the Priory of SS Peter and Paul but also the advowsons of parish churches all over Suffolk and Norfolk. The annual value of the suppressed monastic houses and the appropriated rectories given to the Ipswich college was estimated at £1,000, half the endowment of Cardinal College, Oxford. The statutes of the latter show clearly that Wolsey was intending to build and endow schools in several parts of the kingdom to feed able students to the Oxford college.[34]

Having decided to appropriate St Peter's Church as the chapel of his new college, Wolsey gave the parishioners the choice of attending either St Nicholas or St Mary-at-Quay, the adjoining parish churches. It was probably he that gave the magnificent Tournai marble font in St Peter's its perpendicular base, and without much doubt he was also responsible for the imposing west end, with the two niches which would originally have housed statues of St Peter and St Paul. Much of the chancel was demolished and the double hammerbeam chancel roof was taken down and re-erected on the church of St Mary-at-Quay. This resulted in a large almost rectangular church, very suitable for the kind of ceremonial procession that Wolsey envisaged for the canons, singing men and boys of his college.

The foundation stone of the Ipswich buildings was laid on 15 June 1528 by John Longland, Bishop of Lydda—at that period there were English bishops who took their titles from places in the Holy Land that were at the time inaccessible to Christians. The stone was found in the 18th century broken in two pieces and used as building material in what Clarke described as 'a common wall'.[35] The broken stone was given to Christ Church, Oxford, the resurrected Cardinal College; even in the 18th century Ipswich was anxious to divest itself of its history.

The school or college at Ipswich was to be a community of secular canons headed by a dean. There were to be 12 priests, eight clerks, eight singing boys and poor scholars. There were also to be 13 poor almsmen. All were to pray for the good estate of the king and the cardinal, and for the souls of the cardinal's parents. The first dean was William Capon, who had been head of Jesus College, Cambridge. He reported from time to time to Wolsey, telling him not only what

42 All that survives of Wolsey's college is the brick gateway that probably served as a watergate for people coming by river and St Peter's Church, which Wolsey appropriated as the college chapel. In about 1860, when this photograph was taken, the gate was already showing signs of age; today it suffers seriously from erosion partly caused by passing traffic. (John Wilton)

was being done but about the vestments that were being acquired for the college and about similar matters. On the eve of Lady Day, he told Wolsey in one letter, he and all the college had processed to the chapel of Our Lady of Grace after Evensong in the college church, St Peter's, and there sang Evensong 'as solemnly and devoutely as we cowde'. Present at this celebration were Humphrey Wingfield, the bailiffs and portmen and the Prior of Christchurch (Holy Trinity), 'all the which accompanied us that same night home again to your Graces college with as loving and kind manner as I have seen; and at their coming thither they drank with me both wine and beer, and so that night departed'.[36] Sadly, the dean went on, Lady Day itself (8 September) was 'a day of very fowle wedder and rayned sore contynewally, so that we cowde not go in procession thrugh the towne to our Lady's Chapell accordyng to our statute by your grace made;

but we made as solempne a procession in your grace's College Chirche as cowde be devysed'.

In charge of the college choir at this time was Nicholas Lentall, who seems to have been on secondment from Wolsey's own household chapel, to which he was recalled shortly before Christmas. His place was taken by Robert Testwood, who had been master of the choristers first at the collegiate church of St Mary at Warwick and then at St Botolph, Boston. Lentall's recall at such an inopportune season dismayed the dean, who saw him as the keystone of the choir, but later Capon was to commend Testwood as 'a very synguler cunnynge man' who was making such a good job of training the choirboys that 'I thynke verely there be no better children within the Realme of England'.[37]

The singing men themselves had been carefully chosen, 'very well breasted with sufficient cunnyng for theyr rowmes, and som of theym very excellent', as the dean reminded Wolsey, who was well aware of the prestige to be gained from a really good choir; at his Oxford college the master of the choristers was no less a man than John Taverner, an outstanding composer as well as a most accomplished musician. Wolsey's personal interest was such that he arranged for Taverner to take four of his ablest boys from Oxford to Hampton Court so that the cardinal could himself hear them sing and could choose 'such ij as shall stand with his graces pleasure' for the Ipswich choir.

It is somewhat odd, then, that Wolsey did not pay them better. Capon pointed out to his grace that the singing men at Ipswich were complaining that they had had much better wages 'there from whense they came fro', and that the food was not good enough. 'I feare that theyr commons allowed by your Grace will not suffice theym as yet: for we can make no provysions neyther for beeffs ne for muttons for want of pasture nere unto us,' the dean wrote with some acerbity.[38] One feels it could only get worse, and it did. One man, mourned as 'a very good descanter', died early in 1529 and another had to be dismissed 'for he wolde not come to the quere but at his owen pleasure'.[39]

For just about a twelvemonth the college operated as an educational establishment. In January 1529 the schoolmaster, William Goldwin, sent Wolsey specimens of the handwriting of some of the boys, and expressed the hope that they would soon be speaking Latin in the modern (Italian) manner.[40] As the number of pupils rose Capon referred in the spring of 1529 to an usher in addition to the schoolmaster, and expressed the opinion that the school would have to be enlarged.

Wolsey's fall from power was cataclysmic so far as the Ipswich establishment was concerned. The still-incomplete college was closed down and the materials stockpiled on the site were appropriated by the king. The Exchequer accounts of 1531 record 1,300 tons of Caen stone and 600 tons of flints being removed to Westminster for the benefit of the royal building programme, and many of the completed buildings seem to have been dismantled.

While it is possible to plot the probable extent of the college lands on Ogilby's map there is no sign there of any of the college buildings or of the entrance gateway 'built after the manner of that at Whitehall', which apparently had two broad three-storey towers flanking the entrance arch. The small brick gate, once handsome but now sadly eroded by weather and the spray created by passing heavy traffic along College Street, was no more than a pedestrian access to one section of the precinct, perhaps a watergate used by those who came by river. Had it been completed, the college would surely have formed an imposing group of buildings. Wolsey apparently had plans also to turn Lord Curzon's house in Cole Hill (later renamed Silent Street) into his palace, but those plans too were stillborn.[41]

The Cardinal Archbishop was never to have a home in Ipswich. He died in Leicester, in the Abbey of St Mary of the Meadows, on 29 November 1530, and there he was buried. His hopes of creating a great educational establishment linking Ipswich with Oxford had died before him.

Our Lady of Grace

Wolsey's instructions were that each Lady Day the members of his college should process through the town to the Chapel of Our Lady of Grace in Lady Lane, just outside the West Gate, a nationally recognised place of pilgrimage. It was visited by both Henry VIII and Catherine of Aragon on separate occasions as well as by thousands of lesser pilgrims.[42] Though the royal pilgrims would have attracted plenty of attention as they and their retinue processed to the Chapel of Our Lady, those visits probably did not cause quite such a stir as the visit of a 12-year-old girl, the daughter of Sir Roger Wentworth of Gosfield, in 1516. It was in November 1515 that the girl started suffering violent fits, whether of temper or of some other kind we are not told, and these continued to afflict her until the following Lady Day, 25 March 1516. On that day she had a persistent vision of the Virgin 'in the picture and stature of Our Lady of Grace in Eppeswyche'.[43]

The headstrong youngster demanded to be taken forthwith to the chapel at Ipswich. The implication is that the fits had ceased, but however that might be three weeks later she got her way and arrived in Ipswich, where news of her miraculous cure had preceded her; it is said that a thousand people flocked around to see her escorted to the chapel. Not content with praying in the chapel, the girl sent for Lord Curzon, whose house in Silent Street was one of the finest in the town, and the bailiffs, William Hall and John Wilde, to pray with her. Word got around, and soon Abbot Reve of Bury arrived, having walked all the way from St Edmund's Abbey, and having vowed to do the same every year from then on if only Our Lady would cure the youngster of her fits. History does not record if he kept his vow.

After leading the crowds in prayer the young lady left for her Essex home, making a promise as she went to return. And return she did, aided in her resolve by further fits and some doubtless divinely-inspired rudeness, to be met this time by a gathering of four thousand people, whom she admonished to be 'mor stedfaste in the fayth'. Following her devotions at the shrine she went off to her lodgings and to bed, but at midnight she summoned the bailiffs, the county magistrates, and other top people to her bedside, where she harangued them for two solid hours. When her embarrassed mother told her to take heed to the great clerks and their sayings she made a blistering response, emphasising it by having another fit (of temper?). Lord Curzon ended that fit by pushing a cross into her hands.

That was not the end of that night's events, because an hour later the girl's sisters and a cousin, and then her brother John, began to rave and shout; John had to be taken to the chapel to be cured in front of the image of Our Lady itself. It was a classic example of the hysteria that gave the Church a bad name among reformers. Who was pulling the strings?

While defending its powers, Wolsey did nothing to improve the spiritual life of the Church. Protestant reformers[44] who stressed the central place of the Bible as the only source of God's truth pointed to incidents such as this and to the outward display of religious processions and rituals as examples of what they felt was wrong with the Church, headed by the Pope.

The various religious changes under Henry VIII, Edward VI, Mary and Elizabeth had major effects on Ipswich. One of the leading protestants, Thomas Bilney, was twice 'plucked from the pulpit' while preaching in St George's Church in Ipswich, then arrested by order of Cardinal Wolsey in 1527, and finally burned at the stake as a lapsed heretic. In 1546 two men, Kerby and Roger Clarke, were tried at Ipswich for rejecting the doctrine of transubstantiation and sentenced to be burnt, Clarke at Bury St Edmunds and Kerby in Ipswich.[45] While Kerby was being secured to the stake 'in the market place', presumably on Cornhill, and the wood and straw for the fire were being arranged he defended his view of Christian doctrine in front of a large crowd against Dr. Rugham, a former monk of Bury Abbey.

Protestant ideas were largely imported from the Continent, and since Ipswich was a point of contact with mainland Europe, it need not cause any surprise that the earliest books to be printed in Ipswich, produced in 1547-8 by Anthony Scoloker and John Oswen, were mainly translations of works by such Protestant reformers as Calvin, Luther and Zwingli.[46] In some cases the translation was by Richard Argentine, the master of Ipswich School, who was a vigorous reformer in the reign of Edward VI, a violent Catholic during Mary's reign, and a penitent Protestant in Elizabeth's. It is possible that it was Argentine's influence that brought Scoloker to Ipswich, where he had premises in St Nicholas parish, in mid-1547.[47] Neither Scoloker nor Oswen stayed long in Ipswich. Scoloker had moved to London by July 1548, taking his type with him, and Oswen moved to Worcester in 1549.

Two other 16th-century books have an Ipswich imprint, but neither was in fact printed in the town. The first of them, a work by an obscure 3rd-century Spanish poet, bears the Latin words 'Sold in Ipswich at the fish market by Reginald Oliver' but it was actually printed in Antwerp. The other, the first bibliography of British authors, has an imprint reading 'Gippeswici per Ioannem Overton'; the name John Overton is thought to be fictitious, and the book was printed at Wesel in Westphalia. The reason for this deceit is most likely to be found in the restrictions imposed at the time on the importation of books printed on the continent; the printed sheets were probably brought to Ipswich and disguised with the false imprint before being bound.[48]

Under Queen Mary Robert Samuell, a minister from East Bergholt, was burned at the stake in 1555, followed by two Ipswich women, Agnes Potten, wife of a brewer, and Joan Trunchfield, a shoemaker's wife.[49] William Pikes, a tanner in St Margaret's parish, was known to have an English translation of the Bible and was burned at Brentwood in 1558.[50] In the same year a justice in Martlesham heard that two protestants, Alexander Gooch of Woodbridge and Alice Driver of Grundisburgh, were in Grundisburgh, so he took a search party who used pitchforks to find them hiding in a load of hay. For rejecting the Pope and Queen Mary, Alice Driver had her ears cut off at Bury St Edmunds; both she and Gooch were burned at the stake in Ipswich, praying and singing psalms in defiance of the sheriff and bailiffs, who urged their men to hurry up with the burning.[51]

The Dissolution

Faced with a shortage of cash in the Treasury, partly as a result of expensive wars with France, Henry VIII took a leaf out of his former Chancellor's book by deciding to make use of the Church's abundant riches. Having broken with the Pope and declared himself in 1535 to be the head of the English Church, he used his new-found royal power to dissolve the monasteries, nunneries and friaries. Between 1536 and 1539 the houses of monks and friars were closed and their properties sold to private buyers; the monks were paid pensions, and many became parish priests. In Ipswich, Holy Trinity Priory, the Blackfriars, Whitefriars and Greyfriars were all closed down, and the statue of Our Lady was removed from the chapel in Lady Lane and was taken to Smithfield in London to be burned, although some people claim that it was smuggled out of the country and still survives in a shrine at Nettuno in Italy.[52]

That there were rich pickings to be had is shown by the fact that in 1535 the clear temporal income of the Priory of Holy Trinity was over £69½, spiritual over £18½, giving a total of over £88. Primarily the pickings went to the Crown, but there were others able to pick up a bargain on the way. Two men who benefited from events in Ipswich were Thomas Rush and his stepson and son-in-law Thomas Alvard (Rush married the widow of Thomas Alvard the elder, Thomas's mother, and young Thomas married Rush's daughter by an earlier marriage).[53] Rush had been made the king's serjeant-at-arms in 1508 and continued in the king's service into the 1530s; it may have been his familiarity with the court which introduced his stepson to the service of Cardinal Wolsey at the time he was setting up his college in Ipswich. The friendship of Wolsey's servant, Thomas Cromwell, proved an invaluable investment, for when Wolsey fell Alvard followed Cromwell into the king's service.

Having served as attorney for the college with his nephew William Bamburgh, Rush was able to offer his inside knowledge of Wolsey's affairs to the royal administration; and Alvard was able to do the same. In doing so they were able to pick up some of the spoils. All that survives of Thomas Rush's property in Upper Brook Street is the bressumer beam bearing his badge as serjeant-at-arms, the royal crown, and his initials, erected on the rear wall of a shop following destruction of the timber-framed property in 1970; it is, as Dr. Blatchly says, appropriate, though coincidental, that it overlooks the chapel in St Stephen's Church that Rush built as his memorial and in which he was presumably buried.

The dissolved Holy Trinity Priory was granted to Sir Thomas Pope, founder of Trinity College, Oxford, who sold it in 1545 to Paul and Edmund Withypoll, father and son London merchants. Edmund demolished the buildings and replaced them with a red-brick residence in the latest style, Christchurch Mansion. Some part of the monastic buildings may have survived, for the prospect of Ipswich which formed an insert to John Speed's Suffolk map of 1610 shows a large domed building north of St Margaret's Church and east of the new mansion which resembles nothing so much as the Abbot's Kitchen at Glastonbury. It is a great deal bigger than the garden fountain or ornament which can be seen in the same position on Ogilby's map, though one wonders if the circular garden plot centring on the fountain could represent the foundations of the building. A glance at Speed's picture is sufficient to dispose of the assertion that it is the base of the round tower of Holy Trinity Church, allegedly blown up by gunpowder some time prior to John Kirby's first edition of *The Suffolk Traveller* of 1735. A demolition charge set off in such a position would have done considerable mischief to Christchurch Mansion itself.

When the Catholic Mary came to the throne various people found opportunity to attack Wythypoll. In one case the churchwardens of St Margaret's sent a petition to the Lords of the Council complaining that for ten years he had failed to pay £4 a year to the church as he should have done, had failed to build up the churchyard wall that he had broken down, had 'interrupted' parishioners' use of the churchyard, had 'plucked down' the priest's house and appropriated the land it had stood on, and had merely boarded up the east window after it had been blown out 'by dystress of wynde' instead of repairing it.[54] Clearly some local people disliked the attitude of this incomer. Disputes continued in Elizabeth's reign, and in 1567 Edmund Wythypoll advised the bailiffs not to attend the annual Holy Cross fair which had been granted to Holy Trinity Priory by Henry II, claiming that the Corporation maces had been lodged in the priory during the fair as a recognition that the town had no jurisdiction over it. The bailiffs refused to give way to Wythypoll, and a riot ensued which led to a case in the Court of Star Chamber.[55]

The loss of the religious houses and their endowments proved serious in towns like Ipswich where the majority of the churches had been staffed and run from the two priories. It was all very well to say that the monks could carry on as parish priests, but who was to pay them, and who was to pay for the upkeep of the churches? The town authorities found themselves forced to make provision for the long-term future of the parish churches, and in 1571 they obtained an act for paving the town[56] and also for giving them powers to arrange with the churchwardens for each parish to raise a rate with which to pay a minister and repair the church. They also made provision to appoint a town preacher or town lecturer who preached three sermons a week to the Corporation in St Mary-le-Tower Church.

The dissolution also led to a cessation of the social and charitable work that had been done by some at least of the monastic houses, and in Ipswich it was necessary that steps be taken by the town authorities to fill the vacuum. Christ's Hospital was established by the town to provide a number of social service facilities, and at the same time the endowments of the old grammar school had to be retrieved from the collapse of Wolsey's college and arrangements made for carrying on its educational work. About 1612 the grammar school moved from Felaw's House, on the west side of Foundation Street, to the Refectory of the Blackfriars. After the Blackfriars had been suppressed in 1538, the whole site was bought in 1541 by William Sabyn, a merchant, sometime naval officer, churchwarden of St Mary-at-Quay, and a royal serjeant-at-arms. He sold it to John Southwell.

43   The arms of Ipswich appear on the memorial to Henry Tooley in St Mary-at-the-Quay Church in which Tooley appears with his son on one side and his wife and their two daughters on the other. (John Wilton)

Henry Tooley, probably the richest merchant in Ipswich at the time, died in 1551 leaving instructions for the foundation of almshouses for ten disabled ex-soldiers, with the proviso that if ten such could not be found the places should go to aged and decrepit persons. Tooley's Foundation was established the following year in Foundation Street with five lodgings, each to contain two poor people. As if to prove that charity was designed to benefit the giver, the inmates were required to attend St Mary-at-Quay Church twice a day to say a prayer of thanks for Tooley's bequest. In 1599 William Smart added to the endowments of the almshouses.[57]

When in 1569 the town purchased the Blackfriars from John Southwell in order to establish Christ's Hospital, part of the purchase money apparently came from Tooley's bequest. The hospital was established by royal charter in 1572 for the relief and maintenance of poor aged persons and children, for the curing poor sick persons, and for the correction and employment of vicious and idle poor people.

Tradesmen and Merchants

Tudor Ipswich was a town of business and trade. Besides the various branches of the cloth trade there were a multitude of other businesses large and small established in the town. Even at the beginning of the 16th century Ipswich was already a thriving centre of the malting industry, for on 12 May 1508 the town authorities thought it necessary to publish an edict forbidding 'foreigners', which as mentioned earlier did not necessarily

44   Christ's Hospital was set up by a charter granted by Queen Elizabeth I in 1572, three years after the Corporation had purchased the Blackfriars, of which this building formed a part. In a niche on the wall is a wooden effigy of a Christ's Hospital boy; the school element of this institution survived until 1883, when its endowments were merged with those of the grammar school. (John Fairclough)

mean immigrants from overseas, to carry out malting within the borough.[58]

Barley grown on Suffolk farms was turned into malt in malthouses that were scattered throughout the built-up area. The grain was first steeped in water for two to three days and then thrown out to the 'couch', where it remained for 24 hours or so before being spread on the floor to germinate. As it sprouts enzymes within the barleycorn break down the divisions within the grain and begin to change the starch into soluble maltose, which is turned into sugar in the brewer's mash tun. At the appropriate time the green malt was removed from the floor and loaded into the kiln or kell to be dried; it was this final part of the malting process that proved to be a considerable hazard and was responsible for more than one outbreak of fire. It would seem from the borough archives that some maltsters burnt straw in their kilns. During the course of the 17th century the burning of straw was several times prohibited because it was considered a dangerous practice, but such regulations were difficult to enforce. Presumably other early maltings used wood as fuel; later generations of maltsters used coke, some maltings having their own coke ovens to convert Newcastle coal into smokeless fuel.[59]

G.R. Clarke wrote in 1830 that 'in ancient times the banks on this side the river were inhabited by the principal people of the town: and it is certain that many of their houses have been converted into malt-offices'.[60] Among these 'principal men of the town' were some who made considerable fortunes out of the wine trade with Gascony, the salt fish trade with Iceland, and other commercial enterprises. There was the Henry Tooley already mentioned, who on more than one occasion sent his ship the *Mary Walsingham* 'by the Grace of God Icelandward'. The *Mary Walsingham* had been bought in 1522 by Tooley's factor in Biscayan ports, Simon Cowper, to carry merchandise from Spain to England. He obtained it from the son of a certain John of Koretto for £152 sterling. She was employed both in the stockfish trade from Iceland and the wine trade, which is a bit surprising in view of the statement that when the Iceland ships returned in 1542 even those that had been unloaded 'stink so that no man not used to the same can endure it'.[61]

In the same year that Tooley became owner of the *Mary Walsingham* a commission was issued to a certain John Bertelot to take into the king's service *The Anne of Notyngham*, owned by William Notingham, of Ipswich, and all other ships fit to serve in the war. Sir William Sandys, treasurer of Calais and commander of the rear of the army in Picardy under the Earl of Surrey, wrote to Wolsey from Calais to tell him that he had sent orders to Ipswich and other places for the speedy preparing of victuals. There was, he said, a great lack of beer, something which Ipswich would have been able to supply from its brewhouses.[62] Thomas Rush, who was in 1523 elected to represent Ipswich in Parliament, and Thomas Hungerford superintended the collection of provisions of various kinds at Ipswich for shipment to Calais. Their accounts include the receipt of no less a sum than £1,233 17s. 6d., indicative of the considerable quantities of provisions shipped from the port. Among the accounts are payments not only for provisions but the costs of transport, milling and storage.[63]

45 The room used by the grammar school when it transferred from Felaw's House to the Blackfriars. This print was produced by Walter Hagreen from a painting by Fred Russel. (John Fairclough)

Antwerp in England

It was at this period that two Englishmen, John Johnson and Christopher Goodwyn, promoted a grand scheme entitled 'Ipswich out of England, or Antwerp in England', clearly inspired by Guiccardini's *Antwerp*, published in 1560. Antwerp, forty miles up the Schelde, was a great centre of commerce and a focus of world trade; Johnson and Goodwyn, one a country gentleman and failed merchant, the other a young and wealthy Ipswich merchant, wanted to make Ipswich an English counterpart of the European entrepôt.

The scheme was submitted to Queen Elizabeth's Secretary of State, Lord Burghley, who put it before the Council, but the London merchants saw it as a threat to their supremacy in trade; their hostility ensured that the scheme was shelved. In 1578 the problems the Merchant Adventurers were having with Hamburg and the Hanseatic League led to the scheme being resurrected; Burghley's right-hand man, Peter Osborne, was given the task of examining it and questioning its promoters.

Considering how cosmopolitan a town Ipswich had been in an earlier period it is odd to find Osborne expressing concern that the townsmen of Ipswich might object to having so many foreigners coming to live among them, but it has to be remembered that this was a period when resentment at the success of immigrant weavers was leading to violent incidents in such towns as Colchester, Norwich and London.[64] However, Osborne's concern was soon answered by Johnson and Goodwyn: 'The subjects of this realm have borne and do bear so much already with strangers, and will no doubt bear with and love them also, because they shall profit by them.' Again the idea of a great international port on the Orwell was crushed by the London merchants, who declared that it would spell ruin for the 'whole state of the wealthiest island in Christendom'.[65]

In the 16th century the trade was controlled very largely by the Merchant Adventurers of England, which might have had a branch in Ipswich,[66] by the Merchants of the Staple and by other chartered companies which had strict rules as to who was entitled to trade with certain countries and the ports at which export cargoes should be landed. Ipswich merchants, whether members of the Merchant Adventurers or not, seem to have taken little notice of the rules and rarely concentrated on the staple port nominated by the Merchant Adventurers, spreading their trade much more widely in the Low Countries; in 1574 exports from Ipswich went to Sluis in Zeeland, Flushing on the island of Walcheren, Dordrecht on the lower Rhine, Harlingen in Friesland and Emden on the Ems.[67] Those who traded in defiance of the chartered companies and members of those companies who traded other than in compliance with the rules of those companies were known as interlopers, and the merchants of Ipswich were numbered among them. A contemporary statement of the trade done by interlopers in 1577-8 reveals that they shipped 268 short cloths from Ipswich to Hamburg in that year, a small figure but one that probably does not reflect anything like the complete export trade of the Orwell.

The sacking of Antwerp in 1585 by the Duke of Parma might have provided a great opportunity for Ipswich had it not been for the determined opposition of the City of London. The 1580s were, in any case, troubled years for England, with the launching by the Pope in 1584 of the 'Enterprise of England' to restore the Roman Catholic faith, and the preparations made by Philip II of Spain for an expedition against England, delayed but not ended by Drake's raid on Cadiz in 1587. The town records give much evidence of the preparations made to receive the Spanish attack, with instructions that every portman and each man of the 24 should 'have in readiness for the defense of this Towne' pikes, a bow and a sheaf of arrows, and references to the 'trayning of the Town soldiers'. In 1586 a rate was set 'for providing pouder and matche' for the firearms carried by the trained bands, with a discount for those who paid freely.[68]

As Spanish plans for the Armada to make contact with the Duke of Parma's army, operating in the Netherlands, went ahead, last-minute efforts were made to reinstate the 'decayed' defences of Harwich Harbour; all that could be done on the Suffolk side was to reinstate the earthen banks of 'Langerside Bulwark' and 'Langer Rood', both of which were regarrisoned in 1588.[69] In April of that year Ipswich and Harwich were required to fit out three vessels between them, Ipswich having to bear the lion's share of the cost.[70] What part those vessels played in operations is unknown, but by November they had apparently been demobilised and what was left of their military equipment was being sold.[71]

It seems likely that some of those who manned the three ships were residents of St Clement's parish, a suburb that was largely inhabited by seamen and those involved with the sea at this date. St Clement had been martyred by being tied to an anchor and so was the patron saint of seamen. A one-time resident of the parish was Thomas

46 Sixteenth- or 17th-century houses in Fore Street, photographed in 1929. By the trolleybus pole is a waggon entry giving access to the business premises at the back and probably at the time of building to one of the private quays. The Neptune *public house, a merchant's house which became an inn during the 18th century and continued as a hostelry for 200 years, is on the extreme right.*

47 Another view of old houses in Fore Street which links with the previous illustration. The zigzag chimney of the Neptune *provides an obvious linking point. While many of the houses in these two views have been destroyed the* Neptune *survives, along with the Isaac Lord premises, whose 16th-century gable end and oriel window can be seen projecting over the street.*

Eldred, who sailed with Thomas Cavendish on a two-year expedition beginning in 1586 that took Cavendish's little fleet of three small ships around the world. Cavendish, who came from Trimley St Martin, was thus second to Sir Francis Drake in circumnavigating the globe. Cavendish died on the way home from a second privateering voyage in 1591 during which he was unable to negotiate the Straits of Magellan and so failed in his attempt at a second circumnavigation.

Eldred's house, which lay between St Clement's Fore Street and the churchyard, has been demolished, but between the street and the river there survives an excellent group of timber-framed buildings of the kind once inhabited by merchants taking part in the trade of the port. The group always known today as Isaac Lord's is probably the last surviving example of a 16th/17th-century merchant's house with warehouses at the rear opening directly on to the river. Goods landed at the back of the premises could be stored in warehouses pending distribution or sale in the retail shop on the street front.

Professor W.G. Hoskins describes such places very well.

> This type of house has no direct entrance from the street—or had none originally. It has a long side-passage off which the doorways open to give access to the shop and to the kitchen behind. The passage then emerges into the open at the back into a long courtyard with long ranges of warehouses or lofts stretching back along the site until we emerge directly on to the quay. On the main street the merchant had his tiny shop and behind that came the kitchen and the buttery. The other living rooms were piled up above. At the back door, so to speak, the merchant's ships unloaded straight into his warehouses. At the front door, he was selling pennyworths of goods to retail customers. In between, he carried on the wholesale business that was the mainstay of his livelihood; he covered the whole range of trading, from importer to retail shopkeeper.[72]

A nearby house is dated 1639, but this is the date of modernisation, not of building. It is an interesting example of a hall-house partly of 15th-century and partly of 16th-century date, and was for some 200 years the *Neptune Inn*; it almost certainly owes its survival to George Bodley Scott, a director of W.S. Cowell, who bought the premises in 1947 and spent many years restoring the buildings with his own hands.[73]

Water Supply

The site on which the town grew up gave Ipswich one great advantage; it lay in a basin, and springs in the surrounding high ground provided a constant supply of good water that ran naturally down into the Orwell. This water, running through the streets on its way to the river, not only served for drinking and washing but also for fighting the inevitable fires that broke out from time to time, and so doubtless saved Ipswich from the kind of disasters that struck other Suffolk towns. There were springs all around the edge of the saucer in which Ipswich sits, one of the more important being in the grounds of Christchurch, feeding the fishponds that had supplied fast-day victuals for the monks of Holy Trinity. Water from this spring ran down to the river by way of

Upper and Lower Brook Street, while water from the Cauld Wells to the north-east of the town flowed down Great Wash Lane (Spring Road) and through the Upper and Lower Wash (Upper and Lower Orwell Street). Right down to the present day the street names are evocative of the time when water ran down the thoroughfares and people crossing the junction of The Wash and what is now Orwell Place used the Stepples (stepping stones) to cross the road.

These streams became heavily polluted when used for the disposal of all kinds of household and trade refuse, and both the town authorities and the religious houses took steps to bring clean water into the town by means of bored-out elm trunks, which discharged into large tanks or conduits. 'The conduit' is first mentioned in 1395, and in 1451 two men were chosen to repair 'the conduit and the house',[74] on the site of the later conduit house on the corner of Tavern Street and Cook Lane (St. Lawrence's Street). In 1482 the profits of the conduit were made over to two people 'for the upholding and repairing of the same'.[75] The Blackfriars seem to have made use of the water from the Cauld Wells, bringing it in wooden pipes to a cistern within the friary, while the Priory of St Peter and St Paul took its water supply from a 'fountain' on the Stoke side of the river, the pipes being laid under the river and the mill pond of Stoke Mill. When in 1491 the bailiffs acquired control of the mill and the adjoining marshes the Prior reserved access 'for repairing the aqueduct'.[76] Following the dissolution of

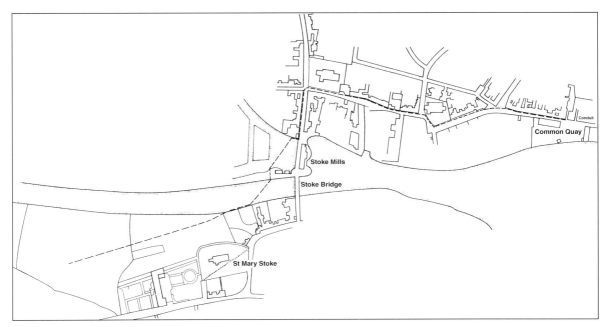

48   The water supply to the Priory of SS Peter and Paul, carried under the river and millpond in a wooden trunk from springs in the vicinity of Stoke Hall. With the dissolution of the priory in 1528 the system was taken over by the Corporation, which extended the pipes along College Street and Key Street to a 'conduit' near the Common Quay, as seen here.

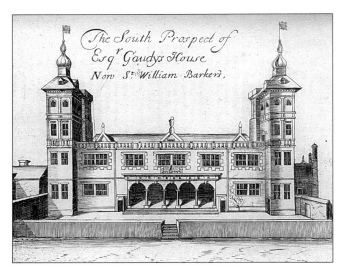

49   *Thomas Seckford's Great Place in Westgate Street, one of the large gentry houses that graced the town in the 16th century. Seckford, who was Master of Requests in Elizabeth's reign, took up the case of John Collins, who in 1574 obtained a licence not only to produce sailcloth in Ipswich and Woodbridge but also to stamp approved pieces of sailcloth with the royal rose and crown. The illustration is from Ogilby's map.*

the priory this water supply and its 'aqueduct' became a public supply, the pipes being extended along College Street and Key Street to a cistern in the vicinity of the Common Quay.

From time to time the Great Court allowed people to make use of the water of the Cauldwell Brook at a small charge, but when in 1555 Edmund Leeche built a water mill on that stream, causing flooding upstream of his mill dam, he was ordered to remove it.[77] Sometimes it seems likely that the water was used for semi-industrial purposes such as the washing of cloth, as when in 1521 John Man was granted permission to 'stopp the water running by Hellens Church, to his own use' for seven hours each day. The wording seems to indicate something more than domestic use.[78] Throughout the 16th century there are many cases of inhabitants being given leave to insert a 'quill' into the water pipe to obtain water; originally it was no doubt a swan or goose quill with the ends cut off that would direct the water into a cistern, from which water could be drawn as required. A small annual charge was levied for this.

William Johnson, shoemaker, was in 1574 made a free burgess in return for undertaking 'to make assurance for the contynuance of the pype belongynge to the conduytt of the late dissolved Black Fryers, now the hospitall, to the use of the bailiffes burgesses and commonalty of the said towne.' It is unclear quite what he was to do, but he was apparently one of those people who can always be relied on to do voluntary work of different kinds.[79] The small rents paid for water must have provided the town with a steady income, so long as they were paid regularly, but money had to be spent on maintenance of the springs and the pipes. Thomas Gleed's account as town treasurer for 1586-7 contains a number of items relating to the work of Thomas Palmer, Thomas Cutberd and Edmond Tayller on repairing the pipes and opening up the springs that fed them. Perhaps lead pipes were already in use, for one item records the payment of two shillings: 'The 26 Januarye to William Gloed for stones, sand and workmanshyp to stope up three holles that the plumer broke upe to mend the conditt pype where it was broken'. Another item relates to a payment to Thomas Palmer 'for casting of on[e] condyte pype ...'.[80]

VI

Stuart and Commonwealth Ipswich

At the beginning of the 17th century Ipswich was a thriving port, with a shipbuilding industry of such importance that it is said the town was known as 'the shipyard of London'.[1] The export trade in woollen cloth made both in the town and in places such as East Bergholt and Hadleigh, although soon to decline, continued to be profitable, and Ipswich merchants grew rich from a variety of commercial enterprises. The cloth industry was being reorganised on a capitalistic basis during the latter part of Elizabeth's reign, and in 1590 a company of clothworkers, shearmen and dyers was set up in Ipswich, partly with the idea of countering the incursions of foreigners into the business. The ordinances of the new company, set down in the General Assembly Book,[2] forbade any craftsman of the company to take apprentices born outside the town without the licence of the bailiffs in writing.

The 45-year reign of Queen Elizabeth I came to an end in 1603, and the Crown passed to James VI of Scotland, great-grandson of Margaret, sister of Henry VIII. English Puritans had hopes that the new king would set about reforming the Church of England in the way they desired, but the Puritan proposals were rejected at the Hampton Court Conference in 1604, disappointing many people in Ipswich. Something of a Puritan stronghold in a county that was noted for its opposition to Roman Catholicism and High Church Anglicanism, Ipswich was to prove a hotbed of resistance as King James and later Charles I endeavoured to impose royal control over the Church. During Elizabeth's reign the Corporation had begun appointing its own town lecturer or preacher, and a succession of Puritan town preachers sought to show the way in which the Reformation should be moved forward. The most notable of these was Samuel Ward, who arrived in the town in 1605. An out-and-out Puritan, he was to prove a controversial figure and was to make a mark on religious life that was to prove well-nigh indelible. A young man of about 28 when appointed town preacher on 1 November 1605,[3] Samuel was the son of John Ward, preacher of Haverhill, and his wife Susanna.

Previous preachers had served for varying lengths of time, but none had stayed for long. Ward, however, remained in his post until his death in 1640. 'If he shall at any time minde to depart, he shall give the town halfe a yeres warning, and they him likewise in case they shall minde to alter' said the entry in the Great Court Book recording his election.[4] As it was the town never did have a mind to terminate his employment; Ward's uncompromising statement of Puritan principles that brought him into conflict with both Crown and Church was approved of by the town authorities who appointed him. For his annual stipend of £66 13s. 4d., together with an additional £6 13s. 4d. towards the rent of a house, he had to preach three sermons each week, on Sunday, Wednesday and Friday, in St Mary-le-Tower, but that was not all; he was involved with the grammar school, and the year after his appointment he was one of three divines appointed to examine the Master of the School, James Leman, to establish 'whether he be worthy and sufficient for the place'.[5] Then on 19 February 1611 the Assembly decided that he and three others should 'examine the Schollers of the Grammar Schole whether there be any fit to be sent to Cambridge or not and to certify which of them (whose parents shall be willing to sende thither) they shal find fittest to be sent for the obteyning of a schollersheppe in Pembroke Hall according to Mr. Smarte his gifte'. William Smarte had endowed scholarships for grammar school boys going up to Pembroke Hall at Cambridge together with a fellowship, often held later by those same scholars.

Two years after his initial appointment Ward was elected town preacher for life, 'if he shall soe long dwell in this Towne', and his salary was raised to £73 6s. 8d. a year. In 1610 it was raised to £90, and then in 1614 to £100 a year. He was considered a great asset to the town.

He fell foul of the Crown when in 1621 he produced a tract for which he himself drew the title-page design, a plate entitled *The Double Deliverance*, a reference to the Spanish Armada and the Gunpowder Plot. Ward was no mean caricaturist; in the middle of the page sit the Pope, the cardinals and the King of Spain in conference with the Devil, while on one side is the Armada being dispersed by the storms and on the other Guy Fawkes approaching the Houses of Parliament, his fell designs revealed by the Eye of God. On the face of it this was a wholly patriotic piece of work, if virulently anti-Catholic. Just at the time of the tract's printing in Amsterdam, however, King James was in negotiation with Spain in an attempt to arrange the marriage of his son Charles to the Infanta Maria, and publication of such anti-Spanish, anti-Catholic propaganda threatened the success of the talks, which were widely unpopular in England. When the Spanish ambassador complained at this affront to his country's dignity, Ward was committed to prison by the Privy Council. From prison Ward petitioned the king for his release, saying that his pamphlet had been written five years earlier and sent to the printers a whole year before. There had been no sinister intention of meddling in any of his majesty's 'secrett affaires', and if allowed to continue his preaching he would, he said, 'be more cautelous for the future'.[6]

Doubtless he obtained his release, but the following year the bishop, Dr. Samuel Harsnett, a determined High Churchman and a man of learning, took proceedings against him in the consistory court in Norwich. Ward appealed to the king, who referred the matter to Lord Keeper Williams. In a biography of Williams published in 1693 Bishop Hacket said that

> the Lord Keeper found Mr. Ward to be not altogether blameless, but a man to be won easily by fair dealing. So he persuaded Bishop Harsnett to take his submission, and to continue him in his lecture at Ipswich … and I aver it upon the faith of a good witness, that after this Bishop Harsnett acknowledged that he was as useful a man to assist him in his government, as was in all his diocese.[7]

Bishop Hacket's informant might have been telling the truth, but Ward continued to get into trouble for his Puritan views. In 1622 the Corporation received a letter from the king inhibiting Ward from preaching the lecture; they referred it to the town's lawyer.

While Puritans sought to build on the Reformation and to remove all traces of what they regarded as popish worship, Charles I sought to establish his control over the Church of England and in doing so to lay down strict rules for worship. Attempts to enforce a uniform liturgy were anathema to Puritans such as Ward, and the Ipswich town preacher spoke out strongly against them. The Puritans believed that the Sabbath should be a day of sermonising and quiet, whereas the High Church party considered that once divine service had been performed the day should be given to innocent recreation. As far as the latter were concerned the young were more profitably employed in archery practice, wrestling or dancing than in listening to sermons, particularly those that were theologically or politically subversive. The clergy were ordered to read the controversial *Book of Sports* from their pulpits; those of a Puritan persuasion, and the lecturers such as Samuel Ward, refused to do so.

Harsnett became Archbishop of York in 1628, to be succeeded as Bishop of Norwich by Francis White, who was translated to Ely in 1631. The good-natured and indolent Richard Corbett came to Norwich the following year and dealt very moderately with the Puritans, much as he disapproved of their sombre way of life and worship—he was himself of a merry temperament, and a practical joker. Bishop Corbett found the measure of Samuel Ward when it became necessary to discipline him. Taking a very moderate line, he obtained Ward's submission, and then sent him, in October 1633, a letter that can only be described as friendly and solicitous.

MY WORTHY FRIEND,

I thank God for your conformity, and you for your acknowledgment. Stand upright in the Church wherein you live; be true of heart to her governors; think well of her significant ceremonies: and be you assured I shall never displace you of that room which I have given you in my affections. Prove you a good tenant in my heart, and no minister in my diocese hath a better landlord. Farewell; God Almighty bless you with your whole congregation.

From your faithful friend to serve you in Christ Jesus.

RICH. NORWICH[8]

One of his fellow-bishops said with truth that Corbett had 'learned the way of that diocese of Norwich, and found that, though it were skittish and would not always come to the pail, yet the Puritan cow gave the best milk'.

One hopes that Corbett's goodwill was reciprocated by the Puritan preacher, though it seems unlikely that Ward would have approved overmuch of some of the practices of the bishop and his two chaplains, Thomas Lushington and William Strode. John Aubrey in his *Brief Lives* tells a delightful tale of the bishop and Lushington, a convivial fellow and much beloved by his patron, repairing to the cellar for a little relaxation. Aubrey describes how 'the Bishop sometimes would take the key of the wine-cellar, and he and his chaplain would go and lock themselves in and be merry. Then first he lays down his episcopal hat—"There lies the bishop." Then he puts off his gown—"There lies the doctor." Then 'twas, "Here's to thee, Corbett," and "Here's to thee, Lushington".'[9]

In 1635 Ward was accused of having 'preached against the common bowing at the name of Jesus, and against the king's *Book of Sports*, and further said that the Church of England was ready to ring changes in religion, and the gospel stood on tiptoe, as ready to be gone'. For this and other offences he was suspended from preaching and sent to prison by the Court of High Commission. The Corporation which had appointed him refused to accept Ward's suspension and petitioned for his reinstatement, pointedly avoiding asking the bishop to allow them another preacher in Ward's place.

William Laud, the leader of the Arminian party[10] under Charles I, became Archbishop of Canterbury in 1633 and immediately set out to impose conformity on the Church, making use of the Court of Star Chamber and that of High Commission to inflict often brutal penalties on those who opposed his edicts. He sent his Vicar-General, Sir Nathaniel Brent, on a visitation of the province in 1634, and in the spring of 1635 Brent arrived in the Norwich diocese. When he came to Ipswich on a three-day visit on 22 April of that year the bailiffs, portmen and 24 rode out to meet him, then entertained him with a banquet.

His report to Laud could not have been pleasing to the archbishop. After remarking favourably enough on the solemn welcome he received from the corporation he went on to say that the town was 'exceeding factious … Mr. Samuel Ward is thought to be the chiefe author of their nonconformity'. He narrated how he had suspended the minister of St Helen's for giving the sacrament to people who would not kneel at the altar rail and had excommunicated a number of churchwardens 'who were soe precise that they would not take their oath. But afterwards they all submitted with protestacon to reforme their opinions, and many doe beleeve that a good reformacon will followe.'[11]

Bishop Corbett died in 1635, his last words being whispered to his beloved chaplain, the companion of his pleasures—'Good night, Lushington.'[12] The new bishop, Matthew Wren, was a very different man, a lover of ceremonial, a rigid disciplinarian and one of Archbishop Laud's most loyal supporters. With a sharp tongue and a peremptory manner of both speech and writing, he had what Clarendon referred to as a 'severe, sour nature'.[13] Few men could have made themselves so unpopular in little over two years as he did while Bishop of Norwich.

Wren quickly turned his attention to Ipswich. Obtaining the king's permission to live for several months at his house in Silent Street, formerly Lord Curzon's house, rather than in his cathedral city, Wren took up residence and began his onslaught on the nonconforming ministers, the lecturers and dissenting churchwardens. He issued 'orders, directions and remembrances' giving detailed instructions on every subject relating to services, parish perambulations, the position of the communion table, genuflection, bowing at the name of Jesus, kneeling for prayers and much more.[14]

Wren's presence in Ipswich, and his actions, provoked rioting in the town and Ferdinando Adams, churchwarden of St Mary-le-Tower, locked the doors against the bishop. The bishop was forced to remove himself for his own safety, and Adams fled to New England, whence he returned in 1640. Far from putting down the riots, the town authorities tacitly encouraged the protesters. It must have been with some feeling that Wren told Laud that Ipswich was proving to be the 'most refractory and styf place' in the diocese.

One of Archbishop Laud's best-known instructions, that the communion table should be set against the east wall of the chancel and separated off from the rest of the church by rails 'reaching across from the north wall to the south wall, near one yard in height, so thick with pillars that dogs may not get in', seems to have aroused particular anger among the Puritans of Ipswich. Alfred Kingston, author of a pioneering work on the period of the Civil Wars in East Anglia, records that the rails around the communion table in St Lawrence's Church were burned by piling furze faggots against them.[15] Since Elizabethan times the communion table had normally stood in the main body of the church, and to the Puritans this Laudian reform smacked of popery. Dogs had roamed free in churches for as long as anybody could remember; at Hadleigh a dog had seized the communion bread and run away with it.[16] As a result of the opposition to his authority Bishop Wren proceeded against the town in the Court of Star Chamber, and in 1637 the Corporation was involved in defending the case.

One of the most notorious pamphlets of the time, *News from Ipswich*, was written not by Ward but by an Oxford-educated lawyer named William Prynne, a strident and vindictive critic of the bishops. The title page declares that the pamphlet was first printed at Ipswich. It was in fact probably printed in Holland, and was published in Edinburgh, where those who later signed the National Covenant were as strongly opposed to attempts to impose conformity on the Protestant Church as were the English Puritans. Writing under the name of Matthew White, supposedly an Ipswich resident, Prynne told of

> our Norwich diocese, where little Pope Regulus hath played such Rex, that he hath
> suspended above sixty of our sincerest, painfullest, conformable ministers, both from
> their office and benefice, so as many of our churches (as the like was never seen since
> King John's days) are quite shut up, and *Lord have mercy upon us* may be written on their
> doors: the people call for the bread of their souls, and their ministers are prohibited
> to give it them ...[17]

For all that he used a nom-de-plume, Prynne was discovered to be the author of this vehement and by no means accurate diatribe and was brought before the Court of Star Chamber, which condemned him to life imprisonment, an exorbitant fine, the pillory, branding, and the loss of what remained of his ears; they had been cropped after an earlier court appearance. It was an horrific sentence.

Released from prison on the collapse of royal power, he sought revenge on Laud by defaming his memory; the archbishop had been executed in 1645. Prynne continued to be a thorn in the side of successive governments, but spent his last years harmlessly and enjoyably as royal archivist in the Tower of London.[18]

Ipswich and Emigration

While some Puritans fled to Holland, others removed themselves even further by emigrating to America, as the Pilgrim Fathers had done in 1620. The bishop's commissary for the Archdeaconry of Suffolk, Henry Dade, complained to Archbishop Laud in 1634 about the increasing emigration of people known to be disaffected by the government of the Church of England, attributing this largely to the discontent created by Ward's preaching against the Prayer Book and set prayer, and to fears expressed by him of changes in the national religion. Another on whom Dade heaped the blame for the spate of emigration was the parson of Woolverstone, 'who is a great stickler for transporting these people'.[19]

As early as 1611 the Corporation had 'adventured' £100 towards the cost of ships to carry settlers to Virginia, where the Virginia Company had founded the port of Jamestown in 1607, but it was only with the *Mayflower* voyage of 1620 to New England that the tide of emigration began to flow strongly. It is within the bounds of possibility that the *Mayflower* was built in one of the Ipswich shipyards, for she was described as 'of Harwich' in 1609 and her captain, Christopher Jones, was a Harwich man.[20]

The Protestant fervour of its inhabitants and of many who lived in the country areas of Suffolk and north Essex which formed the hinterland of Ipswich guaranteed the port a role in the early wave of emigration to New England and other American colonies. Indeed, one of the settlements founded by the Winthrops from Groton and those who went with them in 1630 was given the name of Ipswich 'in acknowledgment of the great honour and kindness done to our people who took shipping there'. Eleven ships carried almost 700 passengers from Ipswich in 1630 in what became known as the Winthrop fleet, since the leader of the party and the inspiration behind the whole operation was John Winthrop, of Groton. Of those 700 passengers, no fewer than 324 were from south Suffolk and north Essex, a great many of them linked by family ties.[21]

Henry Dade's complaints to Archbishop Laud in 1634 led to the Privy Council preventing the departure of two vessels which were to have sailed from Ipswich early in March that year for New England with 80 emigrants in each.[22] It was reported about that time that 'two ships are to sail from Ipswich with men and provision for their abiding in New England, in each of which ships are appointed to go about six score passengers'. These ships, the *Elizabeth* of Ipswich and the *Francis* of Ipswich, both sailed down the Orwell 'bound for New England the last of Aprill', so it might be that the Privy Council did no more than delay their departure.

One of the larger ships sailing across the Atlantic was the 400-ton *Great Hope* of Ipswich, which arrived in America in the middle of August 1635, after weathering a storm which had wrecked one ship and nearly wrecked another. Three more ships arrived on the American coast in June 1637, having left Ipswich some time earlier. They were the *Mary Anne* of Yarmouth, the *John and Dorothy* of Ipswich, and the *Rose* of

Yarmouth.[23] The next year, 1638, the *Diligent* of Ipswich was among no fewer than 20 ships which crossed the Atlantic with at least 3,000 men, women and children. She arrived at Boston on 10 August with about 100 people, most of whom had left Hingham in Norfolk for its namesake settlement in Massachusetts.

The man blamed for encouraging this wave of emigration, Samuel Ward, died on 8 March 1639–40. His widow and eldest son were granted a pension of £25 a quarter by the Corporation, perhaps an indication of the esteem in which the preacher had been held in the town. Ward's daughter Abigail married the Rev. John Ashburne, who became rector of Norton in West Suffolk in 1646 and ran a private madhouse at a time when impoverished Anglican clerics were forced to seek alternative sources of income following the breakdown of the tithe system. One of his patients seems to have been Samuel Ward junior, who suffered from schizophrenia. Ashburne was killed by his brother-in-law in 1661 in an attack that might have been bound up with the ecclesiastical politics of the period.

Suffolk as a whole was strongly Puritan, though the county gentry were split with only a fairly narrow majority supporting the side of Parliament when war broke out, and Ipswich was at the centre of opposition to King Charles's increasing efforts to impose personal and absolute authority and to his moves to enforce conformity in the Church.

Having dissolved Parliament in 1629, Charles ruled personally without a Parliament until he was forced to recall Parliament after the English defeat suffered at the hands of the Scots in the first Bishops' War of 1639. The Parliamentary election of March 1640 was preceded in Suffolk by devious political manoeuvring which included an attempt to remove the shire court at which the elections would be held from Ipswich to Beccles, a 'remote place' which was in the control of the Royalist Sir William Playters. Sir William withdrew from the contest when the attempt was unmasked, and two prominent Puritan sympathizers, Sir Philip Parker of Erwarton and Sir Nathaniel Barnardiston were returned unopposed. They were joined at Westminster by William Cage, a prominent Ipswich Puritan, and John Gurdon, of Great Wenham, who, 'being neither inhabitant nor ffreeman of this towne',[24] gained more votes than Edmund Dey, who had represented the borough at the 1628 Parliament. Cage had already represented Ipswich in six previous Parliaments, being first returned in 1614.

That Parliament of 1640 sat only from 13 April to 5 May, when the king dissolved it on account of the barrage of criticism emanating from it. Cage and Gurdon were again returned for the borough in the autumn and sat in the Long Parliament. The county election held in Ipswich in the autumn of 1640 was an unruly and violent event. The Puritans Sir Philip Parker and Sir Nathaniel Barnardiston were opposed by a gentleman from Mildenhall, Henry North, who was supported by a group of Arminian clergymen. The High Sheriff, Sir Symonds D'Ewes, was accused by North's father, Sir Roger North, in very intemperate terms of having conducted the poll improperly; and on the second day of the election Sir Roger and a number of young men, said to be armed with swords and rapiers, went up and down 'in such a manner on the said

Corne Hill' that Samuel Duncon, one of the town constables, 'fearing that much danger and bloudshedd might ensue', ordered them in the king's name to desist.[25]

Judging by the testimony of Samuel Duncon it would seem that the Norths were throwing their weight about in an attempt to sway the election in their favour, and there was no justification for Sir Roger's allegations. Certainly the poll was interrupted when one of the polling tables collapsed as those waiting to vote crowded around it, and one of the polling clerks had to be replaced when his nose began to bleed, though there is no suggestion that it was a blow that caused his nosebleed. It is true that Duncon was well known in Ipswich as a Puritan, and that D'Ewes was also of that persuasion. Nor was it denied that Duncon took over from the unfortunate polling clerk with the bleeding nose, but the success of Parker and Barnardiston was not subsequently challenged by the Norths. The simple fact was that Henry North had polled only 1,400 votes, each of the other candidates getting more than 2,000, a majority too great to be disputed.

The Civil Wars

When the first Civil War broke out in 1642 the Corporation took stock of the town defences, sending John Blomfield and Samuel Duncon to Colchester to obtain the advice of a military engineer on fortifying the town. At the same time the Assembly instructed the treasurer to purchase 100 muskets and eight barrels of gunpowder.[26] Fears that the king's army might strike into East Anglia from Lincolnshire prompted the Corporation to give instructions in 1643 for the preparation of breastworks and fortifications; the treasurer was ordered to provide 50 or 60 'croudbarrowes or handbarrowes' and baskets for this work.[27] That autumn orders were made for closing up passages over the town walls or ramparts and for the setting of watch and ward: 14 men were to ward by day and 32 to watch by night, particular care being taken that the night watch did not go off duty until the ward was set.[28]

Though Ipswich was stoutly Puritan there were certainly some residents whose loyalty was to the king, and fierce arguments sometimes arose as a result. In 1642 it was necessary for the Great Court to issue an order that anyone interrupting a person addressing the court should be fined 12d., and that all speeches should be directed to the bailiffs.[29] There had been 'great disorder in the Great Court' which disrupted the court's business.

That the Puritans had the upper hand was made clear when John Lany, a Royalist who had taken his deceased father's place as Recorder, was discharged from that position. Peter Fisher and Samuel Duncon, two of the leading Puritan members of the Corporation, were sent to invite Nathaniell Bacon to the town to take over the Recordership. Back came the reply from the Puritan lawyer 'that if the town will please to make choise of him, he will comme and live in the towne', and so he was elected Recorder at a Great Court on 30 December 1642 and sworn in as a burgess not long afterwards.[30] A grandson of Sir Nicholas Bacon, James I's Lord Chancellor, Nathaniell took a very active part in local affairs and wider concerns after becoming a resident of

St Margaret's parish. When Suffolk joined with five neighbouring counties to form the Eastern Association in the winter of 1642–3, Nathaniell became chairman of the Cambridge Committee which ran the association with an efficiency and self-assurance which ensured a success that eluded other similar associations.

His duties as chairman of the Cambridge Committee conflicted somewhat with his work as Recorder of Ipswich, and on at least two occasions the bailiffs had to be requested to postpone local courts so that he might stay in Cambridge because of 'the importance of the present affaires heere'. Presumably the bailiffs, supporters of the Parliamentary cause as they were, agreed without too many expressions of annoyance. When Nathaniell had to be absent from Cambridge his position as Suffolk representative on the committee and his chairmanship were taken by his brother Francis, who was also a lawyer.[31] On William Cage's death in 1646 Francis Bacon was elected to represent Ipswich in Parliament in his place.

50 *Nathaniell Bacon, who was appointed Recorder of Ipswich in 1642 and became chairman of the Cambridge Committee of the Eastern Association. A strong supporter of the Puritan cause, he was nevertheless opposed to the execution of the king and to the proclamation of the Commonwealth.*

Besides Nathaniell Bacon at least eight other Ipswich men served on the Suffolk Committee, and the bailiffs for the time being were also members. There is no doubt that the town played a leading part in the affairs of the Eastern Association, which after 1643 consisted of eight counties. Among those who were active on the Suffolk Committee was one relative newcomer from the north, John Brandling, a coal merchant who was a freeman of Newcastle-upon-Tyne. When he was first elected a portman in 1641 he refused to take the oath, but when elected again in 1643 he 'tooke his oathe of Portman, saving his othe as ffreeman of New Castle'.[32] In spite of his dual allegiance he served as bailiff in 1640-1 and 1642-3, and served twice more in the 1650s.

The second Civil War began in 1648 with Royalist risings at Bury St Edmunds and other places, though Ipswich seems to have been quiet enough. The uprising at Bury came to an end with little bloodshed, but at Colchester a Royalist force took over the town, resulting in a long and terrible siege. Anticipating the threat from the Royalists occupying Colchester, the Ipswich Trained Bands were sent to Cattawade to prevent a crossing of the Stour. In their absence the defence of the town was taken on by seamen, and because the voluntary contributions called for proved insufficient a rate was levied to pay them for their services. At the same time 'a Stronge Warde' was set, and instructions were given that the constable on his rounds at night should be accompanied by three or four men armed with muskets. The Corporation was determined there should be no Royalist agitation in Ipswich.

The trial and execution of King Charles I in 1649 and the proclamation of the Commonwealth was not to the liking of many of those who were involved in the Puritan cause. Nathaniell Bacon wound up his monumental *The Annalls of Ipswiche* in that year with the words 'The last daye of Januarie putts a sad period unto my penn. And thus, by the goodness of Allmightie God, I have summed up the affairs of the government of this town of Ippeswiche under bayliffes whoe are happie in this, that God hathe established their seate more sure than the throne of kings.'[33] Bacon's activities outside the borough could have had an adverse effect on his career as a servant of the town; that they did not is made clear by his election as Town Clerk in 1651 and a claviger in 1653. He joined his brother Francis at Westminster in 1654 when they were both elected to represent the borough in the Parliament that began on 3 September that year, the two brothers being returned in subsequent elections in 1656, 1658 and 1660. Nathaniell continued to hold this collection of offices up to the time of his death, along with a variety of external offices; he was Recorder of Bury St Edmunds, a Master of the Court of Requests and, from 1649, a Judge of the High Court of Admiralty.[34]

On Nathaniell's death in 1660 the body corporate recognised that it had lost a servant of remarkable ability and considerable achievements. At a Great Court on 30 April 1661 it was 'Agreed that Mrs. Bacon shall have a Gratuitie of Five and twentie pounds given her f[m] this towne for the great paynes that her husband, Mr. Nathaniell Bacon, did take in the transcribinge of several ancient Records belonging to this Towne.'[35]

The First Dutch War

The three Dutch wars of 1652–4, 1664–7 and 1672-4 were fought almost entirely at sea, but they nevertheless affected Ipswich to a very marked degree. Not only was the town's maritime trade affected by the presence of hostile fleets in the North Sea but the town became involved in the supply of sailcloth, stores and crew replacements to the English fleet and, in common with other Suffolk towns, received large numbers of sick and wounded men on whose care a large amount of money had to be disbursed by the town authorities.[36]

A clash between Dutch men-of-war and the English fleet in the Channel in May 1652 precipitated both nations into war, and in February 1653 the bailiffs of Ipswich received instructions to impress 30 able-seamen. It should not have been difficult to find that number of men, but it is said that the seamen endeavoured to obtain berths in the colliers where they were free from impressment or else 'took to the plough'. After the fight off the Gabbard, some fifty miles east of Harwich, in June 1653 some of the wounded were taken to Ipswich in the *Tenth Whelp* (the last of ten 14-gun sloops built in 1627, all named *Lions Whelp* and distinguished by numbers), other sick and wounded being landed at Harwich. The bailiffs, Richard Puplett and Nicholas Phillips, received a letter dated 5 June 1653 from Major Nicholas Bourne, a Navy Commissioner and Rear Admiral, in the fourth-rate *Tyger* at Harwich, asking them to make provision for some of the many sick men from the warships ordered into Harwich. At about the same time the Generals-at-Sea, Robert Blake and George Monck (later Duke of Albemarle), wrote ordering the bailiffs to care for the wounded, adding that they would be reimbursed. The bailiffs appointed surgeons to look after the seamen and spent £80 a week on the care of the seamen, but the promised reimbursement was slow in coming.

A naval doctor, Dr. Daniel Whistler, was sent down to Ipswich to care for the sick and wounded men, who numbered at least 80 at Ipswich alone. Dr. Whistler, whom Samuel Pepys found 'good company and a very ingenious man', had studied medicine at Leyden and was the author of the first book on rickets; some years later he assured Pepys over dinner that experiments carried out on dogs concerning blood transfusions were likely to be found of great use to men. The doctor wrote from Ipswich that the number of sick and wounded was 165, presumably at both Ipswich and Harwich, and that 60 more had come since his arrival. 'Harwich is no place for sick men, the air being as bad as at sea … I wish all the sick were sent here, there being very good accommodation.' Most likely some of that accommodation was in Lord Curzon's House in Silent Street, which was turned into a makeshift naval hospital at this time.[37] George Monck, an officer with an unfailing concern for his men's welfare, ordered that the bailiffs of Ipswich and those of Aldeburgh, Dunwich and Southwold should be reimbursed for their outlay on behalf of the sick and wounded men, but still the money remained unpaid. Readers of Pepys' diary will know that this was not untypical of the period.

Eventually there were so many wounded men at Ipswich that it became necessary to send some to Woodbridge and to other neighbouring towns and villages. Monck wrote that he was 'very unwilling to overcharge yor Towne with sick men, no more than needs must', and gave permission for the bailiffs to 'dispose of some of them into the neighbouring Villages which you say bears none of ye burden provided the like Care bee taken of them as where they now are'. In August one of the bailiffs, Nicholas Phillips, wrote to Monck that there were 'neere a thousand sick and wounded soldiers and seamen in the towne' and spoke of the town's 'inability of relieving them, wee have expended all the moneys we could command. . .sent to London and received noe Returnes. We are likelie to see these poore people perish for want of support'. At the end of their year of office the two bailiffs rendered an account to the Admiralty and the Commissioners for the Sick and Wounded showing that they had spent £3,838 9s. 8d. on the sick and wounded between 11 July and 29 September and claiming the balance due of £738 9s. 8d. Their successors as bailiffs had spent another £141 12s. 8d. up to 8 December. The town was having to find a great deal of money for this humanitarian work, and there must have been times when the two bailiffs were worried men indeed as they sought repayment.

The war came to an end in 1654, but this did not remove many of the problems that beset Ipswich, in common with the country at large. In the summer of 1659 the town was still occupied in looking after sick seamen sent upriver by Edward Montagu (created Earl of Sandwich the following year). There were still difficulties in obtaining reimbursement of the money spent in caring for the seamen, and in September 1660 John Maidston, Nathaniell Bacon's clerk, was told to continue his efforts in London to obtain payment.

The Restoration

There were many who were concerned at the increasing part being played by the military in the government of the country, and this concern was reflected in the deliberations of the Assembly, which in 1659 ordered a fast 'to seeke God for the Establishmt of A Governmt that maie be an Incouragemt to trueth righteousnes & Peace'. One concern of the local authorities was to recover local control of the militia and the trained bands. Early the following year the Assembly decided to write to General Monck pointing out that Ipswich was suffering from having so many troops quartered in the town and asking that the unfortunate innkeepers on whom they were billeted should be paid the money due to them. Monck, who believed firmly in the subordination of the military to the civil power, was already engaged in moves that would result in the restoration both of a free Parliament and of the monarchy. The same day that they agreed to send a letter to Monck in Scotland the town's leaders ordered that a day of thanksgiving be held 'for returninge of thanks to the Lord for his Mercies to the Nation in restoreinge of the Parliament to their settinge & soe many changes without blood sheddinge …'.

There is little doubt that there were those in Ipswich who secretly wished for the return of the king. The arms of the Commonwealth had replaced the Royal Arms in the churches, but both at St Margaret's and at St Stephen's someone painted the Prince of Wales's feathers on the back of the panel bearing the Commonwealth Arms, where they remained unseen until the day of Charles's coming, or perhaps rather earlier; Pepys tells how the King's Arms were being set up in London churches in April 1660.[38] Not until 25 May did Charles land at Dover, and not until 10 July did the Assembly gave orders for the painting of the Royal Arms for display in the Moot Hall, an instruction that was ratified by the Great Court on the 23rd. John Brame, limner, was next year paid £20 for painting the arms and other similar work done at the same time.

It is hardly to be supposed that there would have been universal rejoicing at the king's return to the throne in a town with such a reputation as Ipswich, but the authorities gave instructions for the gallery of the Town Hall and the Market Cross to be decorated and for wine and food to be made available on the day the king was proclaimed. Powder was made available to the seamen to fire a salute on the Common Quay and the Trained Bands were to muster, the musketeers being provided with powder and a yard and a half of match so that they too could add to the general rejoicing; their arms were matchlocks in which the smouldering match ignited the charge of powder. As a token of their allegiance the town decided to send a gift of £300 to the king, but had to borrow £250 from four townsmen, who were given a lease of Portmen's Meadow as security. One of those nominated to go to London to present the gift was Robert Sparrowe, who was later to demonstrate his loyalty by including the arms of Charles II in the new plaster front of his house in the Buttermarket.

One of the peers deputed to invite Charles to return was Leicester Devereux, 6th Viscount Hereford, of Christchurch and Sudbourne. Throughout the period of the Commonwealth Lord Hereford had been active as a government servant, but it could well be that by 1660 he, like others who had served the Commonwealth, was prepared to seek the restoration of the monarchy.[39] There were those in the town who could not accept so readily the return of the king, however. In 1662 the Town Preacher, Dr. Brunning, declined to preach at a civic service in St Mary-le-Tower because he felt he could not conform to the Corporation Act which required all who held municipal office to renounce the anti-Catholic Covenant. Nor was he alone in his misgivings, for within months several members of the Corporation had been removed for refusing to sign the required declaration under the same Act, one of them being Richard Hayle who had just previously served a year as bailiff. It might have been in an effort to avoid such an outcome that John Brandling refused to accept office as bailiff with Richard Hayle, pleading age and infirmity.

The argument over the declaration and oath rumbled on for a number of years, with portmen and common councilmen of a particular persuasion refusing to make the declaration and to take the oath, and sometimes refusing to pay the fines levied on them for failing to take up the offices from which they were excluded. It was not only in the field of local government that dissension arose. The 'Merry Monarch' was not seriously involved in religious matters and was inclined to be tolerant of differences of religious belief; in particular he was indulgent to the Roman Catholics to whom he had cause to be grateful for their aid when on the run from Worcester. He was not at first much concerned to further the cause of the Anglican Church, and told a deputation of Quakers, 'Of this you may be assured, that you shall none of you suffer for your opinions or religion, so long as you live peaceably, and you have the word of a king for it.'[40]

51   The interior of St Margaret's Church, showing the Royal Arms over the chancel arch and the magnificent double hammerbeam roof. (John Fairclough)

Alas, this atmosphere of toleration was to be short-lived. The anti-Anglican laws made by the Puritans while they ruled were used as a model for a series of Acts which became collectively known as the Clarendon Code, after Sir Edward Hyde, 1st Earl of Clarendon, Lord Chancellor 1658–1667.[41] Fears that Nonconformist meetings might prove fertile seed-beds of sedition led to the passing of legislation designed to penalise any who sought to worship in other than Anglican forms, and those who suffered most severely under this legislation were the Quakers, a number of whom were imprisoned in Ipswich. One of the buildings of the old Greyfriars apparently passed into Nonconformist use as it is said that in 1672 a group of Presbyterians and Independents were given a licence, after the royal Declaration of Indulgence suspended the persecution of religious dissenters, to meet in 'The Grey Friars' House' in St Nicholas parish.[42]

Nevertheless, the anniversary of the Restoration was annually celebrated in the town with gun salutes and parades by the Trained Bands. In 1665 the Corporation ordered that 11 guns should be fired three times each and two men were 'desired to take Care to gitt the Great Gunns Ready'; the town records show many signs of having been written by speakers of the Suffolk dialect.

The Second Dutch War

Anglo-Dutch maritime rivalry continued unabated and conflicts in Africa and North America culminated in Charles II declaring war on the Dutch in March 1665. It was a war that was to affect Ipswich even more than the earlier struggle with the Dutch, the conflict being brought very close to home when a Dutch force landed on Felixstowe beach in 1667.

To begin with, local involvement was restricted to the impressment of seamen and to caring for wounded men brought ashore from the fleet. Some of those being cared for in Ipswich were buried in town churchyards. The register of St Mary Stoke records the burial in April and May 1665 of men belonging to the *Royal James*, *Royal Oak* and *Henry* and later in the year of men belonging to the *Lyon*, *Monck* and *St Andrew*, that of St Stephen's refers to the burial of 15 seamen who had 'died at the ospele in this parish'. Faced with the extreme difficulty of getting money from official sources the Corporation made use of the proceeds from land bequeathed for the maintenance of the poor to pay for the care of the wounded seamen.[43]

Sir William Doyly was the Commissioner for the Sick and Wounded with responsibility for the eastern counties and was active in dealing with the situation in Ipswich. Pepys met him at Viscount Brouncker's over a good venison pasty on 9 September 1665, 'lately come from Ipswich about the sick and wounded'.[44] That evening he met Sir William again at Captain Cocke's,[45] 'full of discourse of the neglect of our masters, the great officers of State, about all businesses, and especialy that of money—having now some thousands prisoners kept to no purpose, at a great charge, and no money provided almost for the doing of it'. The authorities at Ipswich were not alone in finding it well nigh impossible to get the money needed for looking after the seamen. A correspondent wrote from Ipswich to Sir Roger L'Estrange's *Public Intelligencer* on 31 August 1665 that

> Our Townsmen here have a very remarquable tenderness for the Sick and wounded Seamen, and many of the Principals have propounded the depositing good summes of money in order to their further relief if there should be occasion; divers Tradesmen also offering their commodities without profit to be employed upon that service.

Such altruism seems scarcely credible, and even if the report is correct the Town Clerk continued his attempts to get money from the Commission for Sick and Wounded Seamen. In a reply sent to the Town Clerk in March 1666 Sir William Doyly complained that the inhabitants of Ipswich had made unreasonable demands, and offered to make payment only if they moderated their demands by a half. Possibly that was a desperate attempt on his part to make the available money go further; the Treasurer to the Commission, Captain George Cocke, a man whom Pepys seems to have regarded as untrustworthy, ran into trouble with his accounts and had to face trial in 1670.[46]

English casualties in the Four Days' Battle which began off Ostend on 1 June 1666 were horrific, and Ipswich had to redouble its efforts to care for the wounded. One of those who died in the fight was Captain Philip Bacon, second son of Nicholas Bacon of Shrubland Hall, whose ship, the 52-gun fourth-rate *Bristol*, was brought into Harwich with her masts and rigging gone and as many as 180 enemy shot in her hull. The captain's body was brought upriver to Ipswich, where the members of the Corporation, with the Trained Bands and the county gentry, paid their respects as it was taken to Coddenham for burial.[47]

The English fleet had received something of a drubbing, and a Dutch fleet was soon to be seen off the Suffolk coast, bent on operations that were intended to bring the war to a speedy end. The Council of State, startled out of its complacency, responded to the threat of invasion by giving orders for 'the Plateforms of Landguard Fort' to be repaired and for 'pallisados from Ipswich or Harwich or anywhere else' to be sent to the fort without delay.

The dangers of sending large warships, even those of shallow draught as the Dutch ships were, close inshore, and the fact that the Dutch found the English 'well awake and in a position to put up a good defence', caused operations against the Thames and an alternative assault on Harwich to be abandoned, or at least postponed. Nevertheless, a letter from Ipswich on 5 July stated that '30 of De Ruyter's men in his boat landed on the marshes about Bardsey [Bawdsey] for fresh meat for their general but boat and men were all taken as was some wine going to him', and a couple of days later Edward Suckley reported from Landguard Fort that the appearance of the Dutch fleet had 'put the whole County into armes to attend their motion'.

Alarm turned to rejoicing when at the end of July the Dutch were soundly defeated in the St James's Day Fight, which moved slowly across the North Sea from off the North Foreland almost to the Dutch coast. As the surviving Dutch ships straggled into the Texel there were 'bonfires, guns and bells' of celebration in Ipswich, by order of

52   *The fort at Landguard that successfully resisted the Dutch attack of 1667, drawn by Peter Kent. At the time of the attack it was being reconstructed by King Charles II's chief engineer, Sir Bernard de Gomme, but there had been time only to build a low brick scarp to form a fausse-bray, preventing the Dutch from getting their scaling ladders up against the walls. (Peter Kent)*

the Earl of Suffolk, while Harwich fired a victory salute. Considering the close links between eastern England and the Netherlands it is not altogether surprising to learn that considerable numbers of disaffected English seamen were serving in the Dutch fleet, nor that there were people in Ipswich who were suspected of being in communication with the enemy. In June 1666 Samuel Stannard was elected one of the 24 but was considered unfit to serve on the grounds that he was 'under suspition of holdinge correspondence with our enemies the dutch'.

It was not only the Corporation of Ipswich who suffered from the shortage of money at the time. Money for the navy was so short that it was rumoured the king had decided not to fit his ships out after their normal winter lay-up. The Dutch, on the other hand, seem to have spent the winter refitting their ships and building new ones, and when the spring came plans were made to attack the Thames and Medway. The Dutch penetration of the Medway in June has gone down in history as possibly the worst disaster to strike the Royal Navy until the Second World War. Not only did the Dutch overcome the local defences and burn a number of English warships but they also boldly made off with the *Royal Charles*, formerly the Commonwealth ship *Naseby*, in which Charles II had been brought from Holland at the Restoration.

Much nearer home, a Dutch fleet spread alarm along the Suffolk coast and at Harwich Captain Anthony Deane, Master Shipwright of the Naval Yard, was hurriedly fitting out fireships, of which 13 were merchant vessels belonging to Ipswich that had been impressed by an Order in Council of 16 June. On the last day of June there were no fewer than 70 Dutch warships in the Gunfleet anchorage to the south of Harwich, and when the whole fleet weighed anchor at dawn on 1 July it was expected that an attack was to be mounted on Harwich. Frank Hussey tells how their progress with a north-westerly wind and an adverse tide was painfully slow, 'stretching jangled nerves ashore to limits heretofore unreached'. Instead of turning towards the harbour the enemy sailed away northwards and spent the night at anchor some two miles off Aldeburgh. There was much movement of troops to counter the expected landing, and 100 'brave seamen' were sent from Ipswich to reinforce the garrison of Landguard Fort, at the entrance to Harwich harbour and the Orwell.

Next morning the Dutch ships all weighed anchor and, after standing to the northward for about an hour, tacked on to a southerly course towards Harwich. Watchers on Beacon Cliff and other vantage points saw a number of the vessels come to an anchor in the outer part of the Rolling Grounds, abreast of where the town of Felixstowe is now. They watched anxiously as more than 40 boats and barges were rowed towards the shore with a landing force estimated by one observer at 1,000 men. The intention of the Dutch commanders was to take Landguard Fort and so gain control of Harwich harbour and the Orwell, thus putting pressure on the English to end the war.

The plan might have succeeded if one of the Dutch ships which was to have bombarded the fort from the harbour entrance had not gone aground on the way in and if the fort garrison had not been reinforced beyond the expectations of the attackers. As it was the Dutch were repulsed; they returned to their boats in the evening and, with some difficulty because of the ebbing tide, rowed off back to their ships. There must have been enormous relief in Ipswich when the news came through that the Dutch attack had failed. In London Pepys went to the Council Chamber to deliver a letter and found 'the King and a whole tableful of Lords' considering a case in which an old man complained that his son did not allow him enough to live on. 'This cause lasted them near two hours; which methinks, at this time to be the work of the Council-board of England, is a scandalous thing …' he wrote in his diary. 'Here I find all the news is the enemy's landing 3000 men near Harwich, and attacquing Langnerfort and being beat off thence with our great guns, killing some of their men and they leaving their lathers [ladders] behind them; but we had no Horse in the way on Suffolke side, otherwise we might have galled their Foot.'[48]

From Harwich Lord Oxford sent a dispatch to Lord Arlington, the Secretary of State: 'My Lord, This night with the young flood, the enemy shipped the remainder of their beaten party, and this morning the fleet have turned their backs, and are driving away as fast as the dead calm will suffer them.' Proud sentiments, but in fact the Dutch fleet had not gone away, and the port of Ipswich suffered because the colliers did not dare come further south than Yarmouth. One result of the blockade was to inflate the price of coal by a factor of five in only three weeks.

A peace treaty was signed before the month was out, but nobody either in Suffolk or at Court was in any doubt as to the consequences had the Dutch taken Landguard Fort and established a foothold on the Suffolk shore. It is not overstating the facts to say that the future of the monarchy would have been in doubt.[49] Very likely that thought was in the king's mind when he visited Landguard Fort on 3 October 1668, having come over from Newmarket by way of Ipswich. It was a belated acknowledgement of the bravery of the defenders, who had since been sorely neglected. Major Nathaniel Darell, who had been wounded while defending the fort 15 months earlier, took the opportunity to present a petition to the king stating that 'his Company of his Royall Highness the Duke of York's regiment in ye said fort doe only fall sick for want of Bedds, Blanketts, & other accomodation wch he humbly prayed may be forthwith provided'. The king and his brother, the Duke of York, graciously ordered that the fort's requirements 'bee immediately sent and delivered'.

After visiting the fort and crossing to Harwich to see what had been done there the king sailed in the yacht *Henrietta* up the coast to Aldeburgh, where he disembarked next morning and whence he rode immediately back to Ipswich to dine with Leicester

Devereux, Viscount Hereford, at Christchurch. A letter written from Ipswich the following day says that in the town 'they had all the expressions of joy possible, ringing of bells, discharging of guns, the steeples adorned with flags and streamers, the streets strewn with herbs and flowers, and echoing with the acclamations of the people, and prayers for his Majesty's health and prosperity. The bailiffs, portmen, and commoners attended his Majesty, and presented their mace, which they immediately received again, and after dinner, attended him on horseback with the trained bands, out of the town'.[50]

It proved an expensive visit for the town. Although the king had gone on his way almost immediately after his dinner at Christchurch the Corporation had to entertain his retinue who were left behind, and they had to pay—extravagantly, according to G.R. Clarke—for ale, sack and other refreshments for the lifeguards and trained bands who escorted the king. Not only that, the chief gentlemen of the household applied to the bailiffs for 'fees of homage' amounting to £38 12s. 8d. 'Which of course they cheerfully paid, for the honour of kissing the hand of this "merry monarch" who suffered his servants to be as thoughtlessly profligate as himself,' Clarke adds acidly.[51]

Water Supply

At a Great Court on 8 August 1614 it was decided to bring running water to a conduit on the Cornhill and to St Peter's Church, apparently from Caldwell Brook. The town had borrowed £200 for this purpose from William Bloyse, Richard Marten and Tobias Blosse, and it was agreed to mortgage the Portmen's Meadow in order to repay them.[52] This piece of town land was many times used as security for loans of this kind. Later in the year it was announced that householders could have water out of the Cornhill Conduit for a £5 fine provided they paid the fine within 21 days, and those who came later had to pay annual rents as well as fines. Of course there were people who sought to get their water for nothing by inserting unauthorised quills into the pipes, and almost annually searches were instituted for such illegal abstractions. In 1644 it was agreed that 'Suits shall be brought against such [as] take water wthout the Town licence, by private fastning of Quills to the main conduit'.

Various improvements were made in the course of the 17th century, and while oak and elm pipes continued to be used to carry the water lead piping was increasingly employed. Joseph Palmer agreed in 1659 to make 'A good & substantiall Leaden Cisterne ffyve ffoot square & three foote & twoe Inches in Height and Soder all the Pipes that bringe the water into the Conduit' in return for his being granted the freedom. No doubt Palmer was a plumber by trade. It is probable that at this period Ipswich had as good a water supply system as any provincial town in the country, and one that was better than most.

Fire Precautions

Fire was always a great danger in any town with buildings largely of timber and with thatched roofs, and in spite of the readily available water supply Ipswich was as vulnerable as any other similar community. As a fire precaution it was ordered in July 1616 that nobody should thatch any new house or use thatch in any alterations made to older houses,[53] and two years later an additional order was made that all thatched buildings in the town should be reroofed with tiles.[54] At the same time the Corporation decreed that each parish was to make available 12 leather buckets which were to be kept in the parish church ready for use. It could be someone pointed out that a mere dozen buckets to a parish was a rather meagre allowance, but anyway in 1609 it was decided that every portman should provide four leather buckets and every man of the 24 should provide two for use in case of fire. In addition every freeman and able foreigner was to have one available, and to ensure that this regulation was observed the constables were instructed to make a search to see if the buckets were provided as they should be.[55]

Like so many regulations, it was probably honoured mainly in the breach, for in 1614 it was felt necessary to set a deadline for the regulation to be obeyed. Most likely there had been an outbreak of fire that had shown up a deficiency in the fire precautions, since the treasurer was told to provide four ladders and four iron crows or crowbars. Two of each were ordered to be chained under the Town House and the others to be chained in the Gallery; some town official presumably had a key to release them from their chains when they were required.[56] Constant vigilance seems to have been needed not only to guard against fire but to ensure that the regulations regarding buckets were obeyed. In 1619 a committee was appointed to deal with the matter,[57] and then two years later the 24 were told to make a search to observe if the regulation of 1609 was being observed.[58]

Having presumably provided the four ladders and four iron crows in 1614, the treasurer was instructed in 1631 to provide two long ladders and 'two Great Cromes with iron hookes to serve uppon occasion of ffier'.[59] Since the purpose of the cromes was to haul burning thatch from a roof it is apparent that the earlier prohibition on thatching had been ignored. Indeed, in 1652 Robert Colby, a brewer, was ordered not to thatch his barn and to take off the thatch he had already laid on.

There was a serious blaze in the town in 1654 which doubtless showed the need for more effective firefighting equipment than leather buckets and cromes. However, it was not until 1663 that the Corporation decided to 'gitt an engine for this towne to be used about the Quenchinge of fire (if anie should happen)'. Later the same year John Wright was paid 'Thirtie Powndes ffower shillings & tenn pence wch he Layd out for the Inginn ffor the towne'. Judging by those early fire engines which have survived in other places this would have been little more than a wooden tank mounted on four small wheels, with a manually operated pump to project a feeble jet of water on the flames.

It seems that the 1654 blaze broke out as the result of the carelessness of men working in a maltkiln using straw to dry the malt. The use of straw kilns was immediately banned by the Great Court, and all maltsters using them were told to change their kilns into cockell kells (kell is the Suffolk pronunciation of kiln), kilns with a fire-chamber using a solid fuel. Some brewers were also using straw as fuel, and they too were told to stop doing so. Little notice seems to have been taken of this prohibition, too, for in 1659 the Great Court heard that a number of straw kilns had caught fire, and the instruction to maltsters to cease using straw was repeated, as was the earlier ban on the use of thatch on buildings. Even then some maltsters ignored the orders of the Great Court, which in 1663 told the bailiffs and the justices to suppress their maltings if they continued to use straw kells. It would seem that the dictates of the Great Court were as widely disregarded as the laws regarding speed restrictions and cycling on pavements are today.

Sickness and Health

With its open sewers flowing down the streets and its Cold Dunghills piled high with putrefying refuse it is no surprise that Ipswich was as unhealthy a place as most 17th-century towns. The foreign trade of the port was often blamed for introducing infection, and occasional epidemics spread quickly through the narrow streets.

The Great Plague of 1665–6, whose impact on London was so graphically described by Samuel Pepys in his diary, hit Ipswich in common with many other provincial centres. The Corporation decided in July 1665 to look for a suitable place to build houses to accommodate sufferers, and the following month orders were given that a 'warding' should be organised to keep out anybody coming from a place infected with the plague. At the same time searchers were appointed to seek out sufferers from the plague, and orders were given for all wandering dogs and cats to be killed and for all hogs to be removed from within the town walls. It was feared that the infection could be harboured in the animals' fur.

In spite of all these precautions plague did reach Ipswich, and the pest houses built on Maiden Grave Farm[60] were soon receiving the first victims. The consequences can be traced through the parish registers; in one week 34 out of 64 burials were of plague victims. Those who could afford to do so fled into the surrounding countryside in an endeavour to escape the infection, and this presented the town authorities with yet further difficulties. Because a large part of the inhabitants—the well-to-do part—were out of town it proved impossible to collect the rates. The Great Court agreed in October 1665 to borrow £300 from Robert Sparrow, John Wright, Henry Gosnold and Robert Clarke and to use the Handford Hall lands owned by the Corporation as security. Moves were also made to persuade the justices of the peace for the county to impose a rate on people living within five miles of the town.[61]

The pest houses were specifically retained in case of a further epidemic when Samuell Jacob was given a seven-year lease of Maiden Grave Farm towards the end of 1666. His rent was to be £12 a year, except that the first year was 'to be given him for his service done in the time of the great plague'. When three years later it was agreed to sell the farm to John Ford the Corporation again reserved 'the pest house & soe much grounde as the houses stand uppon to build other pest houses upon iff itt shall please God to visit this towne with the plague'. Happily the Great Plague of 1665–6 was the last major epidemic of plague in England. It was not, however, the last time plague was to strike in the immediate vicinity of Ipswich, for four people died from the disease at Freston in 1910. Eight years later two people died of the same disease at Erwarton in what was the final outbreak of plague in England—apart from a single case contracted in a laboratory at Porton in 1962.[62]

VII

Celebrating the Glorious Revolution

With its history of Protestantism and of outspoken opposition to High Church Anglicanism as personified by Archbishop Laud and Bishop Wren, Ipswich was not inclined to accept James II's espousal of Roman Catholicism or his endeavours to return to the absolute rule of the early 17th-century monarchy. No doubt the town would have been happy to receive William of Orange had he landed in the Orwell in November 1688; he was welcomed to Ipswich in 1693 and was entertained by the Corporation.

That the fleet convoying the Prince of Orange to Britain did not take the shortest route across the North Sea and upriver towards Ipswich might have been due to the presence at the Gunfleet anchorage just south of Harwich of a British naval squadron of 40 men-of-war, 18 fireships and three smaller craft; the Dutch could not have known that discontent at the actions of James II had by that time sapped the allegiance of many of the officers in the fleet. Both officers and men were, as a body, strongly opposed to Roman Catholicism and had been antagonised by James's appointment of a Roman Catholic, Sir Roger Strickland, to the command of the active fleet.[1]

Ipswich was thrown into a state of alarm not very long after the accession of William and Mary by a mutiny of Scots troops in the town. The regiment concerned was the Earl of Dumbarton's Regiment, later The Royal Scots (nicknamed 'Pontius Pilate's Bodyguard'), which had transferred (or been transferred) to William following the landing in Torbay. In March 1689, consequent upon the outbreak of war with France, the regiment was ordered with nine other battalions to the continent. All might have been well had William not appointed the Duke of Schomberg to command the regiment; reputedly one of the finest soldiers in Europe, Schomberg had even fought by the side of the regiment in more than one action, but he was not a Scotsman. With much grumbling the Scots soldiers marched as far as Ipswich, and then, apparently at the behest of some Jacobite officers, they mutinied.

Seizing four guns, they set out to march north to Scotland, to the great alarm of the authorities in London. William sent a considerable force in pursuit, and the mutineers were overtaken near the Lincolnshire town of Sleaford. According to Clarke some of the officers were prepared to make a stand, but finding the situation hopeless the men laid down their arms. They marched back to Ipswich and in due course sailed for the Maas, where, we are told, the men deserted by scores, and even by hundreds.[2] A few of the ringleaders in the mutiny were arrested and taken to London, where they were lodged in Newgate Prison; it seems that they eventually received a royal pardon. In December 1690 information was sent from Ipswich to the Commissioners of the

Admiralty concerning Peter Cook, 'late an officer in Lord Dunbarton's Scottish regiment', who was said to be on his way to France with another person carrying letters to the late king.

When in 1695 news broke of an abortive plot to murder the king the Great Court in Ipswich drew up an address expressing outrage at the conspiracy, sealed with the common seal of the town, which was sent up to London to John Sicklemore, the Recorder, for him to present to the king. The High Steward, Lord Cornwallis, was asked to assist in the delivery of the address.[3]

Six years after William and Mary came to the throne men were working on the decoration of the interior of the roof of St Margaret's Church with painted panels which symbolised the loyalty of High Tory churchmen of the period. The rectangular panels inserted between the rafters bear a heraldic tribute to William and Mary, with the addition at the east end of sentiments which would have been on the lips of all true blue English men and women, 'Feare God, Honour the King'. Behind the installation of the panels, which represent an extraordinary memorial of the Glorious Revolution, were Devereux Edgar, a member of an important Ipswich family with a home in Tower Street, and Cave Beck, a Royalist agent in the Civil War and Master of Ipswich School. Beck was perpetual curate of St Margaret's and St Helen's from 1657 until his death in 1706.

The Toleration Act of 1689 gave religious freedom to all who accepted 36 of the 39 articles in the Book of Common Prayer; it did not, however, give any freedom of worship to Roman Catholics, who remained an object of suspicion and sometimes downright hostility in Ipswich for many years to come. Clarke records that when a Catholic priest, L'Abbe Louis Pierre Simon, first arrived in the town in 1793 Catholic residents were subject to a good deal of animosity and had to meet together secretly.[4] For dissenters like those who had been meeting in Ipswich under the leadership of the Rev. Owen Stockton and, after Mr. Stockton's death in 1680, the Rev. John Fairfax, the Toleration Act meant an end to the cat-and-mouse worship in secular buildings that had been normal for a number of years. The habit of posting a lookout to warn of interference from the authorities seems to have lingered, for when that congregation decided in 1699 to have a meeting house built they inserted into the east door a spy-hole giving a clear view of the approach to the premises from St Nicholas Street.[5]

A piece of land was bought in Friars Street, or Boat Lane as it was known at the time, in the name of Thomas Bantoft, a mercer; it cost £150. Possibly Thomas was a relative of the Rev. Samuel Bantoft who was ejected from the living of Stebbing, in Essex, and subsequently found a home in Ipswich, where he died in 1692. A contract was then drawn up and signed by six members of the congregation and Joseph Clark, house carpenter, for the building of a meeting house. It was dated 5 August 1699, and the building was to be completed by 16 October the same year, though in fact the target was not met; the opening sermon by the Rev. John Fairfax was not preached until 26 April 1700.

The galleries were not mentioned in the contract; they cost another £96, which was paid in instalments. Another additional item was the handsome pulpit, with its magnificent carving in the style of Grinling Gibbons; it is generally assumed to have been the product of one of the great carver's pupils.

Architect Keith Pert, who was honorary architect to the Unitarian Meeting House for a quarter of a century and superintended what he called 'a continual battle against wet and dry rot, death watch and furniture beetle', has theorised that as Sir Christopher Wren frequently worked with the aid of Gibbons it is possible that Wren or one of his apprentices might have had a hand in the design of the Ipswich building. Certainly it is similar in layout to Wren's City churches and contains a number of features normally employed by him.[6]

53   The Presbyterian Meeting House of 1699-1700 in Friars Street, seen in a photograph by William Vick. In the course of the 18th century the congregation became avowedly Unitarian, and today it is the Unitarian Meeting House.

Much as it resembles some of Wren's City churches, the meeting house is very different from the medieval parish churches of Ipswich. Mr. Fairfax in his sermon at the opening of the meeting house seemed to indicate that there was no doctrinal reason for the difference:

> I would not be mistaken, let none think that I have spoken a word to the Derogation of those Stately, Magnificent and Sumptuous Structures, our Publick Churches, which the Christian Piety and Liberality of former Ages Erected for the convenient Assembling of particular Congregations in their parochial Districts every Sabbath day, together with their indowments. No, no. Blessed be God, who hath made such Provision for his Church, and for his Solemn Worship. Had we the liberty of those places, we should seek no other; But these Doors being shut against us, it is our necessity and not our choice to Worship God as conveniently as we can in meaner places with a good Conscience.

It is interesting to see that of the six people who signed the contract on behalf of the congregation two, Edward Gaell and Robert Snelling, were described as gentlemen, but the other four were traders. Thomas Bantoft was a woollen draper, John Groome a linen weaver, John May a clothier and Thomas Catchpole a brewer. When, 11 years later, a trust deed was drawn up the first trustees included as well as the minister and the surviving founders three gentlemen, two maltsters, a linen draper, a woollen draper, a hosier, a woolcomber, a tallow chandler, a schoolmaster, an ironmonger, a chairmaker and three who were described as yeomen, that is small farmers cultivating their own land.[7] It would appear that the Presbyterian congregation was composed largely of tradesmen in a fairly modest way of business.

The trust deed did not lay down any doctrine, and in the course of the 18th century the congregation gradually moved away from the doctrine of the Trinity and by the end of that century was avowedly Unitarian. At that time penalties were still threatened, though not always enforced, against those who denied the Trinity; the threat was removed in 1813 by an Act of Parliament.

The Presbyterian congregation in their Friars Street meeting house had a rival in the Independent congregation who met in a hired building in the Green Yard in the neighbouring parish of St Peter's. In 1686 this congregation invited the Rev. John Langston to move to Ipswich and become their first minister. He remained pastor of the congregation in the Green Yard until his death at the age of 64 in 1704. In his first year he saw the building of a new chapel, which came into use on 26 June 1687. His work was carried on by the Rev. Benjamin Glandfield, who became Mr. Langston's assistant in 1702.[8] The preaching of these two men attracted new people to the Independent congregation not only from Ipswich but from many of the surrounding villages and even from as far away as Harwich, East Bergholt and Dedham, Needham Market and Woodbridge. By 1718 it had become necessary to look for larger premises, and in that year the congregation bought a house in Tankard Street (now Tacket Street) for the minister and a large piece of ground behind it on which to build a meeting house capable of seating nearly 800 people. The roof of this meeting house is said to have been supported by two wooden masts from an old warship, given by the Ipswich shipbuilder John Barnard, whose family were members of the congregation over several generations.

Sadly, Mr. Glandfield died on 10 September 1720 after a long and painful illness—just a week before the opening of the new chapel, which in the 19th century gave way to a fine building of Kentish ragstone, a material much used by the Victorian church-builders of Ipswich.

The first Quaker meeting house was a timber-framed building on a site just to the west of St Mary at the Key, built in 1700, probably by the same Joseph Clark who was responsible for the Presbyterian Meeting House in Friars Street. The Quakers were strongly established in Ipswich, in spite of the persecution they had faced in earlier years, and by the end of the 18th century a new red-brick building had replaced the little timber-framed structure, which was retained as the women's hall. The Quakers came to play a very significant role in the development of Ipswich in the 19th century and took a leading part in business and industry, the Alexanders and the Ransomes being particularly notable in this respect. Clarke in 1830 paid them a well-deserved compliment:

> They are distinguished by a rigid correctness in their dealings, and a mild simplicity of manner; and, notwithstanding the singularity of their costume, and their determination to keep their heads covered in high places, no one can deny, that, as a body, they rank amongst the most respectable members of civil society; and, as such, they have long flourished at Ipswich.[9]

When Celia Fiennes visited 'Ipswitch' in 1698 she commented that 'this town has many Dessenters in it', though she did not go into the detail about them that she had at Colchester. Ipswich she described as 'a very clean town' but 'a little disregarded'. On inquiry she put the poor state of the place down to 'pride and sloth, for tho' the sea would bear a ship of 300 tun quite to the quay and the ships of the first rate can ride within two mile of the town, yet they make no advantage thereof by any sort of manufacture, which they might do as well as Colchester and Norwitch, so that the shipps that bring their coales goes light away.'[10] No doubt she had been listening to the sort of people who are always keen to tell a ready listener what other men should be doing. The truth was that the river was no longer deep enough to bring ships safely up to the town quays, and it was necessary for the larger vessels to be unloaded into lighters some distance below the town.

The silting of the river was the result of a reduction of the tidal flow which had hitherto scoured out the mud from the channel, tortuous as it was in the upper reaches. The reason for the reduction was that marshes had been embanked both above and below Stoke Bridge to provide new grazing land.[11] Altogether some 120 acres was reclaimed above Stoke Bridge and about half that area between the bridge and Nova Scotia, and a glance at Ogilby's map suggests that most if not all of this reclamation had been completed by the end of the 17th century.

The Coal Trade

Daniel Defoe, that most inquisitive of travellers, recorded a decline that he found distressing when he wrote his account of a tour through the whole country of England and Wales in the 1720s. In former times, he says, Ipswich had been the greatest town in England for large colliers employed in the Newcastle-London coal trade. Ipswich built the best and biggest ships for the trade, he reckoned, adding that 'They built also there so prodigious strong, that it was an ordinary thing for an Ipswich collier, if no disaster happened to him, to reign (as the seamen call it) forty or fifty years and more.' These 'prodigious strong' vessels were known as catts, this name being used for ships that were built with closely-spaced timbers for extra strength. Some twenty years after the publication of Defoe's book an Ipswich-built catt, *The Good Ship Humphry* of 300 tons, was for sale at Lloyd's Coffee House in Lombard Street, London. She was said to carry about twenty keels of coals; that is, her spacious hold would take the cargoes of twenty of the Tyne keels which brought the coal downriver from the collieries.[12]

Defoe went on to tell how each winter the colliers were laid up in the Orwell with their sails sent ashore and their topmasts struck, 'under the advantages and security of sound ground and a high woody shore, where they lie as safe as in a wet dock'. When he first knew the town, about 1668, he had been told there were more than 100 colliers belonging to the port, most of the masters and many of the men living in Ipswich when they were not at sea. In winter, he said, there were probably 1,000 more men in the town than in summer.[13] It is interesting to see that the indentures of those apprenticed to the sea sometimes reflected the seasonal nature of the trade. An Ipswich lad, Robert

King, was promised the relatively high pay of £4 a year in the first two years of his apprenticeship, £5 in the third and £6 in the final year 'towards the findeing and provideing himselfe linnen and wollen hose, shoes and other necessaryes the said term, and keeping himself in the winter season ... the tyme the shipp lye upp'.[14]

'The loss or decay of this trade accounts for the present pretended decay of the town of Ipswich,' wrote Defoe,

> ... the ships wore out, the masters died off, the trade took a new turn; Dutch fly boats taken in the war and made free ships by Act of Parliament thrust themselves into the coal trade for the interest of the captors, such as the Yarmouth and London merchants, and others, and the Ipswich men gradually dropped out of it, being discouraged by those Dutch fly boats; these Dutch vessels which cost nothing but the capture, were bought cheap, carried great burthens, and the Ipswich building fell off for want of price, and so the trade decayed, and the town with it; I believe this will be owned for the true beginning of their decay, if I must allow it to be called a decay.

Perhaps there was something in Celia Fiennes' scathing comment, for the introduction of these war prizes dealt the Ipswich shipbuilders a blow from which they seemed unable, even unwilling, to recover. Shipbuilding went on at Ipswich, as we shall see, but the building and owning of the collier fleets moved to the north-east coast, to Whitby, Scarborough and the Tyne itself.

Coastwise Trade

The coasting trade went on, however. To a great extent it was a trade with London, that Great Wen that according to Defoe sucked the vitals of the surrounding counties. He comments that 'this whole kingdom, as well the people as the land, and even the sea ... are employed to furnish something, and I may add, the best of everything, to supply the city of London with provisions.' And many of those provisions reached London by sea. At Ipswich a whole community of windmills and watermills turned out flour not just for local consumption but for export to London and elsewhere. When a post windmill at Halifax, on the west bank of the Orwell not far from Bourne Bridge, was for sale the advertisement noted how conveniently situated it was for the export trade.

Though there were men in Ipswich who owned and operated fleets of vessels engaged in the coal trade and in other trades, the distribution of ownership was wider than might be expected. It was not only the well-to-do families that invested in the town's shipping, for shares were held by many small investors, tradesmen and farmers among them. Ordinarily the ownership of a vessel was divided into 64 shares, and while 32 or more of these might be held by one man the remainder might be distributed among several different people; it was common for the master of the vessel to own one share, or perhaps more. A vellum bill of sale signed by Samuel Parker, mariner of Ipswich in 1696, records the purchase by a Woodbridge merchant, John Bass, of one 'two and thirtieth part of all that shipp or vessel lately built by Mr. J. Wm. Hubbart att Ipswich

54 *Looking upriver from below Woolverstone Park in the 18th century, with Freston Tower in the centre. Though the Orwell appears to be a fine expanse of water in this engraving (after a drawing by a member of the Berners family, owners of Woolverstone Hall), the shipping channel was narrow and tortuous; possibly the ship on the right is following the twisting channel. (John Wilton)*

called the Prosperous Mary of burden 300 tunns, Samuel Parker master'. The price paid, noted on the back, was £82 3s. 4d., indicating a total value for this ocean-going merchant ship of some £2,600.[15] As late as 1720 it was noted that at Ipswich 'the greater part of the inhabitants of that town are either owners of Parts of Ships, or masters of Ships, chiefly employed in the Coal Trade, or in the Fishery'.[16]

The Poor and Poor Relief

How truly it has been said that the poor are always with us. In his delightful *Drayneflete Revealed* (1949), a spoof history that every researcher into local history should read, Osbert Lancaster provides sketches of his fictitious town at each stage from the Roman period to the 20th century, and in every drawing there is a one-legged beggar holding out his hand or his hat.

In Ipswich the decline of the cloth trade created particular problems, as it did in other parts of Suffolk that had once waxed prosperous on woollens. Defoe might well point out that the poor people were employed in spinning wool for those other towns such as Norwich where the trade survived, but poverty remained a problem, not only for the poor. John Woollward, the wherryman killed by lightning in 1708, was one of the inhabitants of St Clement's parish assessed for a rate 'for & towards the Reliefe of the Poor' in 1697; he paid 4s. over the 13-week period of the rate compared with three of the more affluent parishioners who paid over a pound.[17]

Under the Poor Law Amendment Act of 1662 only those poor people who could prove 'settlement' in a particular parish were entitled to receive relief from that parish. Settlement was acquired by birth or, for a woman, by marriage. A further Act of 1691 decreed that if a person moved from one place to another settlement could be gained by proving that he or she had rented property for £10 or more a year for at least a year, had been a hired servant in the parish for at least a year, or had contributed to the parish rates for the same period. Serving an apprenticeship could also provide a person with settlement. The law was complicated and both difficult and cumbersome to implement. It has been described as 'the origin of DSS red tape'.[18] Attempting to prove settlement involved making a sworn statement to a Justice of the Peace, who was often more sympathetic to the parish overseers of the poor than he was to the person involved.

In 1710 Ann Fryett appeared before Cooper Gravenor and told him how her late husband Edmond had lived in Hemingstone, where he paid poor rate and church rate, until they had moved into Ipswich about three years earlier.[19] They had spent some 2½ years living in St Mary Tower parish before moving to St Matthew's, where her husband died, and in neither parish had he paid any rates. 'Nor no other Taxes since they came from Hemingston,' Mrs. Fryett added in confirmation. One thing that is quite clear from the examinations is that there is little or no truth in the assertion so often made that in days gone by ordinary people normally died in the town or village in which they had been born. Towns like Ipswich attracted people not only from all over Suffolk but from much further afield: in 1764 John Bromley, a flaxdresser, told the two JPs examining him that he had been born and apprenticed in Chipping Campden, Gloucestershire.[20]

That the system caught up some people who might not have been expected to be numbered among the poor is proved by the examination of Othinel Smith, who had himself served as Overseer of the Poor while mine host of the *Griffin* in the parish of St Mary Tower.[21] He had been at the *Griffin*, which he hired from William Trotman, common brewer, at £22 a year, for about eight years, and had also kept a number of other public houses both in Ipswich and in the country, but had presumably fallen on evil times when examined before the justices in 1772.

Not unnaturally, the parish authorities were disinclined to give relief to poor men and women if they could avoid it, and it was not unknown for unfortunate people to be passed on from parish to parish. There were cases of pregnant women being hounded out of parishes because the baby would gain settlement wherever it was born—and no parish wanted another poor mouth to feed. Examined in 1768, Susan Durrant told how while the family was living in St Matthew's parish, her husband Edmund contracted smallpox.[22] Before he was taken into the parish workhouse, where he died, he was examined as to his settlement and he said he came from Cockfield, some miles north of Lavenham. Following her husband's death she and her two-year-old son were ordered to be removed to Cockfield, but they were then sent back with a settlement certificate to Ipswich, where she was still living in St Matthew's. There were arrangements by which the parish of settlement could reimburse the overseers of the parish in which the person was living, and this was possibly done in Susan Durrant's case.

The disadvantages of the system were analysed by Henry Fielding, novelist, playwright, barrister and originator of the Bow Street Runners:

That the Poor are a very great burthen, and even a nuisance, to this kingdom; that the laws for relieving their distresses and restraining their vices have not answered those purposes; and that they are at present very ill provided for, and much worse governed, are truths which every man, I believe, will acknowledge. ... Every man, who hath any property, must feel the weight of that tax which is levied for the use of the Poor; and every man of understanding must see how absurdly it is applied. So very useless, indeed, is this heavy tax, and so wretched its disposition, that it is a question whether the Poor or the Rich are more dissatisfied, or have indeed greater reason to be dissatisfied; since the plunder of the one serves so little to the real advantage of the other ...[23]

It would be surprising if the disadvantages of the system were not greatly apparent in a port town where seamen might find themselves in distress. The Mayor of Harwich, James Clements, examined John Rogers, who declared that he had lived with his parents in the parish of St Nicholas, Ipswich, until he was 10 or 11 years of age, and that soon after he was impressed on board one of HM ships. When after some eight years at sea he was discharged at Chatham he returned to Ipswich and married.[24] Another Ipswich seaman, Samuel Shearman, told how he had been impressed aboard a warship about eight years before he was examined in 1768, and that on leaving the Navy he had gone one voyage to Barbados, 'and from thence came home to the sd parish of Saint Clement and has been since relieved by that parish'.[25]

Public Buildings

The best possible picture of Ipswich in the late 17th, early 18th century is to be had from John Ogilby's map, engraved and printed by Thomas Steward in 1698. Ogilby made his survey in 1674, two years before he died, but its later publication is an indication that it portrays the turn-of-century town very adequately. Ogilby was one of those people who succeed at anything they tackle, and he was an excellent mapmaker as well as writer and publisher. John Aubrey, in his *Brief Lives*, tells how he lost everything in the Great Fire of London in 1666: 'He had such an excellent inventive and prudential wit, and master of so good address, that when he was undone he could not only shift handsomely (which is a great mastery) but he would make such rational proposals that would be embraced by rich and great men, that in a short time he could gain a good estate again; and never failed in anything he ever undertook, but always went through with profits and honour.' It was he who arranged the coronation procession for Charles II.[26]

At the heart of Ipswich is the Corn Hill, a quadrangular open space with the Town Hall on its southern side and the Market Cross towards the other side. In the middle had been until 1676 the bull ring where bulls were baited by dogs; in the middle ages this was not just a sport, for it was thought that baiting improved the quality of the meat and those who failed to have their bulls baited for at least an hour before slaughtering them were fined by the town authorities. The Town Hall had begun life as St Mildred's Church, which seems in the late 13th century to have been appropriated by the Priory

55   The Hall of Pleas with its two-storey oriel window, built between 1435 and 1445, can be seen in this print of the Town Hall in 1810. The outside steps lead up to the Moot Hall.

of St Peter and St Paul.[27] In 1393 the Prior of Holy Trinity granted a piece of ground 24 feet by 18 feet with its north end abutting on the Corn Hill, and this land possibly served as the site for the subsequent building in 1435-45 of an extension at the east end of St Mildred's. This extension, sometimes called the Hall of Pleas, was constructed in red brick with a diaper pattern in blue brick on either side of a stone oriel window extending to two storeys.

For several hundred years this was the centre of local administration in which the Great Court was held. It was also the scene of the feasts of the Guild of Corpus Christi and of the entertainments which the bailiffs were expected to arrange; in 1566 Thomas Gooding was fined because he had failed to entertain during his year of office.[28] The lower part of the building served as a kitchen for use on such occasions.

The first Market Cross was given to the town by Edmund Daundy in 1510, the year he served as bailiff. A well-to-do merchant living in St Lawrence's parish, Daundy was also well connected, for he was a relative of Cardinal Wolsey. It has been suggested both by Glyde and by Dr. J.E. Taylor that this cross was of stone and was intended as a preaching cross,[29] but whatever it was that first cross was replaced about 1628 by an octagonal structure with an ogee-shaped lead-covered roof and a lofty central post. The building was partly financed by a bequest from Benjamin Osborne, who had in 1610 left £50 towards the erection of a new cross; it seems to have taken nearly twenty years for the Corporation to persuade his executors to stump up the money, and then only £44 was handed over. In 1723 Francis Negus, one of the borough MPs, presented to the town a statue which, suitably equipped with a sword and a pair of scales, was erected on top of the cross as the embodiment of Justice. Previously, in his garden at Dallinghoo, she had represented Flora.

To the east of the Town Hall and facing out towards the cross was the Shambles, a timber-framed building carried on wooden posts and arches; the butchers' stalls were set out on the open ground floor. It has often been said that the Shambles was built by Cardinal Wolsey, or by his father, but no evidence has ever been produced to support this tradition. Indeed, the only known connection between the Shambles and the Wolsey family is an item in the chamberlains' accounts in 1583 recording a payment of 20s. 'to Mother Wolsey for her paynes in clensinge the Corne Hill, the Butcherage, and the New Keye, for her whole yere's wages.'[30] The probability is that she belonged to another Wolsey family altogether and was not directly related to Robert and Thomas.

The street pattern on Ogilby's map is basically that we know today, but many of the names are unfamiliar. Running west from the Cornhill is Bargate Street, which becomes Gaol Gate Street as it nears the West Gate, at this time used as the borough gaol. Running northwards from opposite the West Gate is Great Bolton Lane, 'leading to Gt Bolton and ye Gallos'; Little Bolton Lane leading out of town from St Margaret's Green is today's Bolton Lane. In Great Bolton Lane (which had by 1740 become George Lane[31] and is now George Street) is the old St George's Chapel, which had ceased to be used for worship in the mid-16th century and was used as a barn when, in 1764, the hay and corn

56 *The Market Cross, seen here in 1785, was erected in or about 1628 to replace an earlier cross that might have been a preaching cross rather than a market cross. It was repaired and altered from time to time, as when in 1745 it was 'Ordered that a Committee do examine whether the repairs done to the Market Cross by Mr. Henry Bond, late town treasurer, were necessary, and the charge for the same reasonable'.*

stored in it caught fire as a result of a boy knocking his torch against the adjacent fence. He had, Clarke tells us, been attending a funeral, 'for, at this time, it was customary to bury the dead by torch-light—and, in consequence of this accident, it was recommended that the custom should be abolished'.[32]

The highway leading from Stoke Bridge to the Cornhill is most emphatically named King Street by Ogilby throughout its whole length; in more recent times it has been split into Bridge Street, St Peter's Street, St Nicholas Street and Queen Street. Branching off towards the Timber Market (now Old Cattle Market) is Colehill, which later acquired the name Silent Street. In the Middle Ages 'le Colhel' had been an ill-defined area stretching from King Street through to the Timber Market.[33] The name Colehill is sometimes confused with the Cold Dunghills, which lay further to the east; a lane on the line of the present-day Waterworks Street is named by Ogilby as Dunghill Pound Lane, a reminder that in the 16th century a pound for stray animals had been built in Warwick's Pits. A reminder of the permission given to two men to set up tenters for

57   *The Shambles or Butchery is mentioned in the town records as 'newly built' in 1378, but in 1583 it was ordered that it should be 'new builded', oaks being felled at Ulverston Hall, Debenham, for that purpose. Possibly this was a drastic rebuilding of a structure already more than 200 years old.*

stretching cloth in Warwick's Pits appears on the map in the shape of Tenter Field on the south side of Great Wash Lane (St Helen's Street). The production of cloth is not the only industrial activity to find its place on the map, for near the end of Rope Lane is 'Claypitt for Brick and tyle' and Rope Lane itself took its name from the rope walk that ran parallel to the lane on its southern side; in 1625 Thomas Gallant was given the use of 'ropers lane' for ropemaking at an annual rent of ten shillings.[34]

Another ropeyard is marked alongside the river just to the south of the shipyards, on one of which can be seen a ship on the stocks. Between 'the way to Brightwell' (Back Hamlet) and 'the way to Nacton and Trimly and ye Fort' (Fore Hamlet) is a third ropeyard, the number of these places serving as a reminder of the amount of cordage absorbed by the vessels built in and operated from the port; many fathoms of rope in a variety of sizes were required for the standing and running rigging of a sailing vessel even of modest tonnage. Other maritime trades fail to show up on any map, but they were present nonetheless. Sailmakers had their premises in the lofts of quayside buildings, mast and block makers operated in yards opening off the quay and in the shipyards themselves, and shipsmiths produced specialised ironwork, and the tools used in the shipyards, in forges not far from the waterfront. All of them contributed to the prosperity of the port.

VIII

The Georgian Town

When Queen Anne died in 1714 the Stuart dynasty came to an end, and the Elector of Hanover became King George I. An address from the Corporation of Ipswich was ordered to be presented to the new king on 21 September 1714, but George I never came to Ipswich. In 1736, however, his successor did visit Ipswich on his way to London, having landed at Lowestoft from the packet that had brought him from Hanover.

Though the 18th century began with Ipswich somewhat run-down, its trade was later boosted by a number of enterprises, one of the less successful being a short-lived whale fishery based on Nova Scotia, a shipbuilding site now obliterated by the West Bank Terminal. Two ships, the *Ipswich* and the *Orwell*, were fitted out by Cornwell, Mangles and Co. for whaling in Greenland waters in 1786-7 and subsequent years, but although the *Orwell* caught seven whales on her first voyage and returned to Ipswich with 4 cwt. of whalebone and 150 butts of blubber the venture was not a success.[1]

Salthouse Street, running from Fore Street to the Common Quay, provides a reminder of a trade that flourished for many years. The salt house in which imported salt was stored and refined stood not far from the quay and was in the early part of the 18th century occupied by Robert Hall, one of the leading merchants taking part in the trade. He was succeeded by Edward Clarke, who advertised that he was selling 'the best sorts of Refined and Newcastle Salts'. North and South Shields at the mouth of the Tyne were at this time the greatest centre in the country for the manufacture of salt, with nearly 200 saltpans in which seawater was evaporated using the cheap local coal, and a large proportion of the salt cargoes brought into Ipswich came from that area. More than a third of the salt cargoes brought into Ipswich between 1718 and 1731 came in the *John and Sarah*, master John Scott, and 10 of them were probably loaded in the Mersey. These consisted of rock salt from Nantwich in Cheshire, used for cattle licks and also in the preservation of hides.[2] Towards the end of the century the import of salt was largely in the hands of the Peckover family, who might well have been connected with the Wisbech family of the same name.

The export of corn was encouraged by a government bounty, leading to a thriving overseas trade through the port of Ipswich. As so often happens, the payment of the bounty led some exporters to attempt to fiddle the system, and in January 1742 the customs stopped three vessels that had just been laden for Dutch ports; all three vessels were found to be carrying rather less than was stated on the manifest.[3] Vessels returning from Rotterdam and other Dutch ports brought a variety of goods including tiles, iron, paper and cloth. From Norway and the Baltic came timber, deals and laths; some of the timber went to the shipbuilders whose yards lined the Orwell at this period.

Shipbuilding

Ipswich had long been a shipbuilding centre, with a number of yards mainly in St Clement's parish. Most important of the 18th-century shipbuilders was undoubtedly John Barnard, who operated yards both at Ipswich and Harwich and built a succession of vessels for the Royal Navy as well as merchant ships. Born about 1705, he was the son of John Barnard, a shipwright, who was admitted a freeman in 1711 for a payment of five pounds.[4]

The outbreak of war with Spain ('the War of Jenkins' Ear') in 1739 brought about a sudden need for warships which could not be met by the naval dockyards, and orders were placed with merchant builders for a number of sixth-rates. John Barnard received a contract for the *Biddeford*, the keel being laid on the St Clement's Yard on 6 November 1739. She was launched on 16th June 1740 and towed downriver to the Navy Yard at Harwich for fitting out,[5] as can be seen in John Cleveley's painting now in the National Maritime Museum at Greenwich. In the background of the painting can be seen a fourth-rate ready for launching. This has to be the *Hampshire*, ordered little more than a month before the launching of the *Biddeford* and built not at Barnard's yard in the town but at John's Ness, more or less opposite Freston Tower, from which site this large vessel could be launched into Backagain Reach. The fact that the keel of the *Hampshire* had probably not been laid when the *Biddeford* was towed downriver presented little difficulty to an artist who, by employing a minimum of licence, could also include a third Barnard vessel, the bomb ketch *Granado*, whose keel was laid on 18 November 1741, four days after the launching of the *Hampshire*.[6]

Between 1742 and 1782 Barnard built 26 further warships at Harwich, two at Nova Scotia yard, Ipswich, and another at John's Ness, but in 1781 he suffered the same fate as so many shipbuilders before and since, being declared bankrupt. Clearly he was a victim of cash flow problems;[7] his failure could hardly be seen as a reflection of any shortcomings as a shipbuilder or as a businessman. Other members of the Barnard family moved to

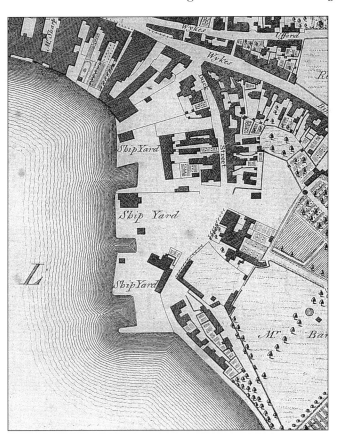

58   A section of Joseph Pennington's map showing some of the town's shipyards as they were in 1776. Among the waterside buildings were workshops used by tradesmen connected with the shipbuilding industry, such as sailmakers, shipsmiths and block and sparmakers.

the Thames and carried on shipbuilding there, but in Ipswich there were others to carry on the tradition of building wooden vessels that, as we have seen, dated back at least to the 13th century. Little more than the names of the other 18th-century shipbuilders have survived, and nothing is to be seen today of the yards in which they worked.[8] They can, however, be seen on Pennington's map, several of them ranged along the east bank of the river in St Clement's parish on what is clearly reclaimed land. Another lay on the south bank just below Stoke Bridge, and further downstream on the same side was Nova Scotia, where John Barnard's son William and William Dudman built a number of merchantmen in the 1760s.[9] Even further downstream was the Halifax yard, from which Stephen Teague launched the 18-gun brig-sloop *Cruizer* in 1797; she gave her name to the most numerous class of warships built in the age of sail. Nine of this class were built at Ipswich by Jabez Bayley between 1806 and 1813, and two more at Mistley Thorn.[10]

The Wherries

Communications with the packet port of Harwich were carried on by wherry, small sailing craft carrying passengers and light goods from and to, presumably, Wherry Quay. These boats bore no resemblance to the wherries of the Waveney and the Norfolk rivers; the appearance of a Norfolk wherry in a painting of Ipswich quay by Fred Russel is artistic licence or artistic error. The Orwell wherries shown on John Cleveley's paintings of the river were boats of about 20ft. in length with two masts, fore-and-aft rigged; small schooners, in fact. Naturally enough there was no regular timetable, for they sailed according to the tide, going down to Harwich on the ebb and returning on the flood.

Day-by-day routine caused no comment, but in July 1708 an upward-bound wherry was struck by lightning and the master, John Woollward, and three of the passengers were killed.[11] Woollward was buried in St Clement's churchyard, under a gravestone which described him as 'master of the wherry'; one might assume from the inscription that there was but one such craft, but in fact the probate inventory of Woollward's effects includes '2 Wherrys with masts, sails, anchors and cables' and also '2 small boats with oars'. Later members of the same family seem to have kept up the connection with the wherries, but they had no monopoly of the trade, for it was Joseph Cole, 'Wherry-Man', who in 1753 advertised a new wherry for the Harwich service.[12] In 1761, however, Joseph Cole and James Woolward went into partnership.[13]

Busiest period for the wherries was during the French Wars when Ipswich, Harwich and the whole area was filled with troops. In 1793 it was reported that the wherries going to Harwich were crowded to such an extent that every day passengers were left behind, and Clarke tells us that between 20 and 30 open boats had been known to leave Ipswich in a single day with passengers for Harwich.

The wherrymen were no doubt both worried and contemptuous when in 1815 a steamer was put into service on what had for so long been their route. The steam packet *Orwell* had been built by James Lepingwell at Yarmouth, and her original steam engine, which proved to have insufficient power, had been constructed in the Norwich foundry of Aggs & Curr; another engine had to be ordered from London, and it was not until August 1815 that the steamer entered service. She operated for only a few weeks before being withdrawn, leaving the Ipswich-Harwich service to the wherries.[14] Future steamships were more successful, however, and soon the wherries were so far forgotten that Fred Russel made the mistake of thinking they were Norfolk wherries.

Joseph Pennington's Map

One obtains a very good idea of the late 18th-century town from the map made by Joseph Pennington, of Needham Market, a busy and widely travelled surveyor who at various times was acting as an Enclosure Commissioner in Derbyshire, Gloucestershire and Wiltshire. The first intimation that he was considering publication of a town map was the appearance of an advertisement in the *Ipswich Journal* of 14 June 1777:

> Proposals for publishing by subscription, A MAP of the town of IPSWICH, from a new and actual survey by Joseph Pennington, of Needham Market, land-surveyor. In which will be delineated not only the streets, lanes, public buildings and bounds of the parishes, but likewise the plan of every private building, yard and garden; thus executed, it will be interesting and useful to every person who is either an inhabitant, possessed of property, or in any other way, connected with the town. The size of the map will be about 2 feet 6 inches.
>
> Subscription Half-a-Guinea; 5s. to be paid on subscribing, and the remainder on delivery of the map.
>
> The work will be begun when 400 have subscribed and finished as soon as possible.

The map was produced, although the subscription did not reach the 400 that Pennington had called for, and was published in 1778. The first thing that strikes one is the rural aspect of much of the town, with spacious gardens occupying a large proportion of the built-up area. Only between the Buttermarket and Tavern Street and in the riverside commercial area are the buildings so closely spaced that there is little or no room for well-laid-out gardens with flower beds and paths, trees and shrubs; the kind of garden in which ladies and gentlemen could take a pleasant walk in the heat of the day.

John Kirby did not overstate the facts when he wrote that

> One favourable Circumstance is almost peculiar to this Place, which is, that most of the better Houses, even in the Heart of the Town, have convenient Gardens adjoining to them, which make them more airy and healthy, as well as more pleasant and delightful.[15]

Not all the gardens were purely pleasure gardens, however, for opposite the Presbyterian Meeting House there was a 'physick garden' adjoining the house of Dr. William Beeston, who was, said Defoe, 'exquisitely skilled in botanick knowledge'. It was started in 1721 by Dr. Beeston, who sent plants to the first Professor of Botany at Cambridge when he was laying out the university town's botanic gardens.

The map shows how the ramparts and the River Gipping continued to give shape to the town, with Tower Ditches and St Margaret's Ditches following the line of the

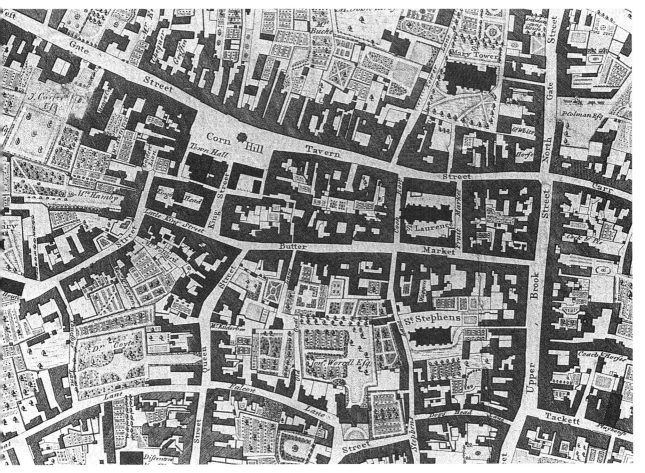

59 *The many gardens are apparent in this section of Pennington's map showing the centre of the town. The medicinal garden which Dr. William Coyte inherited from his uncle can be seen at lower left in Boat Lane.*

town ditch, and Clay Lane (now Crown Street) and Rotten Row (now St Margaret's Street) following the same line outside the ramparts. The extra-mural parishes of St Matthew's, St Margaret's and St Helen's all contain scatters of houses mainly along the principal roads, but little more, while the riverside parish of St Clement's and the hamlets of Wykes Bishop and Wykes Ufford alone show clear signs of urban expansion beyond the bounds of the early medieval town.

Pennington's Ipswich was still a fairly tight community, with streets much as they had been laid down in Saxon times, and there is little to indicate the changes that were to come. All over the town there were relics of its medieval past: in George Street are the remains of St George's Church, not completely destroyed by the 1764 fire, and at the junction of Great Whip Street and Austin Street is what is left of St Augustine's, turned into a barn or stable, according to John Kirby. Between West Gate Street (the modern name has come into use since Ogilby's 17th-century survey) and St Matthew's Street is the old West Gate, but not for long. In 1781 it was decided at a Great Court 'That Saint Matthew's Gate in this town be sold to the best bidder to be pulled down'. And pulled down it was, the last of the gates that once guarded the entrances to the town.

Rebuilding and Improvement

The collapse of the woollen cloth trade had left Ipswich a good deal less prosperous than it had been in earlier centuries. At a time when the property owners of many towns were pulling down their old timber-framed dwellings and replacing them with fine brick houses in the latest style, even the more affluent of Ipswich people were content to modernise and rebuild their 15th- and 16th-century homes.

A favourite manner of improving an old house was to build a new front wall, giving the house a modern appearance without the expense of a total rebuild. The cheapest method of doing this was simply to advance the lower wall level with the front of the jetty, but many owners chose to add an entire front wall, often taken up above eaves level to hide the lower part of the old roof. Whichever method was chosen, it caused an encroachment on the highway. Such encroachment was brought to the attention of the headboroughs, town officials who at this period appear to have been early incarnations of 20th-century planning officers. In many cases they assessed a fine which the houseowner should pay in consideration of being allowed to encroach on the street, but in the case of the Rev. Thomas Bishop who in 1753 wanted to build 'the Front of his House to catch part of the Jetty above being about Fifty-one feet in length' they decided that 'the sd Encroachment is so trifling in Width that the sd Mr Bishop ought not pay any Fine therefore, the same being an Ornament to the street aforesd'.[16]

The Changing Cornhill

In the Georgian period the old St Mildred's Church still served as the Town Hall. This 'homely, uncouth specimen of architecture', as G.R. Clark described it, was partly demolished about 1812 when the Corporation decided to replace it with a new home.[17] In 1813 William Brown, founder of the Ipswich timber merchants of that name, who practised in the town as an architect, took first place in a competition for a design for the new Town Hall; second place was taken by George Gooding, who had just built the new Corn Exchange and might have also designed it.[18]

Nothing was done to put these plans into execution, however, probably because of a lack of money, and when a new Palladian front was added to the remains of the old building in 1818 it was designed by Benjamin Batley Catt, who was some years later described by the Commissioners on Municipal Corporations as 'a builder, who has received a large sum of money from the Corporation funds, without any settlement of his accounts, and is also a lessee of Corporation lands'.[19] Catt had been elected a Common Councillor in 1815 and was a bailiff in 1828, 1830 and 1832. Although contemporary documents speak of the old Town Hall being 'taken down' and of the Corporation's intention 'to erect a new Town Hall on the scite', it is apparent that demolition was only partial and the scheme undertaken was largely a refronting of the existing building.

It is recorded that the walls of the old building proved very difficult to knock down. Whatever the problems faced in destroying the old, the Corporation seems to have encountered even greater difficulties in paying for the new, and in 1830 Clarke observed that the proposed alterations had never been completed; 'and, for want of funds, the interior remains in a deplorable, half-finished state—a reproach to the corporation', he added.[20]

60 & 61   The changing Town Hall, seen below about the beginning of the 19th century with the Market Cross and the Rotunda, both of which disappeared in 1812. The presence of a number of soldiers is indicative of the town's military importance during the wars with France. Right is Benjamin Catt's 'new Town Hall' of 1818, which in spite of appearances was little more than a refronting of the former St Mildred's Church. It is seen here in a photograph by William Vick after further modification in 1841. The last vestiges of the former church were lost when a truly new Town Hall was built in 1867. (John Wilton)

In spite of periodic repairs the old Shambles was by the time of Pennington's map showing distinct signs of decay, though it was only in 1794 that the building was dismantled to make way for the Rotunda, which Dr. Pat Murrell describes as 'a failed Georgian shopping centre'. The first stone of the Rotunda was laid by the bailiffs John Kerridge and William Norris on 10 February 1794, and such was the speed with which the erection was carried out that 500 people attended a concert and ball in the building on 12 August the same year. This circular market house was designed and built by George Gooding on the model of the Halle au Blé in Paris. Facing outwards was a ring of butchers' stalls and shops with living accommodation on two floors behind, while the central space formed a market hall in which traders set out their stalls. The wooden roof and dome structure was assembled and fixed without the use of nails, a fact of which the architect is said to have been very proud.[21]

Alas, nails or no nails, the structure does not seem to have been well built. In addition, Gooding had failed to provide adequate ventilation, and even to 18th-century men and women the smells proved offensive. After only 16 years of life the Rotunda was condemned as a nuisance and was bought by the Corporation for demolition.

On the site George Gooding built the town's first Corn Exchange. To the regret of some of the townspeople the Market Cross, too, was demolished in 1812, and the figure of Justice given by Francis Negus was transmogrified into Ceres with her horn of plenty and erected above the pediment of the Corn Exchange. In that same year a long tradition of cattle sales on the Corn Hill came to an end, the cattle market being transferred to a new site at the top of Silent Street, close to the new provision market which had opened a year or so earlier. To this day the area is known as the Old Cattle Market; the site of the quadrangular provision market with its central fountain is now occupied by the Buttermarket shopping centre.

The Paving Acts

There was a suggestion in 1777 when Pennington's map was advertised that a subscription should be raised to pay for street names to be put up in the town,[22] but if the work did begin at that time it was not completed for lack of money. One of the clauses in the Ipswich Paving Act of 1793[23] empowered the commissioners to be appointed under that Act to cause houses to be numbered 'if they think fit' and also 'to cause to be painted, engraved, or otherwise described, on a conspicuous part of some House or other Building, at or near the Corner of every street, Passage and Place' the name of that thoroughfare. Needless to say, the commissioners seem not to have thought fit, and nothing was done in that respect.

The first stone of the new paving was laid on the corner of Corn Hill and Westgate, which used to be known as the Bell Corner from the *Bell Inn* that stood there.[24] Quite a lot of money was spent in the process, and in 1797 a further Act was obtained, followed by others in 1814 and 1837, empowering the commissioners to raise additional money and at the same time adding to their powers.[25] In the case of Ipswich the commissioners were to comprise the High Steward, the bailiffs, the recorder and deputy

62 *The Town Hall has been refronted and the statue of Justice from the Market Cross has become Flora on the Corn
Exchange which has replaced the failed Rotunda in this view of 1830. (John Wilton)*

recorder, the portmen and common council members, together with every inhabitant
who possessed a house or other property to the annual value of £40 or personal estate
to the value of £800. All the proceedings of the commissioners were to be entered in
books and properly signed, according to the Act, but all the books before 1845 have
been lost. It is interesting that the town authorities, having opposed the appointment
of the paving commissioners, managed to ensure that they themselves, every man Jack
of them, became commissioners.

Military Matters

The continental campaigns of the Duke of Marlborough undoubtedly had their
repercussions in Ipswich, for the town was a convenient port of embarkation for troops
being sent to replace the numerous casualties that occurred in battle. At Malplaquet
the Allies lost one man in four, provoking Tory outrage at the 'butcher's bill'.

Successive invasion scares in 1744, 1756, 1759 and 1779 brought about a
concentration of troops in and around Ipswich. There cannot be much doubt that
when there were large numbers of troops in the area billeting could be at the very least
an inconvenience for innkeepers. However, when in 1803 the innkeepers of Ipswich
submitted a petition to the Secretary of War complaining that 'the number of Soldiers
is so greatly increased that many Innkeepers who have no other means of support must
leave their present situations, unless some speedy relief be given them,' they received
a very dusty answer.[26]

In 1795 a permanent barracks for cavalry was built in St Matthew's parish on a site to the north of the point where St Matthew's Street split into the London road and the Norwich and Bury road, a junction that not surprisingly became known as Barrack Corner. Erected by Richard Gooding, the brick buildings of the barracks stood on three sides of a square, the officers' mess to the north and barrack rooms for the men to east and west.[27] The first regiment to move into the Horse Barracks, as they were generally known, were the 2nd or Queen's Regiment of Dragoon Guards, who earned the title of the Queen's Bays when in 1762 they were for the first time mounted on bay horses. Other cavalry regiments succeeded them until at the end of the 19th century the barracks was taken over by the Royal Horse Artillery, who like their predecessors took a prominent part in the life of the town.

The threat of a French invasion led to a wave of patriotic fervour and to the raising of volunteer regiments in various places under an Act of Parliament passed in April 1794. On 27 May that year Sir Robert Harland took the chair at a meeting in the Town Hall at which it was decided to raise The Loyal Ipswich Volunteer Corps for internal defence, an 18th-century 'Dads' Army'. A Corporation proposal that same year to raise an Ipswich Regiment of 32 serjeants, 30 corporals, 22 drummers and 600 men was, like so many grandiose official schemes down the years, not carried into effect.[28] The enthusiastic Loyal Ipswich Volunteers, on the other hand, had a long and apparently useful life. They received new colours on the renewal of war with France in 1803 and offered to undertake garrison duty if needed. The following spring they marched to Hadleigh for three weeks' permanent duty, and then in 1805 they spent a similar period on duty with the Ipswich garrison.[29] Other volunteer units likewise reinforced the Ipswich garrison from time to time. In 1818 the 1st Regiment of Suffolk Yeomanry Cavalry, some 300 strong, did duty in the town and spent some time exercising on Rushmere Heath, the usual training ground for cavalry.

On the outbreak of the Napoleonic Wars a large riverside maltings close to Stoke Bridge was converted into barracks to accommodate some of the regular troops, and a temporary hutted camp was built on the Woodbridge road just outside the town to accommodate some 8,000 men. It is said that 2,000 workmen were employed in the construction of the hutted barracks, which extended to both sides of the road and cost some £200,000 to build.[30] The hutted camp was used as a military hospital in 1809 to accommodate some of the thousands of soldiers who contracted fever during the Walcheren expedition. Dr. J.B. Davis, who was posted as a temporary physician to serve in Ipswich by the Physician General to the Army, wrote that 'every patient had a separate bed with comfortable bedclothes, and the attendance was entirely adequate'. When the first batch of 92 patients reached Ipswich on 10 September four were dead on arrival. By 6 October more than 400 sick men had arrived in Ipswich without any further deaths, and by the end of the year the total reaching the hutted hospital exceeded 600.[31] The mortality rate in the Ipswich hospital was high. The burial register of St Margaret's Church shows that 218 men died between September 1809 and the following February, the incumbent adding a note that 'No account of the ages of the above men could be obtained. They are those who came sick from the island of Walcheren and died in the military hospitals in this place.'

St Helen's Barracks, the hutted camp on the Woodbridge Road, seems to have closed about the same time as the Stoke Barracks was sold,[32] though some of the huts remained, occupied by extremely poor squatters who proved a burden on the parishes in which they were living. Parishes is in the plural, for though the camp was largely in St Helen's some of the huts were in a detached part of St Stephen's parish, 'so strangely do some of the parishes in this town intersect each other', as Clarke put it.[33]

Not only did the troops become a familiar part of the town scene, not least when parading to St Matthew's Church on a Sunday morning, but the local social scene benefited greatly from the attendance of the officers. Ceremonial occasions and events like the opening of the new Custom House in 1845 profited from the attendance of the regimental band. In return the local people showed a concern for the welfare of the men quartered in the town, as when in 1795 the Ipswich Musical Society held a concert in the Rotunda to raise money for a treat on the King's birthday for the men of the 1st King's Dragoon Guards and the 33rd Regiment of Foot, both of which had not long before returned from the continent. In 1830 Clarke observed that 'The military are very partial to Ipswich, as quarters; for they, generally, are much noticed by, and associate in a friendly manner with, the gentry of the town and neighbourhood.'[34]

The Social Scene

The officers of regiments based in the town might be seen at the theatre, which in the 18th century was still striving, not entirely successfully, to escape from the restraints imposed during the Commonwealth. The Licensing Act of 1737 not only introduced control of theatres and censorship of the plays but enacted that anyone who for reward performed any stage entertainment without Letters Patent from the monarch or licence from the Lord Chamberlain 'shall be deemed to be a Rogue and a Vagabond', thus providing a title for Elizabeth Grice's story of the East Anglian theatre.[35]

Ipswich in the early 18th century had two main venues for plays, a booth at the *Griffin Inn* yard in Westgate Street and the Shire Hall in Foundation Street, built in 1699 primarily to accommodate the Quarter Sessions. The booth in the *Griffin* yard saw such entertainment as that offered by Signora Violante, an Italian rope dancer, as well as plays by visiting companies of players from London. There was also a temporary booth used by some visiting companies. That there was still strong opposition to plays and the theatre from some quarters was proved when this booth collapsed in 1729 in the middle of a performance; a pamphlet entitled *A Prelude to the Plays* was promptly published hailing the accident as 'a rebuke of divine Providence upon those that attended these plays'.

Disregarding the pamphleteer's warning, Henry Betts, an Ipswich brewer, had the town's first permanent theatre built in 1736 adjacent to his *Tankard Inn*, formerly Sir Humphrey Wingfield's house. It was on the stage of this Tankard Playhouse that a young man going under the name of Lyddal made his debut in 1741. He had come to

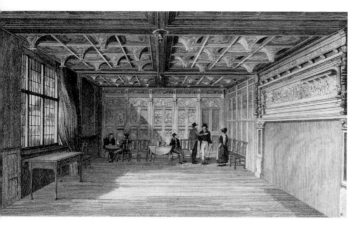

63 Sir Humphrey Wingfield's house in Tacket Street became in the 18th century the Tankard *public house. It contained this remarkable room with a ceiling bearing numerous coats of arms. (John Wilton)*

Ipswich with a company of comedians brought to the town from London by William Giffard, manager of Goodman's Fields theatre. The fledgling actor, who was known to his friends as Davy Garrick, appeared as the African slave Aboan in Thomas Southerne's tragedy *Oroonoko*. Garrick's biographer, Thomas Davies, tells how 'under the disguise of a black countenance, he hoped to escape being known, should it be his misfortune not to please'. He need not have worried, since 'in every essay he gave such delight to the audience, that they gratified him with constant and loud proofs of their approbation'. Garrick never returned to Ipswich, yet the influence he had on the acting tradition was to be felt in the town just as it was in London and elsewhere.

It could be said that he brought a new and civilising discipline to the theatre, reforming by example rather than by decree. When he mounted the stage, anonymous in his black makeup, actors were considered by no means respectable and audiences were frequently ill-behaved, to say the least; probably nobody did more than Garrick to change that situation. From Elizabethan times members of the audience had been accustomed to sit or stand on the stage, even though this often impeded the actors in their performance. Preventing the public from strolling about the stage during performances was perhaps the most revolutionary of all Garrick's improvements. It was with the idea of barring access to the stage that the management of the Tankard Street theatre introduced boxes at the side of the stage when the theatre was remodelled in 1754.[36]

From 1759 onwards the Norwich Company formally leased the Ipswich theatre for £70 a year, and they were regular visitors, especially when the races were being held. Whereas the performances were normally advertised to begin at six o'clock it was not unknown for the summer plays to begin 'as soon as the Race is over'. The races, run on heathland between the Felixstowe and Nacton roads, naturally attracted the officers of cavalry regiments stationed in the locality as well as gentry from a wide area of Suffolk. They were held each June from at least 1710, and acquired status in 1727 when they were allocated a Royal Plate worth 100 guineas. Although the number of races was limited, each race was run in several heats over the two-and-a-half-mile course. Any horse that failed to reach a 'distance post' 240 yards from the winning post by the time the winner had passed the winning post was 'distanced' and thus barred from further heats.[37]

In the early days there seems to have been no accommodation for the crowds who flocked to the races and sometimes spilled over on to the racecourse itself, but in 1775 a 'substantial gallery' was built, and the following year a covered stand was erected with inscribed over it in golden letters 'The Gentlemen's Stand'. Admission to the former was sixpence, but places in the Gentlemen's Stand cost a whole 2s. 6d. To keep the crowds amused there were sideshows of various kinds as well as booths at which refreshments, mainly of the intoxicating kind, could be bought. In 1795 the main subsidiary attraction was an elephant which was put on exhibition with a collection of other exotic animals at a shilling admission, servants being allowed in at half price.[38]

64   *The interior of the theatre, in one of William Vick's photographs.*

Cockfighting with gamecocks, their wings clipped and metal spurs strapped to their legs, was a sport that attracted many of the gentry; wagers on the result added interest to the fight. Edmund Orford, of the *Bear and Crown* in Westgate Street, in 1755 announced a main of cocks between the Gentlemen of Cambridgeshire and the Gentlemen of Norfolk and Suffolk on the two race days. A new cockpit had been constructed there in 1752. Some years later the cockpit of the *Cock and Pye* in Upper Brook Street was the scene of another raceday main: 'The Cocks will be pitted at 11 o'clock, and immediately after the Race is over'. A Frenchman, Francois de La Rochefoucauld, who visited Ipswich in 1784, did not approve of cockfighting. 'It is a game of cruelty, a relic of barbarity, unforgivable in a nation like theirs,' he wrote in his journal.[39]

Such entertainments were for the better classes—the shilling charge for viewing the elephant was well beyond the reach of the 'lower sort'. Indeed, the town authorities were frequently occupied with the necessity of ensuring that ordinary working people were not tempted to indulge their time in sport or gambling of any kind, even the seemingly harmless game of skittles being stamped on because it could be the subject of betting. In 1785 more than 30 ten-pin and skittle grounds in the town were destroyed by the authorities, it being said that they had 'done inconceivable mischief to the lower ranks of this town, by enticing them to spend their money, whilst their numerous families are in want of the common necessaries of life; and those who have not families, contract such habits of idleness and gambling, as perhaps may never be irradicated'.[40]

For all that Ipswich was rather less a centre of social activity than Bury St Edmunds, there were balls during the races, and on other occasions such as the King's birthday that attracted the better class from both town and nearby country. Francois de La Rochefoucauld enjoyed these events during his Suffolk visit 'because I found a large number of people there and was able to talk to people I was able to see only rarely, and partly also because my vanity was tickled'. In France, he explained, he was considered one of the worst dancers, but the English danced so badly that they regarded him as a good dancer.[41]

Many of the balls were held at the Assembly House kept by Benjamin Crocker, which in the 1740s was in St Peter's Street opposite the tower of St Peter's Church. A room in Mr Crocker's house next door to the Assembly House served as a waiting room for the men-servants, who were called when needed to accompany their masters and mistresses home.[42] More than 300 gentlemen and ladies were at the opening concert and ball on 8 November 1753, when a new Assembly House was opened in a more central part of the town. It was adjacent to Dod's Coffee-House on the corner of Tavern Street and Tower Street, one of those fashionable meeting-places that became popular towards the end of the 17th century.

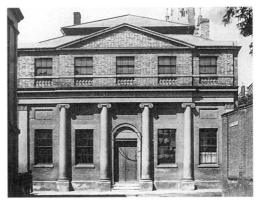

65   *The Assembly Rooms in Northgate Street, opened in 1821 with a ball and supper attended by 'nearly 200 of the Nobility and principal Gentry of the county'. The building now houses a night club.*

A syndicate of ten shareholders leased the premises to one Daniel Bamford, who came in conflict with the law in 1772 when he was disqualified from holding a victualling licence for three years after being convicted of allowing gaming in his house; he had permitted his customers to play billiards, which was a popular game at that time. The Coffee House sold not only coffee and tea but was licensed as a tavern. Fortunately for Bamford the Court of King's Bench quashed his conviction; he later moved to the *Great White Horse*, which he seems to have run until his death in 1806. The Coffee House and Assembly Rooms were bought in 1798 by Ipswich brewer John Cobbold, who spent a good deal on improvements to the premises.

From time to time Ipswich people compared their own amenities with those of fashionable Bury St Edmunds, where the Assembly Rooms (now known as the Atheneum) were 'elegant and universally admired'; with improvements, such as the widening of Tavern Street, going on all around it could not be long before a scheme was brought forward to provide better facilities. Sir William Middleton, of Shrubland Hall, took the chair at a meeting in 1818 at which it was decided to raise money to build a New Assembly Rooms in Northgate Street.[43] Between £3,000 and £4,000 was raised at the meeting, and it was expected that more would quickly be forthcoming, but the scheme was to meet with many difficulties. For a start a case was brought in the Court of Chancery seeking to prevent the owners selling two houses to the subscribers, and although the case failed it proved an ill omen.[44] William Brown's plans for the New Assembly Rooms were approved in August, and before long builder George Mason was at work on the white brick façade. The side wall of the *Great White Horse* facing Northgate Street was similarly rebuilt in Suffolk whites.

The new establishment was opened with a ball and supper in January 1821 attended by 'nearly 200 of the Nobility and principal Gentry of the county', who danced the night away until four in the morning.[45] The ballroom was 54ft. long and 27ft. wide, and under it was a room designed for use as a public library; there were also anterooms for both ladies and gentlemen, a supper room, card room and reading rooms. Alas, the funds collected by the subscription were insufficient to pay for the work, and in 1825 the New Assembly Rooms were put up for sale, with the suggestion that they would with little alteration make a fine family home.[46] In spite of the enforced sale the Assembly Rooms continued to be frequented by the better sort, though in 1827 James and Robert Ransome complained that they had never been paid for ironwork ordered by the architect in 1819. In a letter beginning 'Respected friend,' they wrote of 'a building, raised at the expense of the different tradesmen employed, upwards of seven years ago, none of whose bills, we are informed, up to the present moment are paid!'[47]

Caring for the Poor

Each of the 12 parishes in Ipswich had its own workhouse for accommodating people who could not, or would not, support themselves. The St Clement's parish workhouse in Fore Street was composed of five former houses given by Mary Wright in 1698; it was demolished in the 1830s.[48] Maintaining these workhouses, along with their inmates, was costly to the parishes; it was reckoned that the poor rate in Ipswich in 1821 alone totalled more than £13,000, an enormous sum by the standards of that time.[49] Nor did the parish poorhouses prove particularly effective in operation. Sarah Durrant, singlewoman, was apprehended in Colchester as 'a Rogue and Vagabond' and 'as a lewd Idle and disorderly person lying about in Outhouses and having no visible way of maintenance' in January 1786 and was given a vagrant's pass to reach St. Matthew's parish in Ipswich, which it was deemed was her place of settlement. There she was lodged in the workhouse, but one night in March she and another inmate walked out after stealing items of clothing belonging to other paupers.[50]

The idea of the workhouse was that the inmates should earn their keep so far as possible. The Ipswich Assembly Book[51] contains an order of May 1687 that the beadles were to take up poor children who begged around the town and to put them in the House of Correction, where they should be put to work. 'And if they cannot keep themselves by theire work the parish to which they or any of them belong shall pay the keep of the sd house what their worke fall short of paymt.' Poor children were generally indentured by the Overseers of the Poor to tradesmen such as blacksmiths, gardeners, tailors and brickmakers; in 1795 John Badley was apprenticed to an Islington chimney-sweep—one hopes he did not become stuck in the chimney.[52] The girls were usually bound out as maidservants. Many of the boys were sent to sea as apprentices either to mariners or to fishermen; in 1705 Thomas Harris was apprenticed to George Jackson, of Whitby, master of the ship *The Friends Goodwill* of that port,[53] and in 1747 Peter Grimes and another Ipswich boy were indentured to Capt. John Beall, of Scarborough.[54] The sad and terrible life led by some of these youngsters is portrayed in Benjamin

*66   'That's the way to do it!' It is not only children who are attracted
to a Punch and Judy performance in St Mary Elms, the area known as
The Mount.*

Britten's opera *Peter Grimes*, for which both the name and the story were borrowed from the Aldeburgh poet George Crabbe; where did Crabbe get the name?

The dozen workhouses in the town were mainly former dwelling houses which had, as a report of 1822 explained,[55] been 'engaged by the parish officers as occasion required, without regard either to situation or convenience'. For the most part they were too small for it to be possible to separate ages and sexes. Improvements made to two of the poor houses, those of St Margaret's and St Matthew's, had by 1822 'remedied the most disgusting and promiscuous intermixture in the sleeping rooms'. In the St Margaret's workhouse the aged and infirm as well as the women and young children had been separated from the boys and able-bodied men both during the day and at night, but it was stated that this was 'the only attempt made at classification in the workhouses in Ipswich'.[56]

'Poor houses' was a much better description than workhouses, since it was said to be impossible to find employment for those of the poor who were able to work. There seems to have been rather more concern given to the fact that the poor were not supporting themselves from their earnings than to the obvious fact that, as the old saying has it, the devil found mischief for idle hands.[57] The committee set up to consider provision for the poor recommended in 1822 that the parishes should unite and build one large workhouse to hold 500 inmates, who could be properly 'classified' and usefully employed. The Bosmere and Claydon Union Workhouse at Barham was quoted as a model, but nothing was done to implement the recommendations of the committee for some 12 years.

Some of the obvious deficiencies of the system were made good by private individuals or groups of philanthropic men and women. It was not uncommon for people to leave a sum in their wills to be invested for the benefit of the poor, or to leave land from which the income was to be devoted in some way to relieving poor families. In St Clement's parish in 1685 Captain Samuel Green left £50, to be spent in buying land, for the relief of widows and children of seamen, and in due course his widow added another £10;[58] the rent of the land purchased in Westerfield, which in the 1840s amounted to £17 a year, was distributed each year on 28 November.[59] Then in 1719 Captain Robert Cole left £50 with instructions that it should be used to buy bread to be distributed each fortnight to poor widows of seamen.[60] Others left similar bequests, one donor stipulating that the profits of the investment of his £100 should be distributed among poor seamen's widows and children and other poor not receiving parochial relief.

The inefficient and slapdash way in which these parochial charities were administered would certainly not satisfy today's Charity Commissioners. Trustees died, having failed to arrange for the transfer of property to a new set of trustees, and in some cases which ended up in court, legal expenses swallowed up more than the original bequest. Captain Cole's legacy, instead of paying for land from which the income was to be used to buy bread for widows, as he had directed in his will, was laid out in repairing St Clement's Church, the bread that was distributed once a fortnight being paid for out of the church rates.[61]

An example of more organised assistance was the formation in 1795 of the Ipswich Lying-in Charity which provided assistance and the loan of linen to poor married women at the time of giving birth—those conceiving out of wedlock were specifically barred from benefiting from the charity. In its first 21 years this institution assisted no fewer than 6,130 poor women. A similar organisation was formed by the members of Stoke Green Baptist Chapel.[62] More general help to the poor was offered by the Ipswich Benevolent Society For Visiting and Relieving Poor Persons when under Affliction, formed in 1799. 'The design of this Institution is … to afford some temporal relief to the distressed of every denomination; and especially to communicate instruction to the ignorant, and promote their spiritual welfare, by appointing suitable persons to visit them.'[63]

Traders and Craftsmen

The Georgian town was very much a self-supporting community. Boot and shoemakers, harnessmakers, whitesmiths, plumbers, peruke makers, silversmiths and clockmakers, glovers, tailors, cabinetmakers and printers could all be found within the town, yet there were still people who looked to London for what they thought was quality with cheapness, notwithstanding that the stage waggon that set out from St Nicholas Street on Monday afternoon with 'four able horses' arrived at the Cross Keys in London's Leadenhall Street only on Wednesday morning.[64]

Traders were anxious if they could to advertise some connection with the metropolis. Jacob Milner, muffin-maker, who set up at the *Crown Inn* in St Matthew's in 1764, was anxious to let it be known that he was 'from London', and so was Edward Sheppard who set up as a linen draper, haberdasher and mercer in Tavern Street opposite the Coffee House in 1778. Alas, within six months Sheppard's stock of linens, cottons and muslins was for sale 'for the benefit of his creditors'; a London background was no guarantee of success.[65] Not everyone who moved into the town came from London, for in 1756 coppersmith William Norris advertised that he had come from Norwich to take over the shop of Thomas Crawley near the *Great White Horse*, 'where all persons may depend upon being served as cheap as in London'.[66]

The name of Curriers Lane survives as a reminder of those workers who treated leather with grease mixtures to make it pliable for use in footwear and harness. Leather was produced by tanners such as the Abbotts in their tanyard close by Handford Mill, clearly marked on Pennington's map, and in another tannery in St Peter's parish. In

67 *Dial Lane and the tower of St Lawrence's Church in a print reproduced in Pawsey's* Ladies' Fashionable
Repository *for 1868. Earlier known as Cook Row, this narrow thoroughfare took its modern name from the clock
which projected from the church tower. (John Wilton)*

these hides were first stripped of fat and then cleansed in pits filled with lime and
various noxious liquids; it was a smelly and unpleasant process, but a very necessary
one. That the trade was of considerable antiquity in this part of the town seems to be
indicated by the name of the thoroughfare leading from Friars Bridge to Handford
Road, Tanners Lane, which is to be seen on both Pennington's and Ogilby's maps. The
lane and the name survived until the construction of Civic Drive in the 1960s.

Much of the leather produced by the tanners and curriers went to saddlers and
harnessmakers, of whom there were a baker's dozen in the town about 1830. In 1767
William Adams, saddler and capmaker, advertised that he had saddles of all kinds at his
shop near Dod's Coffee House;[67] such tradesmen were much in demand when transport
depended on the horse. The *Great White Horse* nearby had stabling for 46 horses.

In spite of the shortcomings of the roads, especially in winter, Ipswich was by the
middle of the 18th century beginning to find itself at the hub of a network of waggon
and coach services. Travel was slow and expensive, but for those who could afford the
costs it was possible to obtain goods from London; many tradesmen seem to have made
use of the carriers to bring fashionable stock for their shops. In 1744 Thomas Shave
advertised that he took in goods at the *Nag's Head* in St Mary Elms parish for London,
his stage waggon leaving on a Monday morning and arriving in Leadenhall Street on
the Wednesday, returning with parcels for Ipswich on Thursday.[68] The waggons were

cumbrous vehicles with heavy, broad-rimmed wheels that were thought to roll the road material down but in fact broke up the surface to a considerable extent. When the turnpike trusts began building improved roads—the Ipswich-Claydon road was turnpiked in 1711—they tended to impose heavy tolls upon such vehicles, and it became necessary to weigh the waggons and their loads to assess the toll.

For this purpose weighing machines or steelyards similar to the one that survives in New Street, Woodbridge, were constructed either by the trust or by others, the Claydon trust having one in that village. There was another on St Margaret's Green, and about 1770 Isaac Brook erected one 'entirely of his own projecting and correcting. . .for the more convenient, and much more exact, weighing of Hay, Clover, Straw, Waggons (loaded or empty) that use the Turnpike-Road, or other Things of any Weight'.[69] Like so much else, it is there on Pennington's map, towards the west end of Clay Lane (now Crown Street).

The deficiencies of the roads, which were rutted and poorly made up at best, and often completely impassable in winter, meant that most goods and not a few passengers used coastal shipping. The improvement of roads in the 18th century, however, led to the relatively short-lived ascendancy of the stage coach, which changed its team of horses at convenient inns along its route. As early as the 1740s the Ipswich, Saxmundham and Beccles Flying Stagecoach was running in summer from the *Cross Keys Inn*, Gracechurch Street, in London to Ipswich in one day. It set out at three in the morning and arrived at Ipswich at an unspecified time that night; the vagueness of the arrival time is perhaps explained by the cautious postscript 'Perform'd (if God permit) by Thomas Johnson and Richard Dove'.[70] Travel by coach was, however, thoroughly uncomfortable, particularly for those who rode outside, and it was also too expensive for all but the well-to-do. For most people who were moving around there was no real alternative to tramping.

Smallpox

Travel, by whatever means, could be, and all too often was, a means of spreading infection through the country. Although plague virtually disappeared following the epidemic of 1665-6 smallpox continued to be a disfiguring and often fatal illness, a particularly virulent strain afflicting people of all ages and all social backgrounds in the later part of the 17th century. Queen Mary fell victim to the disease in 1694. A thoroughly unpleasant illness that often had a lasting effect on the sufferer, smallpox was so common in the early 18th century that very few people escaped infection at some stage in their lives. Inoculation, which used the smallpox virus itself to give subsequent immunity through a mild attack of the disease, was introduced to England in 1721, and it was a Suffolk family, the Suttons, who did a great deal in Ipswich and elsewhere to develop a milder and safer treatment than that originally used.

There was a common fear that inoculation created the very epidemics it was intended to counter, and when Dr. William Beeston, he of the physick garden, inoculated three people in Ipswich in 1724 his action provoked a violent reaction. Dr. Beeston wrote that

> The practice of Inoculation in this Town, has so inflamed the angry passions, and stirred up the bitter Zeale of the bigotted high Churchmen, and Dissenters to such a Degree that they Sentence to Damnation, all that are in any way Concerned in it. They say the practice is Heathenish, and Diabolical, it is distrusting Providence, and taking the Power out of God's hand, it will draw down Divine Judgements … but reason they do not, upon the subject.[71]

Robert Sutton, who had worked as a country doctor in Kenton for a number of years, began to take an interest in inoculation after his eldest son almost died after being inoculated by 'a surgeon of his acquaintance'. After a series of trials that 'convinced him he had made some valuable discoveries' he advertised in the *Ipswich Journal* in April 1757 that he had hired 'a large commodious House for the Reception of Persons who are disposed to be INOCULATED by him for the SMALLPOX'.[72]

By 1763 the Suttons had a well-established and profitable business. In that year Daniel Sutton left his father's practice to set up for himself in Essex, and it was he who in 1767 set up an inoculation house at Freston Tower, overlooking the Orwell just four miles from the centre of town. An Ipswich surgeon, Mr. Bucke junior, who resided at Holbrook, was engaged as 'an Assistant in his singular and *most* successful Method' and was placed in charge of the Freston branch of the business, which was well placed to attract patients from the town.[73]

68   Freston Tower, a Tudor prospect tower conveniently remote from the populated area of Ipswich, in which Daniel Sutton set up an inoculation house in 1767.

Opposition in Ipswich still continued, in spite of the success enjoyed by the Suttons. In 1772 a general meeting of the inhabitants was held at the Town Hall at which the bailiffs, portmen and the churchwardens of the 12 parishes 'determined to set their faces against inoculation, as tending to encrease the small pox, by reason of the probability of contagion'. At the same time the town's principal surgeons agreed to refrain from inoculation so as to avoid people coming into the town for the purpose.[74] The introduction of vaccination with cowpox virus in 1798 provided another weapon against the disease, but inoculation continued until it was made a criminal offence in 1840. Yet in 1815 Ipswich was again suffering an epidemic of smallpox, 'notwithstanding the benefit of vaccination',[75] and endemic smallpox was not eradicated in Britain until 1908.

Printing and the News

For the whole of the 17th century printing was largely confined to London, and it was only in 1720 that John Bagnall moved to Ipswich on completing his apprenticeship in London, probably taking over the bookselling business in St Mary Elms parish that had been operated by Henry Truelove junior. In that year he founded the *Ipswich Journal*, which was to remain in publication until the beginning of the 20th century. The extent of Bagnall's business may be judged from the advertisement he placed in his own newspaper in 1721:

> John Bagnall and Company.
>
> Printers and engravers from London at the Printing Office in St. Mary-Elms in Ipswich, Suffolk. Prints all sorts of books, bills, bones, indentures, sermons, proposals, catalogues, warrants … as well and as cheap as in London. … Note. All booksellers, chapmen, hawkers, peddlers, or others, may be furnished with all sorts of little books, songs, large and small pictures in wood or copper, plain or coloured, by wholesale or retail.[76]

Bagnall's business was taken over in the mid-1730s by Thomas Norris, who in 1735 printed the *Ipswich Weekly Mercury*; the issue of 22 February 1735 carried the imprint 'Ipswich: printed by T. Norris, in the Cross Key Street, near the Great White Horse Corner; where advertisements are taken in …'.[77] In 1739 the business passed to William Craighton, who had earlier been a bookseller in Debenham. When he died in 1761 the business was carried on by his sister Elizabeth Craighton and her nephew William Jackson.

The *Ipswich Journal* had a somewhat topsy-turvy career after Elizabeth sold it to her nephew in 1769. William became bankrupt in 1774 and the issue of 17 December was printed by William Bailey 'for the benefit of the creditors of William Jackson'. Part of the agreement between Elizabeth and William at the time of sale had been that he was to pay her an annuity of £30, but on William's bankruptcy the trustees refused to continue this payment, offering only £20. While the *Ipswich Journal* continued to be published for the benefit of the creditors, Elizabeth, then a lady of 70, retaliated by publishing the *Original Ipswich Journal* with the help of John Shave, a former apprentice of her brother's who had acquired the bookselling and stationery side of the business from his former master in 1759. The two papers came out side by side from 24 December 1774 to 22 March 1777, when the creditors' paper was discontinued; Elizabeth then dropped the word *Original* from the title of her paper, which continued to be published by her and Shave and another nephew, Stephen Jackson.[78] Elizabeth must have been a strong-minded lady, for she continued to be associated with the *Ipswich Journal* until 1779, when her name ceased to appear on the imprint. She died in 1796 at the age of ninety-two.

In the 1820s the *Ipswich Journal* took a step forward by engaging Robinson Taylor as a reporter. In the election of 1837 Taylor and the proprietor of the *Journal* were so confident that the Tories would reverse the disasters of 1835 that readers were promised the results in a special issue printed in blue ink; the Tories were successful, but the use of blue ink was found to be impracticable.[79]

Malting and Brewing

The malting trade was thriving in the 18th century and was, according to John Kirby, growing so fast that the Ipswich maltsters were unable to obtain all their barley supplies from within the county and were obliged to import some from Norfolk.[80] The complicated and restrictive rules applied to the trade by those responsible for levying the Malt Tax held back men who sought to improve the technology of malting, but nevertheless changes were made from time to time. When the extensive riverside premises occupied by Jeremiah Byles up to 1777 were offered to let in 1782, it was specifically mentioned that the malting had 'a kiln built upon a new construction to save cinders'.[81] The premises also included a cinder-oven in which coal was coked to provide smokeless fuel for the malt kilns, or kells as they were invariably called in Suffolk. At that time the hard Welsh coal that provided fuel for later malt kilns had not come into use and to avoid spoiling the malt it was necessary to drive off the volatile matter from the bituminous coal by heating it in coke-ovens at high temperature. The buildings stretched along the river some 130 feet, and as some of them were right on the bank it was possible to load bulk grain or malt into vessels lying alongside by way of spouts.

Among the 18th-century Ipswich maltsters was Thomas Cobbold, who in 1723 turned to brewing, opening up a brewery close to St Nicholas Church at Harwich. Born in 1680, Thomas was a descendant of the Robert Cobbold, yeoman of Tostock, whose death is recorded in 1603. Robert's grandson Reynold died at Rattlesden in 1666 at the age of 102, and it was Reynold's grandson John who was Thomas's father.[82]

Thomas Cobbold's brewing venture was undoubtedly successful, but the local water at Harwich was brackish and for his 'liquor', as the brewer terms it, he had to turn to supplies from Suffolk. The story is told of how he transported water from the crystal-clear springs of Holywells, an estate close to the River Orwell just below Ipswich which was in the hands of the Cobbold family; in fact the evidence shows that his water came not from Ipswich but from Erwarton, on the Shotley peninsula. To carry the water across the harbour to Harwich he employed a water-sloop, a little vessel equipped with a tank and a manual pump to discharge the liquid cargo.

For some twenty years Cobbold operated in this fashion, but the need to carry water to his brewery was an overhead that no businessman could contemplate for long. In 1743 he took over an existing brewery in Ipswich, but at the time said that he intended to sell his beer only in Harwich; it seems he was dipping his toe in the water, or perhaps getting a foot in the market:

> HARWICH, January 12, 1742/3
>
> By Request of the Innholders in HARWICH, I shall next week begin, and continue (God willing) to Brew at IPSWICH, in order as well to furnish them with IPSWICH as HARWICH BEER, and the Tap-House in the King's Ship-Yard will as well as all other my Houses in Town, be furnished with both Sorts. This I do for the more agreeable accommodating the large Number of Workmen, and all such Persons as may come down from IPSWICH, tho' I must observe it is not in the Power of any Person to Brew better elsewhere than at HARWICH; for tho' we are surrounded with Salt Water, yet I

will maintain I brew with as good Water as any in the County of SUFFOLK, which is known by all Persons who know ERWARTON Canal, my Water being conveyed from thence by Pipes into my Water-Sloop, in which Sloop is fix'd a square Fatt, intirely tight as a Bason, and brought over intirely neat as those fine Springs produce it.

I shall make my Malt at BURY, of the finest Barley that Country will produce, in order to Brew at Ipswich for the obliging my HARWICH Friends, and such as shall favour us with their Company: but I have no present View of interrupting any Brewers in Ipswich, not intending to dispose of any Thing in IPSWICH but my Draynes; and as I have taken Mr. Harvey's Brewing-Office, there being no other in Town but my own, it shall be the more my Endeavour to oblige all Ship-Masters who come into the Harbour, and all Persons, by serving them the better, rather than according to some People's construction, who would think it would be otherwise. THOMAS COBBOLD[83]

Whatever the truth of his intentions with regard to brewing in Ipswich, in 1746 Cobbold moved the entire brewing process to Ipswich, to a riverside site at The Cliff right below the Holywells, from which the water was piped straight into the brewery. He had competition, for there were other brewers operating in Ipswich, some of them brewing just for their own public houses and some in a larger way of business supplying 'the trade', but by building on a green-field site and by using a source of pure water Cobbold was able to rise above the opposition. It might seem strange from a 20th-century perspective that several breweries could trade in a town with a population of no more than 10,000, but it has to be remembered that ale or beer was the normal drink for a very large part of that population. Even the children drank 'small beer' at a time when much of the water supply was grossly polluted.

The new brewery at The Cliff had been in existence a mere six years when Thomas Cobbold died in 1752, but the business was carried on by his son, another Thomas. It was to continue as a family business for another 200 years and more.

The younger Thomas had five children, born between 1742 and 1750, and it was the third of these, John, who took over when Thomas died in 1767. Thomas was buried in St Clement's Church, and on the flagstone that marks his resting place he is described as a common brewer—one who brewed for the trade rather than for sale on his own premises. Like his father, John was a maltster as well as a brewer, doubtless

69 *Thomas Cobbold, who moved his brewery from Harwich to Ipswich in 1746. (Tollemache & Cobbold Brewery Ltd.)*

producing in his maltings in St Clement's Fore Street and at the Cliff much of the malt that went into the brewery's mash tun.

The Cobbolds also had other interests in the town, for they were corn and coal merchants and also shipowners engaged in trades that took their ships to far parts of the world. Before very long they were as prominent in the public life of the town as they were in its business community. [23] John Cobbold, who lived to the age of 89, was clearly a man of considerable energy. His first wife, Elizabeth Wilkinson, died in 1790, leaving him with 14 children, of whom the eldest, John junior, was then 16. He then married the young widow of William Clarke, the town's controller of customs, a woman 20 years his junior. Elizabeth was able to more than match her new husband's energy, for she not only brought up the children of his first marriage and herself became the mother of six sons and a daughter but still managed to make the family home at The Cliff and later at the Manor House on St Margaret's Green a centre of local artistic life.

During the time the family was living at the Manor House on St Margaret's Green a certain Margaret Catchpole was taken on as a servant in the Cobbold household. The true story of Margaret, a strong-willed countrywoman who seems to have had a habit of getting herself into serious trouble, is almost inextricably confused with the work of fiction that was written by one of Mrs. Cobbold's six sons, Richard. There can be little doubt that it was from his mother that Richard gained his own literary leanings. A generation after its first publication, the Rev. Richard Cobbold's novel was declared to be 'the best read book in Ipswich, if not in Suffolk', but the tale told in that book of the wilful young girl with a smuggler lover is very different in many respects from Margaret's real life. Far from being a young girl when she stole John Cobbold's strawberry roan, a crime for which she was sentenced to death at Suffolk Assizes at Bury St Edmunds in 1797, she was then a woman of 35. The death sentence was commuted, and she spent the next three years in Ipswich Gaol, one of the first prisons in Britain to be built according to the principles of prison reformer John Howard. Then in 1800 she escaped from the gaol 'in the absence of the Keeper, who was attending his duty at Bury Assizes' by climbing over the wall with the aid of a clothes line. A description given in the *Police Gazette and Hue and Cry* at the time describes her as '5ft. 2in. high, of a swarthy complexion, dark eyes and hair, broad face and rather large and homely features'—not quite the attractive young girl of Richard Cobbold's novel. She was recaptured, and again the death sentence was passed, later to be commuted to transportation. It is said that Mrs. Cobbold wrote pleading for her life; certainly she carried on a correspondence with her former servant out in Botany Bay.

Whatever his reputation as a writer, the Rev. Richard Cobbold was blessed with a sense of humour as well as a keen imagination. When in his sixties he was fitted with a set of false teeth, quite a rarity in the mid-19th century, and while out walking in his parish he came on two chimney sweeps eating their breakfast. While chatting to them he said how much he envied their nice white teeth, which shone out from their blackened faces. Back came the quick retort that they would change teeth with him for a pound. The rector pretended to tug at his, and finally after a good deal of apparent effort

70   *The clock that gave its name to Dial Lane is clearly seen in this print of 1845 showing the corner of the Ancient House. (John Wilton)*

pulled them out. Greatly alarmed at this, the two sweeps leapt up and rushed off to the nearby *Queen's Head*, where one of them cried out to Mrs. Mary Allen, the landlady, 'Missus, give us some brandy—we've just seen the Devil!' One suspects that this story was retailed with glee by the Rev. Richard himself.[85]

It might have been something more than his sense of humour that caused him to write to the *Suffolk Chronicle* in 1859 claiming that Margaret Catchpole was on a visit to Ipswich. 'Yes, sir, she was in the train with me,' he wrote with the straightest of faces. 'Margaret Catchpole is upon a visit to Mr. Roe's in Brook Street in your town … Perhaps some who remember her may like to see her.' The inhabitants of Ipswich rose to the bait, and following the publication of the Rev. Richard's letter Owen Roe's shop at 2 Upper Brook Street was besieged by the curious. All that they saw was a highly imaginative and not particularly gifted portrait of Margaret Catchpole by her 'biographer', whose sister Roe had recently married.[86] By 1859 Margaret had in fact been dead for 40 years. She had died in New South Wales in 1819, having contracted a fatal illness from a farmworker she had been nursing.

John Cobbold's eldest son by his first wife, also named John, married Harriett Chevallier, a member of the family from Aspall whose name was later to be given to a fine malting barley that had its origin in an ear of corn that a labourer found in his boot after a day's threshing. The fourth generation John was 23 when his first son, John Chevallier Cobbold, was born—in the same year that saw the birth of his uncle Richard. Father and son were to play a leading part in the public life of Ipswich as it grew from market town to industrial centre during the 19th century.

IX

'Ill-regulated republic'

In the 17th century Ipswich Corporation had ruled the town competently at a time of great upheaval and had protected it from the damaging disturbances that had afflicted some other towns not far distant. Its members had also been instrumental in setting up the Eastern Association, a far more effective body than the other local associations established by Parliament in 1642-3.[1] In stark contrast, in the 18th century the Corporation became riddled with political infighting, corruption and negligence, and by the early 19th it was meriting condemnation as 'an ill-regulated republic'.[2] What happened to bring about such a debilitating change in the Corporation?

That worthy lawyer Nathaniell Bacon wrote in 1649 in the preface to his *The Annalls of Ipswiche* that his purpose in compiling it had been

> That by the perusall of this booke, those that mind the governm^t of this Towne may see what their predecessors have donne, and wherein they failed, that thereby a way may be found for a more p'fect rule of a more righteouse and peaceable governm^t, wth truth wthin this Body … wthout wch both righteousness and prosperity, (wch God forbidd) will gett uppon the wing and be gone, and leave this place buried upp in contempt, wch hitherto hath bein the glory of the places round about.

If only those who came after him had borne his words in mind the story might have been different.

The undermining of the old order had already begun at the time Bacon was copying out the borough ordinances for the benefit of his successors, and the process was carried further after the Restoration when first Charles II and then James II manipulated the charters to their own ends, nominating their own officers. Not only did this royal interference mean a loss of self-government but it created confusion that further weakened the ability of the Corporation to control the town's affairs. James's annulment of his charter of 1688 in a last-minute attempt to regain his lost popularity only added to the confusion, and for some years the town relied on its charter of 1665, the first to be granted by Charles II, under which the portmen and the 24 councilmen made their own choice of men to fill their ranks.[3]

One reason for the Stuart kings' manipulation of borough charters was that in some towns it was the Corporation that elected representatives in Parliament. In Ipswich this privilege lay with the freemen, not with the Corporation alone, but this did not save the town from royal meddling. Until 1688 the choosing of two men to represent the town at Westminster had been a relatively simple affair, but on 29 September 1688 three candidates were put forward and a poll was demanded. 'Thus,' says G.R. Clarke, 'the gauntlet of contention was thrown into the midst of the corporation, and many a battle has ensued, hardly fought, and *dearly* won, and, we are sorry to say, that, in several instances, not without the shedding of blood.'[4] Clarke's italicising of the word 'dearly' is a clear reference to the bribery that was rampant at election time in the 18th century.

In 1689 there was a contested election for bailiffs, who up to then had been chosen from the portmen. Six people, four portmen and two free burgesses, were put forward, and it was the freemen who were elected, by a very substantial majority. This election was symptomatic of a struggle arising between the portmen and the 24; in the 18th century the division became more clearly a political one, the portmen being 'Yellows' or Whigs and the 24 councilmen 'Blues' or Tories. For the most part, members of this divided Corporation put the interests of their own pockets and of their political factions before the interests of the town. Mismanagement in every department of the Corporation was compounded by corruption at every level, and Parliamentary elections became little more than an opportunity for the freemen, who were predominantly drawn from the less affluent section of the population, to take bribes from the rival candidates and their supporters.

As the political struggle between the 'Blues' and the 'Yellows' intensified, each faction sought to obtain the upper hand by creating new freemen of their own persuasion. Granting of the freedom became a useful source of revenue to a town authority increasingly short of money; in 1698 the Assembly set a price of £10, and four years later it was raised to £25. In the space of 15 years, 1698–1713, the number of voters doubled from 229 to 468.[5] To a considerable extent this was the result of the 'Blues' initiating a policy of large-scale creation of honorary freemen following the election of Cooper Gravenor and Richard Phillips as bailiffs in 1702. Between that year and 1720 Gravenor served 12 terms as bailiff, and during that period large numbers of freemen were admitted by honorary presentation, far outnumbering those admitted by apprenticeship or paternity; of 584 freemen admitted in the first 15 years of the century 131 purchased the freedom and 267 were admitted by honorary presentation.

Such goings-on naturally aroused protests, chiefly from adherents of the opposing faction, and at a Great Court on 15 June 1711 six portmen and 17 of the 24-men protested against the court's proceedings as being illegal. To reinforce their protest they withdrew—and without more ado the court voted the freedom to 52 gentlemen from the county and from London, including no fewer than seven baronets. Similar protests were made at a Great Court on 7 August that year, when nine people paid £5 each to be admitted and another 35 were voted in as honorary freemen.[6]

While all this was happening the Corporation was in dire straits on account of having to defend itself in various legal proceedings arising out of the way it conducted its affairs. It was, as G.R. Clarke so eloquently put it, 'deeply involved in those mazes of litigation' which were to bring it to its knees. To pay its bills it was having to mortgage corporation properties, even misapplying money from the town charities in a vain attempt to avoid insolvency. By mid-century the charities were reduced, by maladministration and by misappropriation, to as parlous a state as the Corporation's

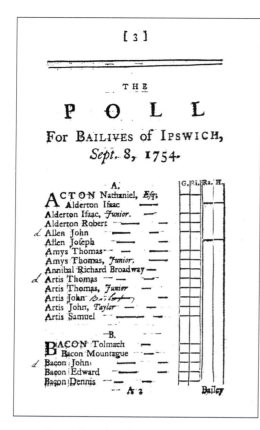

71 *A page from the poll book showing votes cast for the bailiffs (note the spelling 'bailives') in 1754. John Gravenor, the son of Cooper Gravenor, gained 363 and Thomas Richardson 362; the 'Yellows', H. Rant and W. Hammond, polled only 237 and 236 respectively. (John Wilton)*

finances themselves. Indeed, at one stage the Corporation found itself accused of embezzlement in respect of the Lending Cash, a charity which was intended by the several donors to be applied in the form of loans to young tradesmen. As long ago as 1675 the Treasurer had been ordered by the Great Court to take more than £500 out of the Lending Cash at 4 per cent interest to clear the town's debts; not only had the principal not been repaid but the interest was never paid either.

The Great Court made an order in 1743 setting up a committee to inquire into 'what donations have from time to time been given to the Town of Ipswich … and how the same have been paid or applied'. Three years later the court ordered that the 'Report made by the Secret-Committee, appointed sometime since for the Enquiry into diverse Charities belonging to this Corporation' should be printed at the Corporation's expense, but nothing was done. In fact the report was suppressed.[7] If it had not been for the determination of the Rev. Richard Canning, perpetual curate of St Lawrence from 1734 to 1775, to make public the state into which the charities had been allowed to descend the findings of the committee would have been conveniently forgotten. *An Account of the Gifts and Legacies that Have been given and bequeathed to Charitable Uses in the Town of Ipswich; with Some Account of the present State and Management, And Some Proposals for the future Regulation of them*, published anonymously in 1747, was utterly damning. Explaining his reasons for publishing the book, Canning—an outspoken opponent of the Whig majority on the Corporation—wrote that:

> By this we put the People upon their Guard, that whenever the Corporation should grow poor, and come into unworthy Hands, its Leaders may not be suffered to finger any more of it, under the Pretence of borrowing and paying Interest for the sum they take. For this we may depend upon; when they lend themselves Money, they do not intend to pay it … it is done, not so much with Regard to what is past, as with a View to what is to come.

What had been done by the Corporation was to appropriate to itself much of the property left by various donors to provide an income that should have been employed to the benefit of the poor in various ways. To give just one example, Edmund Daundy had in 1515 left lands and tenements in Holbrook so that the bailiffs should pay to the friars in Ipswich on 6 May each year 13s. 4d. for prayers to be said for him and his relatives; the bailiffs were also to make various payments to the poor. Instead of fulfilling the terms of the gift the Corporation sold the Holbrook properties to Judge Clench, and the proceeds of the sale did not apparently go to any poor people. And the Corporation went on mismanaging the charities well into the 19th century.

The Whigs in the Corporation got their revenge on Canning for having made public the scandalous misuse of the charities. When he had book-plates printed for the Ipswich Town Library to ensure that each volume was clearly identified as belonging to that institution, then as now in the care of the master of the grammar school, he was refused admission to the library and spurious reasons were thought up for refusing his book-plates.[8]

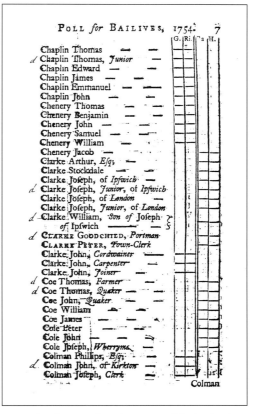

72 *Another page from the 1754 poll book, showing that some of the voters came from London. Towards the foot of the page is the name of Joseph Cole, wherryman, who is mentioned in chapter eight. (John Wilton)*

It is clear that at this period many of the members of the Corporation were neglecting their duties. In 1702 Richard Phillips was fined £100 for neglecting his duty as a portman, and the following year several individuals were fined for neglect of duty or for outright refusal to serve as portmen; Henry Sparrowe was fined £20 and discharged from his office of portman 'for non-attendance and neglect of duty'. The dismissal of Charles Whittaker, who had served both as Recorder and MP for the town, and Richard Puplett, the town clerk, in 1704 led to protracted court proceedings which only added to the Corporation's financial difficulties.[9]

When the Municipal Commissioners made their report in 1835[10] they observed that the manner in which borough elections had been run had resulted in 'persons ill qualified for the office' being chosen, and that the magistrates had ruled the town without enjoying either the confidence or the respect of the inhabitants. The lack of respect for the magistrates was made plain by members of the public who shouted rudely at them not only in the streets but on occasion when they were sitting in court. The refusal of the portmen, 'Yellows' to a man, to appoint new portmen from the ranks of the 'Blue' 24-men led to a steady decline in numbers as the portmen died, and eventually there were only four. In 1820, when the portmen tried to elect two others, it was discovered that since four could not be considered a majority they had lost the power of electing new men to make up their numbers. It seemed that the political division was certain to bring about the dissolution of an integral part of the Corporation.[11]

Not only was the Corporation utterly corrupt and inefficient, but the real power had fallen into the hands of a political organisation known as the Wellington Club, whose members decided to a very large extent what the Corporation should or should not do. Without its support members of the Corporation were powerless to do anything, and there were occasions when a proposal that gained general approval at the Assembly was voted down at the Great Court, members changing their vote because of a decision of the club. This all-powerful organisation had its genesis in the fear of the freemen that if there were a coalition of the 'Yellow' portmen and 'Blue' councilmen they would lose not only the bribes that were paid them at elections by the two parties but also the paid work that was provided by the Corporation and all the other inducements that were offered for them to give their votes to this or that candidate. The various charities controlled by the Corporation, including Tooley's Charity and the Lending Cash, were used to the full in influencing the freemen and securing their votes.[12] The Duke of Wellington, whose name had been appropriated by this infamous club, was put forward without either his consent or his knowledge as a candidate for the honorary office of High Steward in 1821. At the subsequent election, however, he was soundly defeated by Sir Robert Harland, of Orwell Park, Nacton.

When the Municipal Commissioners held their investigation neither the town treasurer, H.G. Bristo, who was also treasurer of the Wellington Club, nor his predecessor as treasurer of the club, B.B. Catt, would give evidence to the Commissioners. Catt refused on the grounds that in taking the oath as a freeman he had sworn not to disclose the secrets of the Corporation.[13] This was the man who had designed the 'new' Town Hall in 1818 and had apparently received a number of sums from the Corporation for which he rendered no account. The commissioner who penned the report, John Buckle, summed up in a way which, while no doubt tinged with his own particular political views, represents no more than the sordid truth.

> The practical working of the Municipal System may be summed up in bribery, invasions of public liberty, and the destruction of industrious habits among the freemen; the election of local functionaries, by whom official power is abused and official duty neglected; the administration of justice by magistrates, whose authority, acquired by violations of the law, is unsupported by the respect of the inhabitants, and sometimes treated with contempt even by the freemen; an inefficient police, under the control of those magistrates; mismanagement and waste of the town property; misapplication of revenues obtained at the expense of the comfort and security of the inhabitants;

alienations for objects unknown, or for the avowed purpose of thwarting an useful body of local commissioners; hospitals perverted to party purposes; charity funds converted into election funds, and become matters of history.

The result is a general dissatisfaction with the established constitution of the borough.

It is a Constitution, which still presents the appearance of a popular government, but is in reality no such thing. Considered with reference to the Corporate Body only, it is an ill-regulated republic; considered with reference to the local Community, it is an oligarchy of the worst description. It is a government which excludes from municipal rights the most considerable portion of the Inhabitants, whether

SLAVERY!

Capt. **GLADSTONE**, the Tory Candidate, will Deliver an Address from the Hustings, on the Cornhill, this Morning, on the blessings of **SLAVERY**; from the well known Fact that the Proud Aristocratical House of Gladstone owe their wealth from labour wrung from Slaves, the worthy Candidate may be considered completely master of this subject. He will likewise state the amount of Money (upwards of £80,000) received by his Family, paid by the Industrious Classes of this country, in the shape of taxation, as compensation for being prohibited any longer to carry on the unhallowed Traffic in Human Flesh. It having been one of the greatest objects of the Tory Government to keep the people in the most abject state of subjection and degradation, the worthy Candidate will shew the consistency of the Ipswich Tories, in endeavouring to appoint him (a Member of the Slave Dealing House of Gladstone) most fitting to represent their views in Parliament.

N. B.—A Band of Hired Ruffians and Tory Bullies will attend the Nomination, for the purpose of Shouting for their Tory Slavery Candidate.

Ipswich, August 15, 1842.

73 *The involvement of Ipswich men such as the Alexanders in the anti-slavery campaign was reflected in local politics. This tongue-in-cheek handbill made its appearance during the 1842 Parliamentary election campaign.*

considered with reference to numbers, property or taxation; and which disqualifies for municipal office the most respectable, intelligent and independent classes of the community. Nor has it even secured the subordinate end of its existence—self-preservation; for in consequence of the party feuds of the two self-elected bodies, which share its official power, the Corporation is now fast approaching to a legal dissolution.[14]

By the Municipal Reform Act of 1835 the old Corporation did indeed meet with legal dissolution without having to wait for the last two portmen to die off. It was replaced by a new corporation consisting of a mayor, aldermen and councillors, and the charities that the old Corporation had so mismanaged were handed over to trustees.

Did the old Corporation go to its end universally unmourned? Samuel Read, who seems to have come to Ipswich in 1830 to work in the office of the then town clerk, attorney John Eddowes Sparrowe, and caricatured many of the members of the Corporation in his sketchbook before going on to become a pioneer newspaper illustrator, took a nostalgic look back at the old Corporation. Entitled 'Random Recollections of the Old Corporation', his sketch shows a table groaning under a feast of roast beef, fowl, oysters and bottles of wine.

Under the title he adds the inscription, 'Tho' lost to sight to Memory dear'.[15]

X

The Beginnings of Modern Industry

W hat was it that persuaded a 35-year-old Quaker iron founder to move from Norwich to Ipswich in 1789? Why was he attracted to the Suffolk town, to which he migrated with just £200 capital—half of it borrowed from the Quaker bankers John and Henry Gurney—and a single workman? One can only surmise that he saw advantages in obtaining his raw materials, mainly coal and pigiron, in a town that was also a port, even one that was suffering severely from the silting of the river and from one of its periodic economic downturns. Perhaps he considered that the market for his agricultural implements would be better in Suffolk, but he could hardly have foreseen the effects his decision would have on the town's later development.

Robert Ransome was the son of Richard Ransome, a Quaker schoolmaster at Wells, which at the time of his birth in 1753 was a small but not insignificant port on the North Norfolk coast. He was apprenticed to an ironmonger in Norwich and subsequently set up what was reputedly the first iron foundry in the city, and with another in Cambridge the first in eastern England. He quickly gained a reputation as an innovator, obtaining a patent in 1783 for 'iron and other metal plates, for covering houses and other buildings,' and then in 1785 another, much more important, patent for 'making plough-shares of cast-iron, which are tempered after a peculiar manner so as to stand the strictest proof'.[1] He was advertising his cast-iron shares in Suffolk as well as Norfolk as early as September, 1786, one of his agents being at Ipswich.[2]

Whatever his reasons, in 1789 Ransome set up a foundry in premises opposite St Mary-at-the-Key Church,[3] possibly making use of the premises occupied earlier in the century by John Dole, who might well have been the first Ipswich ironfounder. Before long he moved to a former malting in St Margaret's Ditches (now Old Foundry Road); the property occupied a site between the old town ditch and Carr Street, where Robert Ransome and his family set up home in a quite modest house with its front door on the street and its back door opening into the works.

74   Robert Ransome, founder of the town's largest and most important engineering works.

Doubtless he was welcomed to Ipswich by fellow Quakers, whose meeting house in College Street was not far from where he first set up in business on arrival in Ipswich. The timber-framed meeting house had been built in 1700 by carpenter Joseph Clarke,[4] who had a year or so earlier been responsible for the building of the Unitarian Meeting House in Friars Street. Among the others worshipping there were members of the influential Alexander family, bankers, merchants and shipowners. Samuel Alexander had opened a bank at Needham Market in 1744 that was later carried on by his nephews Dykes Alexander and Samuel Alexander at Ipswich, where a branch was established in 1767 after some years of market-day-only banking in the county town.[5] It would seem entirely likely that the Alexanders, whose bank stood in Bank Street close to the junction of Foundation Street and Lower Brook Street, supported Ransome as he laboriously built up his business. Alexanders and Co was known as the 'Yellow Bank', a name which distinguished it from the 'Blue Bank' of Crickitt, Truelove & Kerridge, set up in 1786 with premises in Tavern Street, and at the same time proclaimed the political leanings of the partners.

River Improvements

The Alexanders and Robert Ransome were among the people who, towards the end of the 18th century, called for an improvement in the Orwell. The river had silted up so badly that vessels drawing more than eight feet were unable even to reach the town's dilapidated quays, and their cargoes had to be unloaded into lighters in Downham Reach, three miles below the town, with inevitable loss from damage and pilferage; the annual loss was estimated at £3,000, no small sum at that period.[6] The Committee of Subscribers for the Improvement of the Port of Ipswich, which numbered the Quaker bankers and iron founder among its members, called in a Newcastle engineer, William Chapman, who had been assistant to William Jessop on the Grand Canal in Ireland, had been involved in making improvements to the River Hull and had published *Observations on the Various Systems of Canal Navigation.*[7]

Perhaps it is not surprising, given his background in inland waterways, that in his first report[8] Chapman proposed either a ship canal on the north side of the Orwell or a cheaper scheme of dredging to straighten out the channel of the Orwell and to increase the amount of tide in the upper reaches. The canal would have been entered from Downham Reach by a sea lock with a width of 31ft. and a depth over the sill sufficient to admit quite large vessels, and would have by-passed not only the shallows at Downham Bridge that prevented large vessels from reaching the town quays but also the meanderings of the channel. It would have terminated in a 'proposed bason or floating dock' eleven acres in extent, with a small lock at the upper end to give access to the Stowmarket Navigation, opened just a few years earlier. Freshwater coming down the Gipping would have been taken along a 'proposed New Course of River' very similar to the New Cut that was eventually excavated as part of the dock scheme of the 1830s.

Ipswich Corporation had successfully opposed proposals put forward in 1719 to make the river navigable up to Stowmarket because it feared that trade might pass the

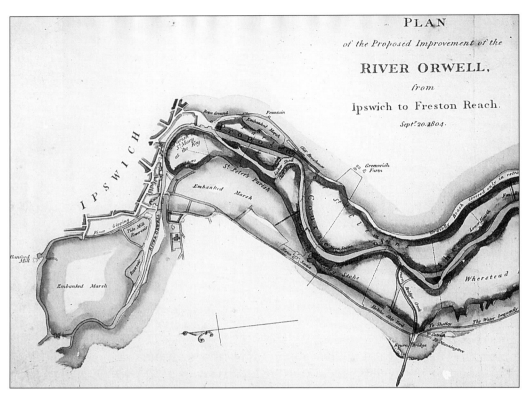

75   *A plan issued in 1804 in connection with proposals to improve the approaches to the town quays. It shows the marshes upstream of Stoke Bridge and between the bridge and Nova Scotia whose embanking had been responsible for reducing the tidal flow in the river, leading to serious silting.*

town by. Towards the end of the century, however, the success of the Duke of Bridgewater's pioneering work in canal-building in the Manchester area led the merchants of Ipswich to accept that the town could only benefit from improved communications, and Ipswich Corporation decided not to contest a Bill promoted in Parliament by a number of Suffolk landowners that would authorise the making of a navigation from Stowmarket to Handford Bridge in Ipswich. The Act[9] received Royal Assent on 1 April 1790, and the navigation was opened in the autumn of 1793.

The improvement of the Orwell that would bring ships safely up to the town quays was another matter. It was an interesting scheme, reminiscent of that much earlier one that resulted in a canal to bring ships up into the port of Exeter, but it did not find favour with the merchants of Ipswich.

As time went on and the merchants and shipowners continued to prevaricate, it became increasingly apparent to many townspeople that action was urgently required to halt the town's decline. Whereas in 1755 it had been calculated that there were 12,124 inhabitants, in 1801 the population had fallen to 11,061, and the town's new industries were being handicapped by the inadequate state of the Orwell. A general meeting of the inhabitants of Ipswich was held at the Moot Hall on 15 February 1803 to consider what ought to be done to improve the situation; the meeting decided to seek Chapman's advice once more.[10] In March 1803 Chapman submitted a report recommending 'the formation of a Wet Dock in front of the town that may accommodate at least 100 Sail of Vessels and of a Canal Communication with it from a Lock near Downham Reach capable of admitting ships of above 370 tons measurement or near 500 tons Burthen with sufficient depth of Water for them to Navigate independently of the tides. This plan. . .does not differ essentially from the first I proposed to you in my former report.'

Alternatively, Chapman suggested merely deepening the river and straightening the channel to enable vessels of 250 tons to reach the quay on spring tides. That would cost a mere £15,000, 'but when done your expences would not cease, because,' he said, there would be 'a considerable annual charge in keeping the River to its depth, of which the advantage of ballasting the ships will form but a small part.' Here he was referring to the monopoly held by the corporation of supplying ballast to vessels leaving without cargo.

In November of the same year he scaled down his earlier plans and suggested a shorter canal from John's Ness, then a year later he presented a further report in which he put forward a further scaled-down canal beginning at the Fen Bight and costing a little over £25,000. His frustration really burst forth when he penned a postscript to his report after he had heard the reaction to his plans at a meeting of the committee on the eve of another general meeting of the inhabitants on 13 November 1804.

> Gents,
> From the bent of the Public opinion appearing to me to be in favor of the expedient of simply deepening the River and Cutting off some of the bends because of the idea that it will be adequate to all the wants of the town and that the superior advantages of the plan recommended would in the general opinion not compensate for the greater estimated outlay. . .it appears to me clearly advisable not to bring forward my report to the General Meeting tomorrow, because by creating a secession from those who are in favor of the only plan likely to be carried into effect, it may prevent anything whatever being done.[11]

Chapman must have despaired of ever seeing anything done at Ipswich, but both the inhabitants and the Corporation set up their own committees to consider a Bill that should be presented to Parliament. The Corporation, anxious as ever to preserve its old rights and privileges and to gain control of the income from shipping dues, proposed that all 41 members of the Corporation should be River Commissioners, leaving only 25 commissioners to be appointed on behalf of the inhabitants. That proposal failed to meet with the approval of those who knew that the Corporation could not be relied on to carry the proposed Act into effect if the powers were vested in them, and the Committee of Subscribers for the Improvement of the Port of Ipswich went ahead and drew up its own Bill to be laid before Parliament.

76   *The River Commissioners' steam dredger is seen at work surrounded by its attendant mud barges in this lithograph from a drawing by the Rev. Richard Cobbold. One of the first of its kind to be brought into use, the dredger proved its worth in deepening and straightening the approaches to the port. (John Wilton)*

Several of the clauses in the Bill drawn up by the Committee of Subscribers were specifically intended to relieve the Corporation of its old powers over the Orwell, prerogatives that had been used merely to fill the Corporation coffers and not for the benefit of the town. When the Corporation petitioned the House of Commons against the Bill 'in order to get those objectionable clauses expunged or amended,' its record of inactivity told against it. The Bill successfully passed through all its stages in Parliament and the Act received Royal Assent from King George III in 1805. This Act for 'improving and rendering more commodious the Port of Ipswich' brought into being a new body of River Commissioners who would act effectively as guardians of the port.

Chapman did not turn his back and walk away, as he might well have done. He stayed to advise the River Commissioners on the purchase of one of the first steam dredgers to be put to work anywhere in England. The 'steam dredge barge', as he called it, not unnaturally attracted some degree of popular attention, for it was only the fourth steam dredger to be put to work in this country. 'Nearly similar machines moved by Horses have long been in use to raise mud,' Chapman reported to the commissioners, 'and the chief difference between those and that now in question is that the latter is moved by Steam and intended to raise Gravel as well as Mud.'[12] He referred in his report to 'the necessity of some alteration, which circumstance very generally attends the setting to work of every new machine.' They were at the forefront of progress, and teething troubles do arise with new technology.

Much of the money for the purchase of the steam dredger and for the work done on the river was put up by individual River Commissioners. Samuel Alexander alone subscribed £3,150 during the first year. New channels were cut through the mudbanks downriver from Ipswich, and valiant efforts were made not merely to keep the navigation open but to improve the approaches wherever possible. In 1820 the commissioners made a cut through Round Ouze, rendering it unnecessary for vessels to use the circuitous and difficult channels round by John's Ness, and the following year they began a further cut to take ships straight across the bank between Hog Island Reach and Limekiln Reach.

Thus were the foundations being laid on which the new port for the Victorian age could be constructed. As so often, though, the foundations were perhaps less firmly laid than they might have been if some of the town's leading citizens had been able to see beyond the ends of their noses and been less parsimonious.

Ploughshare Improvements

While all this was going on Robert Ransome had been making improvements in the ploughs he produced, thus expanding his sales. In 1803 he obtained a patent for making and tempering cast-iron ploughshares and other items for agricultural use; a piece of iron inserted into the sand mould chilled the under-surface of the share and produced a hardened surface.[13] The earlier cast-iron shares wore away too fast, and as the first edge was worn off the share tended to 'lose its hold of the work' and to pass over weeds without cutting them. The new process provided a hard underside about an eighth or a sixteenth of an inch in thickness; as this wore much more slowly than the soft metal of the upper part of the share, a constant sharp edge was provided in everyday use.

No less important was the introduction of the cast-iron plough body. Even after an inventive Suffolk farmer had brought into use a cast-iron plough-ground or bottom, the wooden plough was still an inconvenient and not altogether satisfactory implement. As a later member of the Ransome family wrote in 1843, 'scarcely two workmen would make them alike, and sometimes one plough would work well and easy to the holder, while another made by the same hand would be inferior in these respects.'

What was probably the first steam engine in Ipswich was set to work at Ransome's foundry in February 1807. Erected by a Cornish engineer, it was employed in working the bellows for the smithies and in operating grindstones, lathes and other machinery.

Robert's eldest son James was apprenticed to his father in 1795, but having learnt his trade he went off to Yarmouth to set up his own foundry there. He returned to Ipswich in 1809 to go into partnership with his father, and three years later the Norfolk-born engineer William Cubitt took on the role of engineer to the firm, helping it counter the agricultural depression that came with the end of the Napoleonic Wars by expanding into bridgebuilding and millwrighting. During Cubitt's first four years at

Ipswich work valued at nearly £5,000 was gained which, it was claimed, 'would probably not have been undertaken without him'.[14]

Several cast-iron bridges built by the firm still exist, one of them at Brent Eleigh and another at Clare, but the iron Stoke Bridge built in 1819 to replace the old stone bridge washed away by a flood a year earlier was itself replaced after little more than a century. It is doubtful whether the ironwork for these bridges was cast at the Ransome foundry; certainly the castings for Stoke Bridge were made at Dudley. It might be that the Ipswich foundry was unable to handle such large castings at that time.[15] The bridge destined for the Stoke crossing was actually erected in Dudley, and Cubitt went there to approve its construction before it was dismantled and sent by canal boat to Gainsborough on the Trent, where it was loaded into a seagoing vessel which brought it to Ipswich.

77   *The iron Stoke Bridge built by Ransomes to replace a stone bridge washed away by floodwater in 1818, with the maltings that was converted into a barracks during the wars with France just beyond the bridge on the right. Although the bridge was erected by the Ipswich firm the castings were made at Dudley; the painted marks put on to facilitate assembly were still clearly visible when the bridge was taken down more than 100 years later.*

By the time Ransomes were diversifying into civil engineering there was a second foundry in the town, the St. Margaret's Iron Foundry established by Jacob Garrett, brother of Richard Garrett of Leiston. From this foundry, set up in 1802 in premises that had earlier been occupied by John Cobbold, came the cast-iron milestones for the Little Yarmouth Turnpike, quite a number of which still survive, and those for the road between Darsham and Bungay. Those that have not been replaced by later castings bear both the name and address of the founder and the date, mainly 1818. Garrett also made the cast-ironwork, the columns of the nave arcade and the window tracery, for St Nicholas Church at Harwich, which was built in 1821. Jacob Garrett, who had before opening the foundry been in business as a whitesmith, coachsmith and bell-hanger, also supplied bar iron and other trade goods to blacksmiths, a branch of business that was carried on by members of his family into the second half of the century.

Robert Ransome's second son, the younger Robert, also trained as an apprentice under his father and became a partner in 1818, at which time the firm became known as Ransome & Sons. This title was kept until the elder Robert retired in 1825, when it became J. & R. Ransome, though sometimes referred to unofficially as Ransomes Brothers. A member of the third generation proved just as much an innovator as his forebears and contributed a great deal to the later success of the company. James's son James Allen Ransome was apprenticed to the firm when a boy of 13 or 14, and his acceptance as a partner at the age of 23 resulted in another change of name, to J. R. & A. Ransome. For almost a decade he lived at Yoxford and managed a branch that the firm set up in the village, perhaps in an attempt to compete with the Leiston firm of Richard Garrett on their home ground.

A practical man, he played a leading part in the development of new implements and the improvement of existing ones, and when the Agricultural Society of England (later to be granted the prefix Royal) was established in 1838 he became an active member. Thus it was that Ransomes exhibited at the society's first show at Oxford in 1839, and came away with the society's Gold Medal.

After five years of very active retirement the elder Robert Ransome died in 1830, having seen his grandson begin to play a vital part in the work of the firm. In his retirement Robert had taken up copperplate engraving and had made himself a telescope, for which he ground the lenses himself.

In the year of Robert Ransome's death a very capable engineer, Edwin Beard Budding, invented the cylinder lawnmower. He was employed in an ironworks at Stroud in Gloucestershire which was largely involved in the construction and installation of machinery used in the woollen mills of the West of England, and his lawnmower design adapted the rotating cutting cylinder used in a machine for the shearing of cloth. The circumstances under which J.R. & A. Ransome acquired a licence to manufacture Budding's Patent Grass Cutting Machine are not known, nor

78 One of Jacob Garrett's cast-iron mileposts made for the Little Yarmouth Turnpike Trust. Many still survive along the A12, though others have been lost through road improvements and realignments.

is the name of the far-sighted person who opened negotiations for the acquisition of that licence; all that is known is that the firm acquired a licence in 1832.

Although in the early years the demand for these cumbersome machines with their heavy rollers and exposed gearing was minimal and no more than 70 or 80 machines were produced each year, the implications for the future of the company cannot be denied. By 1866 lawnmower production had reached more than 200 machines a year, and the following year it soared to over a thousand. From then on Ransomes were one of the 'big three' lawnmower makers.

The Ransomes were fortunate in the employees they attracted to their works in St Margaret's Ditches, some of whom spent their entire working lives with the family. In 1835/6 James Ransome compiled a list of about a hundred men in the firm's employ, one of whom was William Rush, son of the workman of the same name who had in

1789 moved from Norwich with the elder Robert. 'William Rush has now lived with us, with only a short intermission, for 42 years. He first worked for my father, he afterwards went with me to Yarmouth in 1804 was afterwards a short time with another Founder in Beccles and then came back to us at Ipswich in 1810 — He is now on the decline, but has been one of our best and most faithful workmen, has been our principal Mould Maker for Shares and Ploughs, and for many years was our foreman in all heavy fittings of Cast Iron Work.' In the margin James added a note: 'W Rush's father lived with RR Nor'ch in 1782 and never left our service.'

A particularly valuable employee was William Worby, who was foreman in the 1830s and rose to be works manager. The Ransomes were quite prepared to allow him to use his initiative, and perhaps it was this that caused problems when a new partner, Charles May, joined the firm in 1836. Whatever the cause, William and the new partner did not get along together. When in 1837 the Ransomes decided that the firm was expanding beyond the capacity of the premises in St Margaret's Ditches the opportunity occurred to separate the two protagonists, but poor William thought he was being given notice to terminate his employment, as he recalled later.

> One morning in March 1837, I was summoned to the presence of Messrs Robert and James Ransome in Mr Robert Ransome's room, which was then an upper room in the offices in St Margaret's Ditches. Mr Robert Ransome told me that they had sent for me to find a place for myself. I asked if they wanted me to leave them, whereupon Mr Robert Ransome said, 'By no means—we mean that you should go and hire malt offices or some such place, where you can take some of the men and some of the work, forming a sort of branch works, as we are getting too thick here, and we do not want you and Mr May together.'[16]

Worby found what he was looking for in a building, possibly a former malting or else part of the St Clement's Shipyard, on the bend of the Orwell a couple of hundred yards below the Common Quay. It is to be seen, between the site of St Clement's Shipyard and an inlet, on the carefully drawn panorama of the riverside produced by Edward Caley when the Wet Dock scheme was proposed in 1837, with 'Orwell Iron Works' painted on the end wall to announce the new ownership.[17] Also visible on the drawing is an iron crane, perhaps made by Ransomes, standing on the adjacent quay. Without a doubt Worby knew just what he was doing; the new dock would provide unrivalled facilities, enabling raw materials to be unloaded right outside the new works and, as trade grew and implements began to be exported, allowing Ransomes' products to be loaded into ships at what amounted to the firm's own quay. It is not to be wondered at that the Ransomes and Charles May were among those who were involved in bringing forward the dock scheme.

The Wet Dock

The River Commissioners managed their business well, paying off the original loan of £8,000, borrowed on security of the rates to be levied on goods entering the port, by

1830. They also managed somehow to accumulate a surplus of £25,000. Among them were men who believed that more should be done to improve the port and make it suitable not just for the coasting trade but for foreign trade as well. They doubtless remembered William Chapman's words that the town would eventually regret not having carried out his original plan for a ship canal and dock.

It was generally believed that the provision of a dock would lead to an increase in overseas trade, for the possibilities had been spelt out quite clearly by advocates of the dock right from the beginning of the century. Jabez Hare pointed to the opportunities in a pamphlet recommending the damming of the Orwell at Downham Reach:

> The natural advantages which Ipswich possesses over any other port on the eastern coast of Britain is mainly owing to the superior accommodation which Harwich harbour presents for the access of vessels of less than 400 tons burthen, under all circumstances of wind and weather. It is no uncommon occurrence for from 100 to 200 sail of the Baltic fleet to lie wind-bound there, 2 or 3 weeks unable to reach the several destinations, Hull, London or Liverpool, whilst with proper dock accommodation in the Orwell they might have delivered their cargoes and sailed again without loss of time.[18]

By 1835 pressure for the next step to be taken to give Ipswich improved facilities for shipping was becoming irresistible. Had Chapman not died in 1832 he would very likely have attended the meeting held in the Moot Hall on 29 January 1836 under the chairmanship of Dykes Alexander 'to take into consideration a proposal for forming a Wet Dock at this Port, and improving the River and Harbour.'[19]

Chief protagonist of the wet dock idea was William Lane, the Collector of Customs for the port and in earlier years a bailiff of the town. Describing his proposals at the meeting, he suggested forming the existing channel of the river from St Peter's Dock to the Ballast Wharf into a wet dock and bypassing it by a nearly straight cut to carry the tidal water. Estimating that the work could be done for between £25,000 and £30,000, Lane suggested that an Act of Parliament should be sought allowing the £25,000 accumulated by the River Commissioners to be used for the purpose. Lane was elected to the committee that was appointed to collect information. Also on that committee were men like the Alexanders, John Cobbold, James and Robert Ransome, George Hurwood, who was then in partnership with a man named Turner, and shipbuilder William Bayley.

79 *Shipping in the Wet Dock about 1860, a view looking north from the vicinity of the original entrance lock. (John Wilton)*

The Dock Committee appointed to collect information on the proposal, which included among its members a number of River Commissioners, sought the help of a prominent London engineer, Henry Palmer, who was asked to report on the viability of a wet dock in which ships could lie afloat at all stages of the tide. Palmer was well known as an engineer; he had been one of the prime movers in the formation of the Institution of Civil Engineers a few years earlier. The proposals that Palmer put to the Dock Committee were certainly ambitious. He envisaged a dock of 33 acres water area that would be the biggest in Britain; none of the docks on the Thames at that time approached the size of that proposed for Ipswich, and those at Hull and Liverpool would be dwarfed by it. Jessop's Floating Harbour at Bristol was a good deal larger, but it could be argued that the concept was somewhat different.

While Palmer worked on his proposal the Dock Committee went ahead with the preparation of a Bill for submission to Parliament. It would enable a new body of commissioners to raise money for the building of a dock, providing facilities for shipping that would enable the town to meet the challenges of the Victorian era. Then, as all seemed ready for the Bill to be submitted to Parliament, a diehard group of River Commissioners headed by Welham Clarke proposed at a meeting of the commissioners that they should pay out of their funds 'all expenses the gentlemen of the Dock Committee had incurred up to the present time, provided they throw the Dock Bill overboard into Deep Water'. Put to a meeting of the River Commissioners on 19 June 1837, this proposal was convincingly defeated.

That proved to be the River Commissioners' final meeting, for on 30 June that same year, just ten days after Victoria's accession, the Ipswich Dock Act[20] received Royal Assent; the future of the port lay with a new body of Dock Commissioners. It was to the Dock Commissioners that Henry Palmer reported later in the year. The scheme that he submitted owed much to both Chapman and Lane; Jabez Hare's idea of a dam across the river near Downham Reach he dismissed as being impractical.[21]

Palmer's plans came up for discussion at a public meeting in the Town Hall on 4 November 1836.[22] Despite his absence from the meeting—he was indisposed at the *Great White Horse Hotel*, having travelled all the way from Wales to attend the meeting—the assembly expressed itself in favour of his 'voluminous and excellent report'. His involuntary absence was unfortunate, and might well have set some of those concerned with the proposals against him; in subsequent days there were complaints that he had treated the Dock Commissioners with contempt by being absent from their meetings. Engineers such as Palmer were involved in more than one scheme at a time and often found it difficult to attend all the meetings at which their presence was demanded.

The scene was at last set for progress to be made. William Chapman would certainly have applauded those who fought for new improvements, for in a report of November 1804 he had stressed the need for boldness.[23] Pointing out the great expense of using the West India Docks and other facilities in London, he had urged the Ipswich merchants to provide the kind of facilities that would attract trade away from the Thames to the Orwell, and had commented that 'the time may shortly come when the subscribers may find the disadvantage of their works not having been executed on a large scale'.

One wonders if Palmer were aware of Chapman's remarks as he worked at his drawings of the dock and the various ancillary buildings. By 23 October 1837 the plans were ready for inspection and it was possible for the commissioners to invite tenders for the work of constructing the wet dock. Although Palmer's estimate for the construction of the dock and the improvement of the river had amounted to £58,100, the lowest tender was one of some £65,000 from a David Thornbory, of King's Lynn, and that was accepted in March 1838.[24] Perhaps the Dock Commissioners should have looked at the tenders more closely and not accepted the lowest, for Thornbory proved to be a thorn in the side of the engineer as construction progressed, and the commissioners had to foot many a bill for extra work during the next four or five years. In the end the matter of Thornbory's remuneration had to be submitted to arbitration.

As part of the dock project Henry Palmer designed and built timber-framed warehouses, which at first-floor level reached out across the quay so that goods could be loaded direct from the warehouses into vessels lying at the quay. In a report on his proposals, Palmer remarks that 'it is proposed to support the front walls of the warehouses upon a Colonnade, the Columns being composed of Cast Iron'. The engineer made it plain that he was anxious that these buildings should be pleasing to the eye and not merely functional, and so they were. These modest yet handsome warehouses were in the course of the 19th century overshadowed by lofty maltings and flour mills filling the space between the quay and College Street, and they have long since given way to other, less attractive buildings, but the cast-iron columns are still there on the quayside supporting new structures.

Near the Custom House on the Common Quay were steps which once provided access from the quay to small boats. In 1837 Caley had found the 'Brick work, piles and steps very bad,' and it seems obvious from the drawing that the steps were unusable. These steps were lost when the new quay in front of the Custom House was formed. The early Custom House was 'a low, ill-shaped, isolated building, supported on the south, next the water, by a numerous range of pillars, reaching the whole length of the front, which is about a hundred and twenty feet, forming a colonnade, under which the masters of vessels and other seafaring people delight to perambulate'.[25] When Henry Palmer made one of his early reports to the Dock Commissioners, he referred to the opportunity offered 'for building a Customs House more in accordance with the new character of the port'. Accordingly the building was demolished and replaced soon after the completion of the dock.

All was not to be plain sailing, for opposition to the dock scheme was beginning to grow in Ipswich. Leading that opposition was the Tory *Ipswich Journal*, whose editorials expressed worries about frost damage to quay walls and fears of the effect of high winds on vessels entering or leaving the lock; correspondence decrying the scheme as ill-judged and spendthrift was published with a regularity that displayed a strong bias against the Dock Commissioners. On the other hand, the *Ipswich Mercury*, with other

80   *On the right of this view of the Wet Dock is the gasworks, established in 1821. It was able to receive all its supplies of coal by sea. (John Wilton)*

political affiliations, expressed itself very much in favour of the dock scheme. The misgivings of the *Ipswich Journal* were reflected within the ranks of the commissioners, for they themselves were very much concerned about the costs involved. At a meeting in April 1838 they indicated that the amount of the proposed contract with Thornbory, together with the cost of other work, 'approaches very nearly to the means at the disposal of the Commissioners', and wondered if it might be 'expedient to ascertain whether the specification can be so modified as to reduce the amount of the outlay without impairing the general effect of the works'.[26]

The commissioners, Palmer and Thornbory got their heads together in an attempt to solve this difficulty, and the Management Committee recommended that the commissioners 'limit the extent of the Dock in the first instance to the Ballast Quay, but under the full assurance that the Commissioners shall complete the Dock according to the original plan as soon as the resources of the Commissioners can be so economized as to enable them to do so'.[27] Palmer pointed out that to build the lower embankment in one place and later to replace it by another embankment further along would cost a great deal more than if they went ahead with the original plan, and it seems that the commissioners had second thoughts. As it was, the quay never proceeded beyond the

Ballast Wharf, and to this day the south-eastern side of the dock slopes into the water, with jetties built out into the deep water by firms whose premises abutted Helena Road.

A contract with David Thornbory was signed on 12 June 1838. Digging had begun three days earlier, those employed on the task being 'fifty labourers residing in the neighbourhood of the town hitherto in search of employment'. Two months later, on 13 August, the first stone of the new quays was laid by the mayor, attorney Peter Bartholomew Long, who was also Clerk to the Dock Commissioners.

The general specifications of the works to be executed, drawn up by Palmer, were detailed and precise, leaving little or nothing undefined.[28] Carefully set down were specifications for the cutting of a new channel to take the water of the River Gipping on its way to the sea; for the building of the lock through which ships could gain access to the dock; and for the erection of a quay along the north side of the dock so that people and goods could for the first time pass along the waterside. There were also specifications for the roadways alongside the dock and the new river channel.

The requirements for the two dams at the upper and lower ends of the dock were particularly detailed, as indeed they needed to be:

> The Embankment at the lower end of the Dock is to be composed of Gravel and Clay uniformly mixed. Within the Bank … a Wall of Puddle, composed of one part Chalk or Clay to 5 parts Gravel and Sand or other materials equally suitable. It is to be formed 10 feet in thickness; it is to be sunk two feet below the natural bed of the River and to extend one foot from the surface of the Bank, the whole of the other part of the Bank is to be well founded or otherwise worked so as to form one compact solid mass.

Nor did the specifications leave any doubt as to the manner in which the quays were to be constructed.

> The Wall is to be built in parallel courses, the bricks to be used in it are to be the best hard Grey Stocks well burnt so that the sand contained in them shall become vitrified. The Mortar to be used is to be composed of Blue Lias Lime or of other stone Lime of good quality which will set well under water and sharp clean Sand in the proportion of one part Lime to three parts Sand. The Lime is to be well burnt and slacked with water and to be well worked with the sand in a rolling mill until an equal and uniform mixture is formed.

It must have seemed that these detailed specifications left no room for argument; the contractor was to carry the work out to the engineer's entire satisfaction, and the engineer's decision was final and binding. With the contract signed and the required standards clearly set out, the work went ahead at a cracking pace.

A year later, on 26 June 1839, the foundation stone of the lock was laid by the new mayor, George Green Sampson. Contemporary reports state that some 15,000 people turned out to watch the mayor process with a bodyguard of police, and accompanied by aldermen, councillors and harbour officials, from the Town Hall to the riverside excavations. It was a hot summer's day, and the populace seems to have regarded the event as a good excuse for a day in the fresh air. The band of the 9th Lancers, their tunics faced with scarlet and blue, played at the dockside to entertain those who awaited the mayor's arrival through a triumphal arch crowned with a model schooner and the motto 'May Ipswich Flourish.' Cannons boomed out, and there was loud cheering from the masses as the civic procession appeared. Thornbory was presented with a purse of money, presumably a token gesture, and the townspeople were treated to a grand firework display.[29]

The entrance lock was placed part way along the New Cut, with the dockmaster's house beside it. Preliminary plans show the lock facing obliquely down the New Cut, but for some unknown reason it was in fact built at a much more obtuse angle so that vessels entering the lock had to turn across the New Cut to line up with the entrance.

As the building of the lock went ahead Thornbory laid plans for a celebration well judged to placate any workmen who were feeling aggrieved at the pace of work expected of them, and no doubt also to gain the support of others who were invited to take part. On 1 October 1839 the contractor provided a dinner for his workmen 'at the bottom of the newly-erected Dock entrance' to celebrate the completion of this part of the works. 'The men were seated at a table extending the whole length of the entrance, having only room for a cross table at the top, at which Mr Thornbory presided, surrounded by several ladies and gentlemen, who were politely invited to partake of his hospitality and among whom the wine was freely circulated', while 'several hundreds of spectators looked down upon the joyous scene from an elevation of many feet …'.[30]

By early in 1840 the New Cut was nearing completion. It was still separated from the river by embankments at each end, and it was to be some time before water would be admitted to the new channel, but work was proceeding well enough. The lock needed only its gates, while some 2,000 feet of the new quay on the north side of what was to be the dock had been completed.[31] With the works largely open to anyone as they were, it must have been difficult to protect them from thieves and vandals. Always aware of the need to encourage those whose assistance he needed, Thornbory 'presented the police with £10 as an acknowledgement of the protection exercised over the property constantly exposed at the works'.[32] Later the Dock Commissioners resolved that 'inasmuch as the duties of the Police will be materially increased by the additional watching necessary at the quay, the Commissioners suggest to the Watch Committee the propriety of adding one man to the established force … the expense of which addition the Commissioners will undertake to defray.'

The great project was proceeding apace, but the *Ipswich Journal* continued its tirade against the dock, hinting in May 1840 at 'a vast increase of expenditure'. Indeed there was; the following year the commissioners had to obtain a further Act of Parliament enabling them to raise more money. There is no doubt that the work was costing far more than had been estimated; in 1860 George Hurwood, who succeeded Palmer as dock engineer, told the Institute of Civil Engineers that the total cost had been £130,000.[33] Towards the end of the year the newspaper suggested that the slow progress of the work might almost be welcomed 'as putting off the evil day when this ill-considered and

81   The kilns of a malting and the gasholders and chimney of the gasworks are prominent in this photograph taken from the river steamer by Charles Emeny, of Felixstowe, in May 1889. Above the lock gates to the left of the picture can be seen one of the town's windmills.

rashly undertaken plan shall be called completed.' In fact it was more than two years before the work was finished. One reason for the delay was that the contractor was found to have omitted the stipulated wall of puddled clay in the lower dam, merely piling up material dredged from the river. The cautious Palmer demanded that the work should be done properly before the lock gates were closed and water impounded in the dock; in the meantime vessels entering and leaving the dock had to contend with the tide rushing in or out through the narrow lock chamber.

Thornbory, however, had ingratiated himself with all and sundry, and the engineer found himself up against a brick wall when he tried to insist on the unsatisfactory work being rectified. Somewhat incredibly, the contractor had even by some means arranged his appointment as a Dock Commissioner. There is evidence enough in the Commissioners' Minute Book to show that Palmer was at loggerheads with some of the commissioners, who more than once accused him of exceeding his authority in making this arrangement or that. On one occasion in 1841 the commissioners actually objected to work done on Palmer's orders 'without consultation with or any direction from the Commissioners or Committee' and ordered the discharge of the men employed on the work. In the Committee of Management Minutes[34] is a report from the frustrated engineer:

> The only part of the Resolution to which I am now replying … is that which refers to my having projected and carried into effect the work alluded to without directions from the Commrs. To this I have only to answer that the nature of the work was such as is usually left entirely to the discretion of the Engineer, and it did not occur to me that the Commissioners would require to be consulted upon a matter of purely mechanical arrangement. With regard to the fourth Resolution I have to regret exceedingly that circumstances made it impossible for me to give such an explanation to the Committee as would have prevented the discharge of the men, whereby one week will have been lost, for it is quite evident that that work must be executed and that no time should be lost in completing it.

Clearly there was a faction within the Dock Commission that was not merely dissatisfied with the engineer but would be glad to see the back of him. When it was announced at a monthly commissioners' meeting that Palmer's contract had run out John Ridley remarked acidly, 'Could they not now dispense with the services of the Engineer altogether?'[35]

The lock gates were operated for the first time on 17 January 1842, when high water was just before four o'clock in the afternoon. Darkness was already closing in as Palmer superintended the closing of the gates. The first vessel to pass out of the lock was the little sloop *Director*, outward-bound for Rochester with grain and goods, which left the dock with the mayor, Dock Commissioner John Chevallier Cobbold, on board. Shortly after the *Director* had slipped through the lock and down the New Cut the collier brig *Zephyr*, which had brought a cargo of coal from Newcastle-upon-Tyne, came upriver. Expecting to have to anchor in the New Cut, for the lock gates had closed against him, Captain Scrivenor had ordered the anchor to be made ready, and it hung just below the hawsehole. The gates were quickly opened and the collier swung to enter the lock, but as she did so the ebb tide caught her and drove her into the lock wall; the fluke of the anchor was driven into the ship's planking, necessitating repairs which the owner undoubtedly found too costly for his liking; the *Zephyr* was very soon advertised for sale. 'Thus,' observed the *Ipswich Journal* tartly, 'after no inconsiderable bungling and delay, the town may be said to enjoy the advantages of a Wet Dock.'

The *Journal*'s views of the event were undoubtedly coloured by its political leanings. Compare the 'bungling and delay' with the comment in the *Ipswich Mercury* that two or three hundred people were present to witness the first operation of the gates, in spite of the dullness of the weather; and that not just the *Director* and the *Zephyr* but a number of other vessels passed through the lock 'without any difficulty or accident having occurred'.[36]

The opening of the Wet Dock undoubtedly had a very beneficial effect on the trade of the port. Whereas between 1820 and 1834 the average navigation dues received by the River Commissioners had been £2,360 per annum, in 1844 the receipts were double this amount, while by 1855 they had increased to £10,000 a year. During the early years of the dock, receipts far exceeded expenditure; and the balance was used for financing further improvements to the river, making it possible for larger vessels to reach the dock.

Between 1843 and 1845 the number of vessels arriving from and sailing to foreign ports more than doubled, and before the end of that decade it had doubled again. Yet even in the 1850s, when the average number of coasting arrivals was some 1,500 vessels a year, the arrivals from foreign ports amounted to fewer than 120 or 130 a year.

XI

Ships and Railway Engines

If the dominant name in 18th-century shipbuilding was Barnard, the family that is synonymous with 19th-century Ipswich shipbuilding is the Bayleys, who are believed to have originated in Kent or Sussex. John and William Bayley began as boatbuilders rather than shipbuilders in Ipswich about 1765, hiring a part of Nova Scotia yard from John Barnard. George Bayley, John's second son, became manager for his mother when his father died in 1785 after a riding accident, and in due course his brothers Philip and Jabez were apprenticed to him.[1]

George was a good businessman and a reliable shipbuilder, able to attract contracts such as that for the 544-ton *Sir William Bensley* for the Honourable East India Company's country service, which was built on the upriver yard just below Stoke Bridge in 1802. By the time of his death in 1807 George had amassed property worth £7,000. Brother Philip was, as his nephew George (son of George, senior) rather tartly put it, 'not overstocked with brains', and he 'remained a working man all his life with a working man's thoughts and habits'. Jabez, on the other hand, was a man of business and a leading figure in Ipswich shipbuilding for many years. Nephew George, with that acerbic character-judgment of his, described Jabez as 'one of those good natured impulsive men on whom one cannot rely with confidence'.[2]

Whatever young George's opinion of his uncle, Jabez was a good enough shipwright to attract orders from the Navy, and between 1804 and 1814 built 31 warships, gaining an excellent reputation for the attention he paid to ventilation and the prevention of rot. Among the vessels he built in those years was HMS *Transit*, a revolutionary vessel designed by Richard Hall Gower, who lived at Nova Scotia House. Gower, who had been an officer in the Honourable East India Company's sea service, was one of those men whose minds are wont to think beyond the conventional; he described himself as 'an officer accustomed to pass his mid-night watch on ship-board, during the quietude of steady weather in considering the imbecility of shipping, and the wants of seamen on the ocean, with the intention of supplying their defects.'[3]

Gower had designed a revolutionary sailing vessel of an entirely new form, both as regards hull and rig, and had persuaded a number of friends to fund the building of the vessel at Itchenor, near Chichester, in 1800. This vessel was rigged as a four-masted barquentine, with conventional square rig on the foremast and somewhat unconventional fore-and-aft sails on the other three; the hull had a beam-to-length ratio of 1:4.7 rather than the 1:4 that was normal at the time. The *Transit*, as she was named, 'has to modern eyes many of the labour saving features which were finally embodied in the American multi-masted barquentines of the last days of sail,' says

Hervey Benham in one of his books on east coast maritime history.[4] The *Transit* proved extremely successful, being much faster and more sea-kindly than any contemporary vessels, either warships or merchant ships, but Gower was wholly unsuccessful in persuading either the Navy or the East India Company to adopt his ideas until in 1809 the government was eventually persuaded to commission a second vessel to the same design. Unlike her predecessor, which was launched 'as rigged and complete for sea', this vessel was towed from Ipswich to Deptford Dockyard to be fitted out, and it is said that alterations made by order of the Navy Board ensured that she did not enjoy the success of the first *Transit*. Gower ignores this vessel in his book, but does mention a third vessel of the same name, a three-master built as a yacht for the Hon. G. Vernon by Jabez Bayley, under Gower's superintendence, in 1819.

In 1821 Jabez Bayley built a much smaller vessel designed by Gower, a lifeboat paid for by a subscription raised in Ipswich, to be stationed at Landguard Fort. When she was launched from Bayley's yard near Stoke Bridge on 4 April 1821 the 29ft. 6in. boat was dropped off the wharf and allowed to fall several feet into the water, apparently as a demonstration of her qualities.[5]

Jabez Bayley is best remembered for the series of East Indiamen built at Halifax Yard, beginning with the *Orwell*, launched in the presence of some 20,000 spectators on 28 August 1817. Under the contract with Captain Matthew Issacks, of London, Jabez agreed to build an East Indiaman of 1,330 registered tons at a price of £22 10s. per ton for the hull complete. It was a price at which he expected to make a handsome profit, but the preparations for launching such a large ship swallowed up all the profit, and rather more.[6] The *Orwell* made eight voyages out east between her building and 1830.[7] She later traded on the China coast, and was broken up in London in 1840.

Convinced that large contracts would restore his tottering fortunes, Jabez secured an order from Captain Henry Templar, of Limehouse, for two more East Indiamen each of 1300 tons. Before they were ready Captain Templar sold his contract with the East India Company to Scott, Fairlie and Hare, of London, and they were launched in 1821 as the *David Scott* and *William Fairlie*, named after the principals of that company. As we have already seen, bankruptcy has always plagued the shipbuilder, and Jabez was adjudged bankrupt some years later. His property, all of which was offered for sale for the benefit of his creditors, included standing trees as far away as Colchester and Ixworth.

Nephew George built two wooden steamers, the *Ipswich* and *Suffolk*, for operations between Ipswich and London, but the service was not a success. Only a handful of steamships were built on the Orwell, including an iron steamer, the *Orion*, built by Read and Page in 1840, but throughout the 19th century local yards continued to turn out sailing vessels including a succession of attractive ketch barges employed in the coasting and short-sea trades.

Smaller spritsail barges were built for trading along the coast, and it is clear that in the mid-19th century a direct trade was being carried on between Stowmarket and London in sailing barges smaller than the spritsail barges that today race each summer on the Orwell but not greatly different otherwise. One such barge was the *Gipping*, an iron vessel built at Ipswich in 1842 by Read and Page and said when advertised for sale in 1847 to have been 'constantly employed in conveying goods between London and Stowmarket'.[8] Another was the barge *Ironsides*, whose master was killed when he fell overboard and was crushed between the barge's hull and a bridge on the Stowmarket Navigation; by an evil twist of fate the man's son was washed off the deck of the same barge only a month later on Christmas Eve, 1841.[9]

The last round-bottomed sailing vessel to be built in the town, the brigantine *Clementine*, destined for the Newfoundland stockfish trade and later registered at St Johns, Newfoundland, came off the ways at the St Clement's Yard just outside the lock gates in 1885. The big barges launched from Ipswich yards included the *Eastern Belle* (1883), *Southern Belle* (1885), *Lord Shaftesbury* (1886), *Lord Iddesleigh* (1888), *Lord Hartington* (1889) and *Lord Tennyson* (1891) for the English and Continental Shipping Co. Ltd. of London.[10]

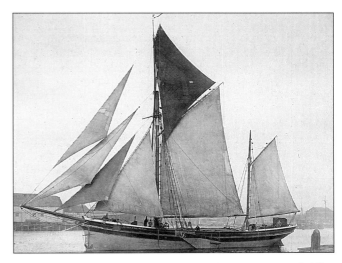

Bargebuilding in Ipswich came to an end with the launching of the *Jock* in 1908 and the *Ardwina* in 1909 by Orvis and Fuller. The former barge spent some sixty years in the fleet of Ipswich maltsters R. & W. Paul; she was named after William Paul's grandson.[11] The Paul family firm was built up by Robert (1844–1909) and William Paul (1850–1928), the sons of

82 The big ketch barge Cock o' the Walk *in Ipswich Dock. The photograph was probably taken in 1899 when she brought a cargo of phosphates from Dunkirk for Prentice Brothers. Many such ketch barges were built in the Ipswich yards, though the* Cock o' the Walk *herself was built at Millwall on the Thames in 1876.*

Robert Paul (1806–64), the expansion of their malting enterprise being linked to the manufacture of animal feedstuffs and flaked maize; as a result of their activities the brothers earned themselves the popular title of 'Maize Kings of East Anglia'.[12]

Malt made in the Ipswich maltings went by coasting vessel to supply the London breweries, while grain grown in the Suffolk fields went not only to London but to many other ports around the British coasts. When the expansion of the malting trade in East Anglia outstripped the supply of home-grown barley sailing vessels brought cargoes from the Black Sea and later from North America, while barges brought imported barley loaded overside from ships in the London docks to fill the garners of the riverside maltings.

Other raw materials were also brought in by sea, including the pig iron that was needed by the town's expanding engineering industries. In the year 1846 more than ninety cargoes of iron were recorded arriving at Ipswich, where Ransomes' and other foundries absorbed a considerable proportion of the 14,000 tons represented by those cargoes. In that same year 10,000 quarters of linseed was imported from the Baltic and the Black Sea to feed the local oil mills, to say nothing of great quantities of both hewn and sawn timber, needed both by local industries and by the building trade, which boomed as the town expanded apace.[13]

The vessels sailing out of the East Coast ports in the earlier part of the century were almost entirely small vessels, many of them brigantine rigged, with square sails on the foremast and a gaffsail on the main; this rig was a development from that of the brig, square-rigged on both masts. Indeed, some brigs were re-rigged as brigantines to make them handier and more economical.

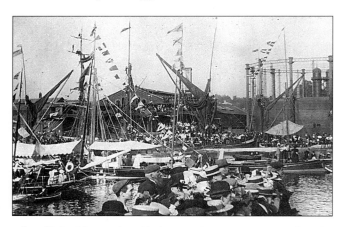

These small ships were dependent on the weather; not only was stormy weather a handicap to trade but a contrary wind might hold up great fleets in Harwich harbour or Yarmouth Roads. In January 1847 it was reported at Ipswich that the number of vessels in the newly constructed dock was 'unusually small, the prevailing south-easterly winds having prevented the arrival of much shipping. At the present period about 500 vessels are wind-bound in the Humber—most of them being colliers. The price of coal in Ipswich has in consequence advanced …'.[14] Later in the month the price of coal dropped as the first of the delayed colliers sailed up

83   Spritsail barges alongside the gasworks quay serve as grandstands from which spectators watch water sports in the dock during a regatta at the beginning of the 20th century.

the Orwell, and then at the beginning of February it was announced that 'there has been a larger number of vessels entered the port this week than at any previous period, there being no less than 41 colliers arrived since our last, out of which number about 30 arrived within the last two days. On Sunday there were not less than 40 sail of vessels under way between the Dock and Downham Reach at tide time.'[15]

The average cargo brought in by these vessels was less than 100 tons. When the barque *Ruth* of Ipswich brought 450 tons in one trip in 1848 her arrival excited comment because of the unusual size of the cargo. This vessel was lost off the Irish coast in 1849 when on her way from Ipswich to New Brunswick for a cargo of Canadian timber—a reminder that those same vessels that sailed week by week in the coasting trade might at suitable times set off for ports in Europe or North America, in the Mediterranean or some other far-flung part of the world.

The many risks they ran ensured that comparatively few ships lasted for very long, but some seem to have borne charmed lives. Some of the men who sailed these vessels were themselves veterans: in the 1850s John Cobbold's little sloop *Endeavour*, built at Faversham in Kent in 1783, had a master aged 79, and the mate and third hand were both 65. The master, John Thorne, had been at sea continuously for 67 years, 17 of them in the Royal Navy. The *Endeavour* had been employed in supplying the fleet at the Nore during the wars with France.

The Coming of the Railway

Coastal shipping was soon to have a rival in the railways that were being built throughout the country in the 1830s and 1840s. In spite of their espousal of the Conservative cause the two Cobbolds, John and his son John Chevallier Cobbold, were favourably disposed towards such projects as the dock scheme and the bringing of the railway to the town. Together with the Rev. Dr. John Chevallier they were among those in Suffolk who spoke out in support of the Grand Eastern Counties Railway, which was, according to the prospectus issued in 1834, to build a line from London to Yarmouth by way of Ipswich and Norwich.

84 John Chevallier Cobbold, businessman, dock commissioner and railway pioneer. (Tollemache & Cobbold Brewery Ltd.)

As far back as 1825 Dr. Chevallier had taken the chair at a meeting in Ipswich Shire Hall at which a scheme for a railway to run from Ipswich to Diss had been discussed, and in 1833 the two Cobbolds had been members of a steering committee which failed to get another railway scheme off the ground. In the case of the 1825 scheme it had been proposed to work the line with 'loco-motive steam engines'; had it been constructed that line would have been among the very first locomotive-operated public railways.[16] All three men became directors of the Eastern Counties Railway Company—the word Grand was dropped before the company's Bill was successfully introduced into the House of Commons in 1836—and once construction of the line began in 1837 they struggled manfully to ensure that the railway extended into Suffolk. Only about one in twelve of the shares were taken up in eastern England, however, and many of the proprietors were from the industrial Midlands and the North; when it came to a fight the Cobbolds found themselves outnumbered.

The directors from outside East Anglia had no interest in where the line went so long as it earned money, and at the 1838 annual meeting it was announced that the line was not to be laid beyond Colchester for the time being. There ensued a power struggle in which the Suffolk and Norfolk directors were ousted and replaced by Lancashire men, and all J.C. Cobbold's legal efforts to force the ECR to fulfil what he regarded as its obligations to Suffolk failed.

Outvoted time after time, J.C. Cobbold realised that if the railway were ever to reach Ipswich it would have to be built by another company. He found an invaluable ally in Peter Schuyler Bruff, a young engineer who had trained under that eminent railway builder Joseph Locke and had worked on the construction of the Eastern Counties line. The Eastern Counties between Colchester and Ipswich as laid out by John Braithwaite was to have been carried across the River Stour by a 70ft viaduct with about a hundred arches just a few yards from Flatford Mill, but Bruff's route took the line across the river at a much lower level just at the head of the estuary; his line was to be constructed at an outlay much less than Braithwaite's estimate. Bruff's plans and estimates were considered at a public meeting held in Ipswich Town Hall on 8 August 1843, Bruff explaining how the line was to be carried in a tunnel under Stoke Hill and up the Gipping valley on its way to Norwich. A branch to Bury St Edmunds would leave the main line near Stowmarket. The cost of the whole 'Projected Eastern Union Railway' would, he said, be less than £16,000 a mile, inclusive of land, stations and rolling stock.

John Cobbold was a member of the committee appointed to carry the project further, with his son as honorary secretary. With the Eastern Union there were to be none of the lavish salaries that had been a feature of earlier, sometimes fraudulent, railway schemes. The Eastern Counties Railway Company was invited to nominate a representative to serve on the committee, but the company declined to do so.

Bruff's original plan had been for the line to follow the north side of the Stour estuary to Holbrook Bay, where a branch would strike off to Shotley, the main line curving away to the north to reach Ipswich by way of Freston. When application was made in 1843 for a Bill, however, the plans submitted showed the route from the river crossing at Cattawade climbing through a deep cutting at Brantham and reaching Ipswich by way of Bentley and Belstead.

Casting his mind back to the power struggle that had ousted local interests from the Eastern Counties board, the editor of the *Ipswich Journal* urged local people to take shares in the new company.[17] Alas, all too few of the readers heeded the editor's words, and it was left for the directors to find most of the capital needed; the rest came from those speculators in the North. J.C. Cobbold was one of the two treasurers of the Ipswich and East Suffolk Hospital; he and his fellow-treasurer Dykes Alexander offered to advance the railway company £600 at five per cent interest, 'on receipt of a temporary acknowledgement for such loan until the Directors were authorised to issue debenture bonds'. As Hugh Moffat says, a modern auditor would not consider this to be a suitable trustee investment.[18]

Although opposed all the way by the Eastern Counties Railway Company, the Eastern Union's Act received Royal Assent on 19 July 1844. Named in the Act were the first directors, eight from Ipswich, one from Stowmarket and two from Huddersfield. J.C. Cobbold was elected chairman and Ipswich draper John Footman became vice-chairman and managing director. Joseph Locke, the great railway engineer who was at that time building railways in France as well as in this country, was taken on as engineer. He appointed his former pupil Bruff as resident engineer, and left all the day-to-day work to him. As contractors Locke brought in the famous Thomas Brassey and his partner,

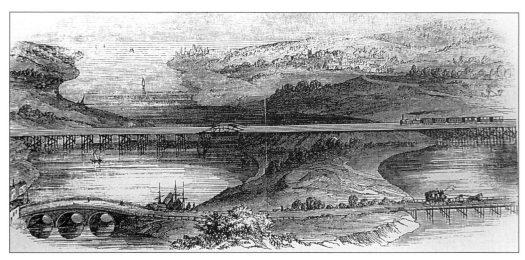

85   *The Cattawade viaducts that carried the Eastern Union Railway over the River Stour on its way to Ipswich.*
Although a coach is seen in this engraving, the stagecoach service from Ipswich to Colchester ceased as soon as the
railway was opened.

William Mackenzie, who were both engaged with him on the French railways. Towards
the end of August 1844, plant and materials were being landed by barge at Cattawade
in preparation for work on Brantham cutting and the two timber viaducts across the
Stour. In local charge of the work for Brassey and Mackenzie was a Scot, Alexander
Ogilvie, who later in his life set up home at Sizewell House, near Leiston.

Working practices were crude and dangerous. Seven lives were lost during the
construction of the Colchester-Ipswich line, and three more during work on the south
side of Stoke tunnel; most of those who died were local men. With the completion of
the Cattawade embankment early in May 1846, the line reached completion. Local
newspapers told the story of how Mr. Ogilvie decided

> on traversing the entire line with a locomotive engine, and on Tuesday morning an
> engine and tender arrived from Lawford at the Ipswich station, about seven o'clock in
> the morning. The engine has for some time been upon the line, having been employed
> in drawing the earth waggons between Ardleigh and Manningtree. At nine o'clock a
> large party left Ipswich by the train which consisted of a number of open luggage wains.
> Peter Bruff Esq., the Company's engineer, took the direction of the locomotive, and
> the journey to Colchester was accomplished in about an hour and a half. At twelve, a
> larger party left Colchester in the train, which now consisted of some new and very
> elegant first, second and third class carriages, built for the Company, and reached
> Ipswich in 1 hour 25 minutes.[19]

The official opening of the line on 11 June must have been a very joyous occasion for
John Chevallier Cobbold, who joined the special train that ran from Ipswich to Colchester
at Bentley. Everywhere along the line the train was greeted by cheering crowds.

By the time the Ipswich line was opened to public passenger traffic on 15 June 1846, the Ipswich and Bury St Edmunds Railway Company was in being and work was in progress both on the tunnel and on the line northwards up the Gipping Valley and towards Bury. John Chevallier Cobbold, John Footman and Peter Bruff were among those on the footplate of an engine named *Bury St Edmunds* when it headed a special train to Bury on 26 November 1846. A local newspaper provided a memorable account of the journey through the tunnel:

> Little time was allowed for reflection—shriek went the whistle of the engine, and amidst shouts of 'Down with your heads, gentlemen', to those who travelled as 'outsiders', the train shot into Stoke Tunnel, and was soon threading its dark recesses. The scene was extremely novel to those who had never before travelled through the bowels of the earth—the shrieks of the engine, the clatter of the carriages, the whizzing of the steam, the shouts of the passengers, mingling together in uproarious and strange confusion.[20]

When the EUR Extension to Norwich was opened in 1849 the Cobbolds had indeed succeeded, against all odds, in making Ipswich a centre of railway communications. Continued hostility from the Eastern Counties, which did all in its power to hamper the operations of the Eastern Union, had a cumulative effect on the smaller company, however, and in 1854 negotiations between Brassey, who had been paid largely in EUR stock, and the Eastern Counties chairman, David Waddington, resulted in the ECR taking over the working of the EUR. Bruff, whose relations with the ECR had not always been good, was employed by that company as engineer.[21]

Within a year or two of the opening of the Eastern Union lines a tramway had been laid to the dock so that cargoes could be loaded from ship to rail and from rail to ship. This line was also to serve a new works that went up alongside the dock.

The Orwell Works

As work went ahead on the construction of the dock, and while the Cobbolds were concerning themselves with bringing the railway, Ransomes made the decision to build a new works on the riverside, to the south of the temporary premises occupied by William Worby's branch works. It was to be known as Orwell Works. Almost certainly it was the increase in trade brought about by the railway work to be described on pages 171-3 that brought about the decision; the firm had long outgrown the somewhat restricted premises between St Margaret's Ditches (in future to be known as Old Foundry Road) and Carr Street. The first of the new buildings were occupied in 1841, and over the next eight years more and more activities were transferred to the new site as further workshops were erected. James Ransome took charge of the new works, Charles May remaining at the Old Foundry in St Margaret's Ditches.[22]

The beginning of the move coincided with the production of Ransomes' first steam engine, a little portable engine with a vertical boiler that was shown at the Royal Agricultural Society show at Liverpool in 1841. Following its return from Liverpool the engine was made self-moving by the addition of a chain drive to the rear axle, and in

86   *The new station at the north end of the tunnel was quite new when this photograph was taken from Stoke Hill; the background appears almost entirely rural. For more than twenty years there was only a single through platform and a dock for the East Suffolk line, the island platform not being added until 1883. (John Wilton)*

this guise it was exhibited at the 1842 show in Bristol. It was not really the forerunner of the traction engine, for it was merely self moving and not intended to haul other vehicles, though it did carry a small threshing machine on a platform.[23] The judges at the 1842 show reported that the little Ipswich-built engine, which was of the so-called disc type patented by Henry Davies (an early attempt at producing a rotary engine), 'travelled along at the rate of four to six miles an hour, and was guided and manoeuvred'—by a horse in shafts attached to the front wheels—'so as to fix it in any particular spot with ease'. They awarded it a prize of £30, but no more is heard of it.[24]

Ransomes exhibited another self-moving engine, made not in Ipswich but at the Railway Foundry of E.B. Wilson & Co. in Leeds to the design of Robert Willis, at the 1849 Royal Show at Leeds. It carried off first prize at the Royal and was afterwards employed in threshing in Suffolk, spending some days on two farms at Bramford and then moving on under its own power to a farm near Freston. Alas, the rough roads of early Victorian East Anglia shook it to pieces all too quickly, and another pioneer disappeared from the country scene.[25]

The firm completed the move to the new Orwell Works in 1849, the event being marked by a dinner given by the partners to some 1,500 guests, including the entire workforce.[26]

By 1850 steam power was becoming accepted in the fields as it had been years earlier in the mill and the factory. 'The use of fixed steam engines, of from four to eight horse power for impelling threshing machines, is now common on large farms in the north of England and the south of Scotland; and the use of both fixed and portable steam engines, of two, three and four horse power, for impelling the several machines of the farmery, is pretty general in many of the best parts of the centre and south of England,' said the writer of *The Rural Cyclopaedia*, published in 1849. At the Great Exhibition of 1851 in Hyde Park, Ransomes showed not just a selection of their farm implements but also a fixed engine and a portable.

In later years the firm was among those that designed classes of engine specifically for service in what would today be termed the developing countries. John Head, who joined the firm as an apprentice in 1848, invented an apparatus which enabled straw to be burnt as fuel in the firebox of portable and traction engines. This development, made in collaboration with a Russian engineer named Schemioth, proved a very useful one in countries where there was no wood available for fuel and where coal had to be imported at great expense.[27]

There came a time when the erecting shops at Orwell Works were full of engines under construction, and engines by the dozen can be seen in various stages of erection in old photographs of the works. Portable engines destined for overseas countries were packed in crates, their wheels, flywheels and various other large components being packed separately before despatch. On arrival at the port of destination it was a small matter to unpack the wheels and axles and fit them to the still-crated engines for onward haulage.

The Quaker Connection

Quaker business acumen, energy and principle contributed to the commercial and industrial growth of Ipswich in many ways. Links through marriage, friendship and religion between Quaker families in different parts of the country did much to assist the evolution of local firms such as Ransomes; not only were they all Friends, but some were family relations by marriage.

The first newcomer to Ransomes was Charles May, who joined in 1836 and shouldered most of the responsibility for the railway work that was so important to the family firm. Between the time of his joining the firm and 1851, when he left it, May took out eight patents, some of them in conjunction with members of the Ransome family. Four of them involved the construction of railways and two were concerned with agricultural machinery.[28] The significance of the railway trade is indicated by the company's balance sheet for 1851 which shows nearly £87,000 for railway and general engineering work compared with only £35,000 for agricultural work.[29]

Following the departure of Charles May the Ransomes invited his nephew William Dillwyn Sims to join the firm as a partner. William's aunt Ann was the wife of Richard Dykes Alexander, the Ipswich banker and philanthropist, and William himself married Eliza Curtis May, while in 1892 old Robert Ransome's great-granddaughter Mildred married John Dillwyn Sims, William's son, so it is possible to see a complex web of relationships growing up. In 1865 another of the founder's great-granddaughters, Mary Ann Ransome, married John Jefferies, who had been an apprentice at Orwell Works, and in due course he too became a partner in the firm. Each time a new partner was taken in the firm changed its name; over the years it had ten different titles, ending up in 1884 as Ransomes, Sims & Jefferies.

It was undoubtedly the Quaker connection that brought a certain John Fowler to Ipswich in the early 1850s. John came of a long line of Friends, for the Fowlers had been among the earliest disciples of George Fox, founder of that religious movement, and it was through family links with the leading Quaker families in the north of England that in 1847 John became an apprentice with a Middlesbrough engineering firm. When the Friends decided in 1849 to send a delegation to Ireland, then suffering severely from the potato famine and the resulting widespread destitution, to discover what might be done to alleviate the situation John was invited to go along to give the delegation the benefit of his engineering knowledge.[30] Realising that economical drainage of the Irish wetlands could increase and help diversify agricultural production, John set out to develop a means of mechanising the laying of field drains, up to then a laborious and expensive manual process. He turned for advice and assistance to Ransomes and to their works manager, William Worby, whom he first met one fine summer's evening on Brighton beach. It is recorded that on that summer's evening the two men spent two hours 'very seriously talking and calculating on the subject and came to the conclusion of its being impracticable ...'.[31] The development work to which Ransomes contributed so much was eventually to lead not just to the successful use of steam power for land drainage but to the evolution of steam ploughing.

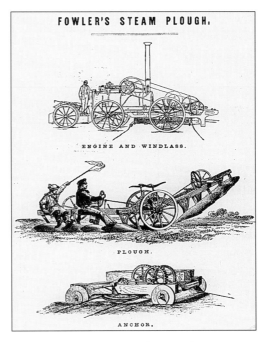

87   *A page from Ransomes & Sims' 1859 catalogue showing an early version of John Fowler's ploughing engine, the balance plough developed in Ipswich, and the anchor to whose development William Worby gave so much thought.*

It was with a Ransome 10 h.p. portable engine and a Ransome four-furrow balance plough that Fowler at last won the Royal Agricultural Society's £500 prize in trials at Chester in 1858. The collaboration between Fowler and Ransomes continued even when the former set up his own works in Leeds which produced its first pair of ploughing engines in 1862.[32]

First works manager of the Steam Plough Works was an Ipswich man, Jeremiah Head, who had been articled to Robert Stephenson & Co. in Newcastle at the age of 17 in 1852. Head, a relative of the John Head who became a partner in Ransomes, had played an important part in the development of the steam plough and had at one point been assigned full time to work done by Stephensons in producing windlasses for Fowler. It has been said that while John Fowler was the team leader and innovator he was greatly indebted to those who worked with him, including Head and Worby.[33]

In view of these local connections it is not entirely inappropriate that the Ipswich Museum should have become the home of a one-tenth scale model of a Fowler 14 n.h.p. ploughing engine made in 1864 to the order of Prince Halim Pasha, who had purchased a number of full-size Fowler engines for use in the Egyptian cotton fields. It seems the model was never delivered, for at the beginning of this century it was rescued from the office loft in Leeds by a Fowler employee, Percy Robinson, who spent many years restoring it to its original condition.

Manufacturing Centre

The extent to which the town had grown as a manufacturing centre is emphasised by a note in a mid-century directory that about forty steam engines were employed in the town's various mills and factories.[34] Ransomes were but the largest and most important of five ironfounders; there were four artificial fertiliser manufacturers, three of whom would in the 20th century combine into a company known around the world; 14 corn millers and 15 corn merchants; nine curriers and leather cutters, one of whom, Conder's, continued in a considerable way of business well into the 20th century; and at Flint Wharf there was Frederick Ransome, a member of the ironfounding family, who had set up as a patent stone manufacturer using a process he had developed for dissolving ground flint in chemical. Frederick and some of his Suffolk workmen migrated about 1860 to Greenwich, where a new works was set up more or less on the site of the Millennium Dome.[35]

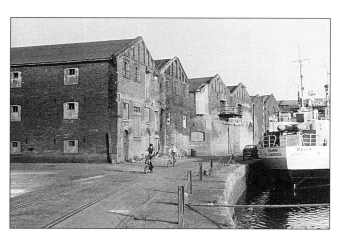

One of the more important engineering companies was that of Edward Rush Turner, whose works between College Street and the river is today recalled by Foundry Lane. Established in 1837 as Bond, Turner and Hurwood, iron founders and general engineers, it was to develop into a nationally known firm of milling engineers, E.R. & F. Turner; one of their horizontal steam engines survives at the Cliff Brewery. Turners also set up the Greyfriars Ironworks, destroyed in one of a series of spectacular fires at the beginning of the 20th century, on the site now occupied by Cardinal Park. A catalogue issued in 1882 shows that E.R. & F. Turner were then producing steam

88   Edward Packard's artificial fertiliser factory, set up around 1850. The street running back from the quay to Duke Street was constructed about the same time and was named Coprolite Street after the original raw material of fertiliser manufacture. The buildings were cleared away soon after this photograph was taken.

engines, oil milling machinery, machines for the preparation of artificial fertilisers, and corn milling plant, to say nothing of chaff cutters, thrashing machines and similar agricultural implements. The firm was among the pioneers of roller milling, as early as 1863 making roller mills for use in conjunction with traditional stone mills in a process of gradual reduction of wheat to flour.[36]

From 1878 onwards the Hungarians were using the roller system to produce flour without employing stones at all, and about that time Turners and a number of other British milling engineers paid a visit to Hungary to study the new process. By 1884 the firm was supplying complete mills

89   The barges which were used by Packard to carry raw materials from Ipswich Dock to the Bramford works are seen on the left of this view of a busy dock in 1923. Only survivor of this fleet is the Yare, *the barge on the outside in the foreground, which is now a houseboat at Pin Mill. (Ipswich Port Authority)*

on the roller system, often providing the engine and boiler to power the mill, though the production of steam engines was discontinued in 1908 to allow for expansion of the milling side of the business.[37]

Turners' manufacture of phosphate-grinding mills, acid pumps and other equipment for the artificial manure industry resulted from the discovery by Prof. J.S. Henslow of the properties of the phosphatic nodules known as coprolite and the subsequent establishment of the artificial fertiliser trade in the Ipswich area in the 1840s. About 1849 Edward Packard (1809–99) set up the first artificial fertiliser factory on the quayside at Ipswich, the new road driven through from Duke Street to the dockside alongside the works being named Coprolite Street. The process involved grinding the coprolite, quarried in the coastal area east of Ipswich, and dissolving it in sulphuric acid in brick pits known as dens; the breaking down of the phosphate resulted in what would today be termed atmospheric pollution, and in 1854 Packard was persuaded to move his works to Bramford,[38] where Joseph Fison, of Eastern Union Mills, Ipswich, also set up an artificial manure works.

The manufacture of clothing was one of the lesser industries that became established in Ipswich, developing from a cottage industry into one that employed considerable numbers of workers in factories in various parts of the town. Ipswich also developed into one of the main corset manufacturing centres thanks to the expansion of what had begun as a cottage industry based largely on outworkers. Having been founded in 1820 as drapers and silk mercers, Footman, Pretty & Nicolson opened a new corset factory of impressive size in Tower Ramparts in 1882. From 1889 the corset-manufacturing side of the business was carried on as William Pretty & Sons, the department store in Westgate Street being known as Footman, Pretty & Co. Perhaps it is not surprising that there should also have been a sewing machine manufacturer,

90   The corset factory of William Pretty & Sons in Tower Ramparts shortly before demolition in the 1980s. It had been built in 1882 by Footman, Pretty & Nicholson, a firm founded in 1820.

George Whight & Co., operating in the Butter Market around 1880, producing what was known as the New Excelsior machine.

It is often advertisements in the local newspapers that give us much of our information about trades and industries, and during the 19th century these publications became more common. *The Ipswich Journal* was joined in 1810 by the *Suffolk Chronicle* and then in 1839 by the *Ipswich Express*, which in 1874 was absorbed into the town's first daily newspaper, the *East Anglian Daily Times*. In mid-century Robinson Taylor, who had been engaged as a reporter by the *Ipswich Journal*, became publisher of that paper. He was succeeded in that position by Henry Knights, who was also part-proprietor of the Bible and Crown Printing Works, set up at 16 Market Lane in 1864. Four years later the Market Lane premises were absorbed by Cowells and the Bible and Crown Printing Works moved to Princes Street, where both steam and water power were used; presumably the water power came from the Gipping. Besides being publisher of the *Ipswich Journal* Knights produced *Knights' Suffolk Almanack and County Handbook* in 1869; under various titles it continued to appear annually right up to 1939, though Knights himself died in 1898.

There can be no doubt that the Craightons have a very special place in the history of Ipswich newspapers, but probably the best-known name in printing is that of Cowell. Abraham Kersey Cowell acquired the bookselling business of Richard Nottingham Rose in the Buttermarket, where his 16-year-old second son Samuel Harrison Cowell was an apprentice, in 1818. The older Cowell was the first pastor of Walton Baptist Chapel, so it seems likely that the printing side of the business was carried on by his son although the father's name was used until the boy came of age.

The circumstances of the takeover were explained in an advertisement in the *Ipswich Journal* of 11 July 1818:

Printing, book selling, bookbinding and stationer.

Old Butter Market, Ipswich.

Mr. R.N. Rose finding it necessary to dispose of his business, A.K. Cowell has been induced to take it, in consequence of his son being apprenticed to him, and begs leave to inform the public, he has employed a competent and confidential person to manage it …

In 1826 Samuel Cowell bought premises in Old Gaol Lane (later known as Old Market Lane and now absorbed into the Buttermarket shopping complex) adjacent to his shop in the Buttermarket and opened a tea, coffee and spice warehouse. Further purchases extended the business until it occupied a large area between the Buttermarket and Falcon Street, and by 1879 the firm was described as wholesale stationers, letterpress, anastatic and lithographic printer, machine ruler, account book and paper bag manufacturers—and wholesale tea dealers.

When Samuel Cowell died in 1875 the business was carried on by his son Walter Samuel Cowell and W.B. Hanson, who had joined the firm as manager in 1866. The business was converted into a limited company in 1900.[39]

The Railway Builders

Always seeking profitable products that would carry the firm through periods of agricultural depression, Ransomes turned to producing a variety of railway materials that went into the construction of lines not only in this country but also abroad. A visitor in the 1860s saw the chairs in which the rails were fixed being cast by what he called 'a quick and ingenious process':

> One part of the floor is occupied by a very narrow semicircular railway on which small wheeled frames are made to travel round the curve from the sand-heap at one end to the pot of molten metal at the other. In these frames the moulds are hung on pivots, so that by a touch they turn upside down at pleasure. A boy reverses a mould and rams it from the under side full of sand. The mould rights itself; the orifice is opened, and a boy at a run pushes it to the opposite end of the railway. There the men with the big ladle immediately pour in the liquid iron, and in a few seconds a solid railway chair is formed. By this time another boy has run up with another mould; and so it goes on all day, filling and casting, and turning out tons of chairs every week.[40]

Trenails for fastening the chairs to the sleepers and keys or wedges to hold the rails tight in the chairs were also produced at Orwell Works, along with much else that was required by the engineers and contractors who were constructing lines across the world. For many years the railway work provided the greater share of the firm's income, at least until the 1860s when there was an upsurge in the export of farm implements, leading the partners to seek space to expand the capacity for agricultural work.

The decision to turn over the railway work to a new company, and a new works on the other side of the New Cut, provided some of the extra accommodation needed at Orwell Works, which was itself being expanded from the original six acres to ten. That decision might also have been influenced by the need to specialise to a greater extent than before, since steel was taking the place of chilled iron and it was vital the railway department should not fall behind the current developments.

In 1862 Richard Rapier, a Northumbrian who had been apprenticed to the Newcastle engineering works of Robert Stephenson & Co., became manager of Ransomes railway department. With the formation of a new company in 1869 Rapier became a partner

with Robert James Ransome, and
Ransomes & Rapier was soon to make a
name for itself that was second to none.
In the 1870s it took a leading part in
supplying equipment for the Welsh
narrow-gauge slate railways, and also for
similar railways on sugar plantations far
across the sea.

Richard Rapier was indeed an
enthusiast for narrow gauge, writing a
book on *Remunerative Railways for New
Countries*, and he had an ambition to build
the first railways in China. That
undeveloped country could, he believed,
be opened up to profitable trade by the
construction of a network of steam-

*91   'Portable Railways are often required for temporary
purposes … These will be found to be most convenient
in lengths of 10ft. or 12ft., because the weight of such
lengths, with their sleepers attached, is well within the
power of two men to lift about …' An illustration from*
Little Railways, *issued by Ransomes & Rapier in
1880.*

operated narrow-gauge railways. Early attempts to break into that little-known country
were frustrated by political and diplomatic objections, but Rapier's opportunity came
when in 1872 the firm of Jardine, Matheson & Co., one of the leading China merchants,
obtained permission from the Chinese authorities to build a quay, jetty and warehouses
at Woosung, on the Yangtse River some twelve miles below Shanghai, and to construct
a road from Shanghai to Woosung. The object was to avoid having to navigate large
ships up the difficult and hazardous reaches of the Yangtse to Shanghai. Ransomes and
Rapier suggested to Jardine, Matheson that instead of building a road they should
allow R & R to lay a narrow-gauge railway along the same route.[41] After much discussion
between the two companies the proposal was accepted, and in the autumn of 1873
work began on the design of a tiny locomotive to be used in the construction of the
line. The little 0-4-0 tank engine *Pioneer* was ready just over a year later, and tests on a
circular track in the Waterside Works yard and on George Tomline's tramway at
Felixstowe showed that though it weighed no more than 1 ton 2 cwt it could do

92   The tiny engine Pioneer, *built in Ipswich by
Ransomes & Rapier and sent to China to help build
the Shanghai & Woosung Railway.*

considerably more than pull its weight;
during the Easter holiday of 1875 it hauled
a train over Tomline's tramway with no
fewer than 80 adults in the open trucks,
and achieved a speed of 12 mph.

All the same, various alterations and
improvements were made before the
Pioneer was shipped off to China; the
original 4in. cylinders were increased to
5in. bore and the gauge was increased
from 2ft. to 2ft. 6in. In the autumn of 1875
the little engine left England in the

steamer *Glenroy*, along with five R & R workers who were to construct and then operate the line. Those five were John Sadler, the foreman; Will Jackson, chief working engineer; David Banks, the second engineer; John Sadler, jnr, second foreman; and his brother George, general assistant.

Conditions in China were by no means pleasant, and severe extremes of weather, the attacks of mosquitoes and long hours of arduous work soon created health problems for the railway builders, but in spite of the difficulties construction went ahead. By 14 February 1876 the *Pioneer* was running over the first three-quarters of a mile of track, and a passenger service began on 30 June the same year between Shanghai and Kangwan, the halfway point, using the Ipswich-built 0-6-0 tank engine *Celestial Empire* and a number of four-wheeled carriages also shipped out from England. A second, similar engine, the *Flowery Land*, was put into service the following year. The conditions under which the

five men were living and working took their toll, and foreman John Sadler became seriously ill; he died on 15 September 1876. Then George Sadler became ill, and it was feared that the coming Chinese winter would end his life. He was sent home to England under the care of his brother John, leaving just two stalwarts to carry on the operation of the line.

93   A goods train on the Shanghai & Woosung Railway, headed by the six-coupled tank engine Celestial Empire.

The agreement for the building of the line had included an option for the local mandarins to purchase it. In October 1877 the mandarins acquired the railway and immediately announced that the line would be closed on the arrival at Shanghai of the 7p.m. train from Woosung that same evening. It must have been with a mixture of emotions that Jackson and Banks left for home early in 1878. For some unknown reason neither of them returned to employment at Waterside Works. David Banks joined the Continental Department of the Great Eastern Railway as a fitter in the Marine Workshops at Parkeston Quay and William Jackson became locomotive superintendent on the Southwold Railway. The stories he told of his life in China must be behind the persistent legend that the engines and rolling stock from China found new life on the line between Halesworth and Southwold; this legend has been embroidered to tell how the engines ran through the Suffolk countryside with Chinese dragons emblazoned on the side tanks—though photographs taken in Shanghai show that they were not decorated in this way at all.[42]

Just what became of the first railway in China is something of a mystery; what is certain is that the engines did not return to Britain. Ransomes & Rapier went on to make equipment not only for railways in Britain but for lines in India and other parts of the world, to manufacture sluices for the Aswan Dam and for other water control schemes, and to build the biggest walking dragline in the world.[43]

XII

Victorian Town

At the beginning of the 19th century Ipswich had a population of 11,277, almost all crowded into the area within the old medieval ditch and bank and into the extra-mural parishes of St Matthew's, St Margaret's, St Helen's and St Clement's. In the course of the century there were to be enormous changes; by 1851 the population had almost trebled to 32,914, and in another 50 years it had doubled again to 66,630.

The young Victoria was called to the throne at a turning point in the town's history, for just ten days after her accession the Queen gave Royal Assent to the Ipswich Dock Act which was to help lay the foundations for the town's future prosperity.[1] Already the town was changing; streets were being widened and old timber-framed houses were being demolished so that much more imposing brick-fronted properties could take their place. Between 1815 and 1818 the *Great White Horse Hotel* and other buildings on the north side of Tavern Street lost their ornate fronts when the street was widened; William Hunt describes how the jettied fronts of the old houses were replaced by new fronts of fashionable white brick.[2] It was in this operation that the Old Coffee House, with its splendid carvings of 'undeniable grossness, and even vulgarity in certain details',[3] lost its façade. John Glyde explains the disappearance of 'so picturesque a specimen of domestic architecture' by pointing to the narrowness of this important shopping street and to the traffic congestion that resulted.[4]

94   *Best known of the Ipswich hostelries, the* Great White Horse *was the scene of Mr. Pickwick's unfortunate encounter with the lady in curl-papers. The timber-framed building acquired its facing of Suffolk whites in the 1820s following the building in Northgate Street of the Assembly Rooms using white bricks.*

At the same time that the main streets were being widened new thoroughfares were constructed through what had in many cases been the gardens of large mansions, while other former gardens and orchards became the sites of courts of little mean houses that provided homes for the newcomers attracted from the countryside by the burgeoning industries of the town. One of the new streets was Great Colman Street, which was taken through from opposite the Assembly Rooms in Northgate Street to Major's Corner in the 1830s; it was probably named after the Colman family, members of which are shown as owners in the area on Pennington's map. The opportunity to construct this new street arose from the sale in 1821 of Harebottle House (as it was then known), a Tudor house built in 1538 by John Harbottle, a successful cloth merchant.[5]

Another Tudor mansion to be lost to such development was Thomas Seckford's Great Place in Westgate Street, shown to advantage by Ogilby.[6] The house and its gardens gave way to Museum Street, named after the museum designed by Christopher Fleury, an Irish-born architect who was also responsible for the mid-Victorian buildings of Ipswich School in Henley Road.

Established in 1847, the Ipswich Museum was certainly not intended by its promoters as a purely middle-class institution. It was proposed from the outset that it should be 'more particularly for the benefit of the working classes', but unfortunately the regular lectures, 'to which tickets for free admission are distributed among the working classes', failed to attract the attention of more than a minority of such people.[7] Museum Street was constructed in the same year as the museum itself was built, and just beyond the pilastered museum building turned to the east; in 1850 an archway was cut through the house in which Lincolnshire banker William Ingelow had lived from 1834 to 1844 to make a way through into King Street. When in the 1850s a junction

95   *Charles Darwin's tutor, Prof. J.S. Henslow, was among the promoters of the Ipswich Museum which gave its name to Museum Street and provided a model for other later establishments of the kind in other parts of the country. In 1881 a new museum was opened in High Street, on the same day that the new Post Office and the new entrance lock to the Wet Dock were also opened. (John Wilton)*

was made between Museum Street and Thursby's Lane the eastern leg of the street was renamed Arcade Street, the name Museum Street being applied to the whole street from Westgate Street to the new Princes Street; the awkward junction between the two sections of Museum Street is thus explained as an afterthought.[8]

The opening of the new railway station at the north end of the tunnel in 1860 necessitated a new link with the town centre. Princes Street had originally been intended to run from the vicinity of the Cornhill to Friars Bridge, but progress was slow and it was still incomplete when the new station opened, a timber bridge being thrown across the river to carry a new Railway Station Road linking Princes Street and Birds Garden with the railway; in due course the whole route became known as Princes Street. Even in 1864, when William Hunt produced his *Handbook*, Princes Street was still unfinished, and 'looks very much like what it is—a street bored through a mass of houses, gardens, streets and lanes diagonally, leaving corners and angles of old buildings, dead walls with the marks upon them of gable ends dislodged, and bits of lanes running off at curious tangents'.[9]

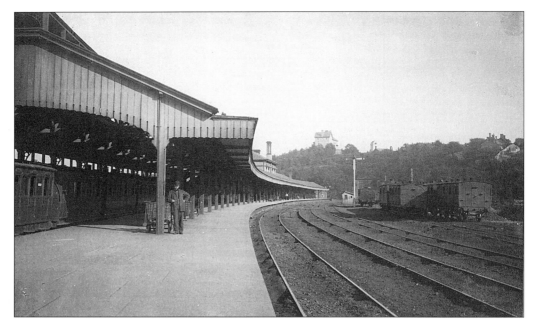

96   *The new Ipswich station looking towards the Stoke tunnel about 1880. Above and to the right of the signal can be seen Stoke windmill, which had by this time lost its sails.*

In 1856 the cattle market moved from what has since been known as the Old Cattle Market at the top of Silent Street to a new site on the marshes between the new Portman Road and Railway Station Road. The surface of the marsh was raised about two feet to provide a firm, dry site for the cattle pens.

Street Lighting

In the Middle Ages the illumination of the streets at night had been provided for by an order that all householders should keep a lantern in their windows throughout the hours of darkness, but such an expedient was no longer good enough for a developing 18th-century town. In 1793 Tavern Street was lighted with three different kinds of oil lamps to enable the paving commissioners to choose the most efficient. Their choice fell on Smythuril's patent lamps, and during the winter of 1793–4 almost 300 lamps were installed throughout the town.[10]

In 1817 three prominent Ipswich businessmen, Robert Ransome, his brother James, and John Talwin Shewell, the Tavern Street draper, put up £2,600 between them to supply Ipswich with gas. Aided by William Cubitt, who was at that time working with the Ransomes, they installed a gasmaking plant in a corner of the foundry in St Margaret's Ditches.[11] The Corporation was unwilling to grant permission for the laying of pipes in the streets, eventually giving consent only for them to be installed in Carr Street, Tavern Street and the Cornhill. The first domestic gas lamp in Ipswich was in due course lit ceremonially, if extravagantly, with a £1 note at Mr. Allen Ransome's home in Carr Street.

The first oil street lights were replaced by gas lamps in 1818, though it was not until 1863 that the last old oil lamp was replaced. There is a story that a chairman of the town council's paving and lighting committee laid down the dictum that the distance between street lamps should be such that a person standing midway between two lamps should be able to read the time by his watch.[12] The people of Ipswich soon saw the advantage of gas light, both for street lighting and for domestic use, and in 1821 the Ipswich Gas Light Company was incorporated by Act of Parliament.[13] One clause in the Act stipulated that gas for public lighting should always be such as to afford a cheaper and better light than oil. The company built a new gasworks on land bought from the River Commissioners beside the Orwell, in a position very convenient for the supply of coal by ship from the north-east coast.

97   *The gasworks was built in a very convenient position for receiving supplies of coal by sea, and towards the end of the 19th century received two hydraulic cranes for unloading vessels lying at the gasworks wharf.*

Dykes Alexander was the first chairman of the company, and the 201 shareholders included no fewer than 18 other members of the Alexander family as well as members of the Cobbold and Ransome families. One shareholder who played a leading part in the progress of the company was Daniel Poole Goddard, who took over as engineer and clerk when Cubitt resigned from the post in 1826. On his death in 1842 he was succeeded by his son Ebenezer Goddard, who in turn was succeeded in 1882 by his son Daniel Ford Goddard.

There were no gas meters in the early days, and the company contracted to supply gas for a given number of hours per night per half-year, the consumer undertaking to extinguish his light at a certain time. If he used the gas for a longer period he was expected to report the fact, and he would then be charged accordingly.[14]

Looking after the Poor

Daniel Ford Goddard had been engineer and clerk of the Ipswich Gas Light Company for only five years when he resigned to devote his time fully to public work, which in his case meant not only membership of the town council and service as Member of Parliament for the town for almost 24 years but the creation and operation of a remarkable social institution in the most deprived area of Ipswich. The Ipswich Social Settlement in Fore Street was an undenominational and non-political social centre which was intended to serve not just as a rallying point for the local community but as an influence which would permeate the whole town. When set up in 1896 it occupied a section of a row of part-medieval buildings, but before very long these premises gave way to a large brick building designed by local architects William Eade and Edwin Johns in what has been described as Edwardian free-style.[15] Not content with having spent a considerable fortune on setting up the Social Settlement and in providing fine modern premises in which its various activities could be carried on, Ford Goddard took a very active part in the everyday running of it.

A staunch member of Tacket Street Congregational Chapel, Ford Goddard declined to attend the usual civic service at St Mary-le-Tower when he was elected mayor in 1891. He also dispensed with the usual mayoral banquet, preferring to distribute dinners to the poor inhabitants.[16] He was knighted in 1907, partly in recognition of his work at the Social Settlement. In his social work Ford Goddard was following the example set by the Alexanders and Ransomes earlier in the century. The former family seemed to have an input into every philanthropic cause, being as lavish with their time and effort as with their money, and not confining themselves merely to local initiatives; Dykes Alexander enshrined their involvement in the anti-slavery campaign in the names of streets in his housing development between London Road and Handford Road.

As early as 1817 Ransomes established a relief society for their workmen which became known as the 'Old Sick Fund' and was succeeded by other similar 'clubs' providing for employees unable to work through sickness or injury. In the late 1840s a workmen's hall was founded at Orwell Works in which those who lived too far away to go home for meals might eat. It also provided a meeting place for the Mental Improvement Society, a form of evening class actively supported by the Ransomes on its formation in 1836. When writing of this society John Glyde commented that 'The employers have very wisely abstained from any interference in the management of the Society. They have sought to cultivate the feeling of self-dependence in the men engaged at the works …'.[17] To what extent were such efforts on the part of the employers appreciated by the workers? 'The ignorance in which the great mass of the working classes is sunk, is frequently and bitterly lamented by the few intelligent working men,' Glyde wrote, pointing out that although Ransomes employed as many as 1,200 men at times the average membership of the Mental Improvement Society was no more than 300, although the subscription was only a penny a week.[18]

The Ransomes were also supporters of the Mechanics' Institute, founded in 1824 for 'the instruction of the members in the principles of the arts they practice … and in the various branches of science and useful knowledge'. A library and reading room for members was set up in a former schoolroom in St Matthew's Church Lane belonging to Richard Dykes Alexander.[19] A year later a move was made to premises in the Buttermarket hired from Jabez Hare, one of the prime movers in the formation of the institution, who became librarian. The library grew largely through gifts from members and well-wishers, but it was found necessary to decline some offers; one particular volume was ordered to be placed under lock and key to prevent members having access to it. Later the committee was persuaded to initiate a museum after receiving from Daniel Poole Goddard 'a specimen of natural history, viz., a cat which was found starved to death in the roof of a building after having been missed five years'. The largest exhibit was the skeleton of a whale that had been stranded near Harwich—an embarrassment because of its size. Further embarrassment ensued when serious complaint was made that the starved cat had been thrown out without the consent or knowledge of the donor.[20]

The Mechanics' Institute made its final move to premises in Tavern Street in 1834, the former shop of Mr. Chapman, chemist, being purchased for £1,000 by a company of shareholders on the institute's behalf. It is still there, though the word 'mechanics' has been dropped from the title. Starting off with 210 members, the Mechanics' Institute grew until by the end of the century its membership approached 1,000. About the same number was claimed by the Working Men's College, inaugurated in 1864 and run by the energetic vicar of Wherstead, the Rev. F. Barham Zincke, in the Old Assembly Rooms further along Tavern Street. For an annual subscription of a half-crown members could attend evening classes in French, German and Latin, arithmetic, book-keeping, chemistry and a variety of other subjects.[21]

98   William Vick's photograph of the Working Men's College in Tavern Street, which occupied the former Old Assembly Rooms. The decorations date from the period when this was a fashionable gathering place not for working men but for the upper classes.

Besides all these there was a host of small organisations seeking to aid 'the deserving poor', from the Ipswich Penny Club whose object 'was to assist the working classes in providing useful clothing for their families' to the St Clement's Self-Help Society and the Society for the Encouragement of Industry. The latter might appear to be a local forerunner of the Confederation of British Industry, but in fact its object was 'to provide needlework during the winter months for poor women at their own homes, paying them for their labour'. There was little employment for local women in the mid-19th century 'except at their own special vocation—using the needle'.[22] However, nearly 1,000 women and girls were engaged in the stitching of stays, earning a pittance for their work.

Working men employed in one of the engineering works might have a steady job, but the labourer who was dependent on casual employment lived a hand-to-mouth existence, and so of course did his family. Temperance speakers might rant against 'the demon drink', but conditions in many homes were such that the companionship to be found in the beerhouse proved all too attractive to many working men. The temperance movement in Ipswich originated in 1835 when three soldiers called a public meeting at which George Greig, a trooper in a cavalry regiment then stationed in the town, called on his hearers to sign the pledge of total abstinence forthwith.[23] In 1840 the

Temperance Hall was erected at the expense of Richard Dykes Alexander on the corner of High Street and Crown Street; it later became an iron foundry where George Abbott made kitchen ranges.

Licensed premises were often the meeting place of the various 'benefit clubs' and friendly societies that sought to look after members in time of sickness or in old age. The aim was an excellent one, but in some cases the 'clubs' proved unequal to their task, the subscriptions being insufficient to meet the expenses; and in several instances the secretary absconded with the funds.[24] The town's seamen, no strangers to shipwreck, were among the earliest to join together to protect themselves against hardship. In 1826 the *Ipswich Journal* carried 'An appeal from the Seamen's Shipwreck Society To the Benevolent Inhabitants of Ipswich and its Vicinity'. Rather than merely appealing to charity the members of this society subscribed to a fund out of which shipwrecked members could be assisted. As time went by the objects of the organisation were broadened to looking after the needs of the widows and orphans of men lost at sea; the large banner carried by members in their anniversary weekend processions towards the end of the 19th century bore the slogan 'Here the widows & orphans find a friend'.[25]

A good deal was done in the course of the century to alleviate the position of working-class men and women, but as Glyde pointed out education was the key to improving what he called their 'moral and social condition'.

101   Trustees and members of the Ipswich Shipwrecked Seamen's Society on the march during one of their anniversary weekends. At the head of the procession two men carry a large model of the sailing vessel Adela.

Schools and Education

Education was important in Ipswich, a town in which in the Middle Ages boys and girls came of age legally when they reached the age of 14 and could count and measure. The grammar school cannot be traced in the town records earlier than 1477, but it seems likely that it had been in existence at least in the early 15th century, for Richard Penyngton (perhaps an ancestor of the 18th-century mapmaker Joseph Pennington) was described as 'late grammar school master of Ipswich' when in 1412 he was sued for assault by a butcher.[26] The grammar school was granted a charter in 1566 by Queen Elizabeth. At the beginning of the 19th century the school, still housed in the Blackfriars, was continuing to provide a classical education; it was left to other schools of less ancient establishment to furnish a practical education for children who looked forward to a career in commerce. A return to a House of Commons committee in 1818 revealed that there were 26 day schools in Ipswich with 1,395 scholars; four of these, including the grammar school, were endowed.[27]

The majority were private schools or 'academies' for girls as well as boys run largely by women, sometimes by a husband and wife jointly. In these schools the children of well-to-do businessmen and up-and-coming tradesmen received at least a semblance of education, either as day pupils or as boarders. Few of those who ran these establishments can have had the advanced views of a Mrs. Flowerdew, who in the early 19th century conducted an 'establishment' for a limited number of pupils at Ipswich and a 'seminary' for young ladies at Bury St Edmunds at which she and her daughters taught a number of subjects including history and Italian. 'Learning, in the usual sense of the word, is by no means necessary,' she wrote; 'we contend for no such thing, but let us regard young ladies as rational and accountable beings.'[28]

Many of the people who ran schools at that period would have scorned such a reasoned basis for their work, had they even been capable of taking it in. Worst of all were the day schools opened by 'persons not merely wanting the ability efficiently to instruct the young, but in many points totally unfitted'.[29] John Glyde characterised some of them as 'dame schools', and wrote of how their proprietors 'by means of a large cane and other injudicious modes, succeed in frightening the poor little things into keeping their tongues and limbs still for hours daily'. By the 1850s a number of clergymen and other philanthropists had set up infants' schools that were proving so successful that the dame school operators complained bitterly of 'ladies and gentlemen who try by large schools to prevent honest women from obtaining a small income'.[30]

102   The wooden statue of a Christ's Hospital boy was transferred when in 1841 a move was made from the old Blackfriars to premises on the Stoke side of the river.

There might or might not have been an Ipswich counterpart of Dotheboys Hall, but there can be no doubt that the teaching at some of the town's charity schools tended to be entirely practical. At Christ's Hospital, which from the time of Elizabeth I had been primarily concerned with 'maintaining, educating, bringing up, and apprenticing of poor boys', the pupils were set to spinning as a means of earning their keep. During the 18th century the administration by the Corporation of Christ's Hospital, which still occupied premises in the old Blackfriars, was as inefficient and lax as was so much of the Corporation business, but with the passing of the Municipal Reform Act this and other charities were placed in the hands of a board of trustees. In 1841 the trustees spent a considerable sum on repairs and alterations to Chenery Farm in Great Whip Street, a property belonging to the charity, and moved the major part of the school to those premises. There 40 boys were instructed in the Three Rs, and were 'occasionally employed in cultivating the extensive gardens attached to the hospital', leaving 16 boys in the Blackfriars where they seem to have received a somewhat inferior education.[31] Christ's Hospital School continued its work until 1883, when its endowments were merged with those of the grammar school, which had by then moved to new buildings in Henley Road. The foundation stone of the new school was laid by the Prince Consort on 4 July 1851, when he came to Ipswich to attend a meeting of the British Association for the Advancement of Science.

Early attempts at providing an education for poor children were very much bound up with religion, and those schools promoted by members of the Established Church excluded nonconformists. Earliest of these was the Grey Coat School for boys in Curriers Lane, opened in 1709 by 'several worthy gentlemen and clergymen. . .who considering that nothing in all human probability can contribute more to revive the practise of Christianity amongst us, than a careful instruction of youth in the grounds of their faith and duty … very generously contributed large sums towards the erecting and maintaining the schools'.[32] The associated Blue Coat School for girls was opened in 1710, but the education the girls received can only be described as second best. In 1737 a resolution was passed that 'Whereas the girls have for some years past been taught to write at considerable expense, without the written order of the Governors, it is now ordered that no girls henceforth be taught to write at the expense of the Society'.

103   The premises for Ipswich Grammar School in Henley Road, designed by Christopher Fleury in the Elizabethan style, were relatively new when this photograph was taken,though the ivy is already giving them an appearance of antiquity. A postman is obligingly posing for the photographer on the right. (John Wilton)

The success of the Grey Coat School depended less on the financial support of worthy gentlemen and tradesmen in communion with the Church than on the devoted service of James Franks, who was master for 43 years. For part of that time his wife Elizabeth was in charge of the Blue Coat School. James resigned in January 1874 'from failing health and strength' and died six weeks later.

A considerable proportion of those attending the Grey Coat School went to sea; in 1747 it was said that out of 68 boys who had left the school since 1739 no fewer than 29 had done so.[33] About 1840 a former pupil who had risen to master mariner bequeathed the charity £500, and it was decided that the interest on that sum should be devoted to teaching navigation to boys set on a career at sea. From then on James Franks was additionally teacher of navigation, with the promise that when the funds permitted he should have £3 for every boy taught navigation—they never did permit.

Excluded as they were from the charity schools and the various church schools, the dissenters set up their own. The Red Sleeve School was established at some time in the early 18th century by the Presbyterians and Episcopalians and the Green Sleeve School in 1736 by the Independents and Presbyterians, these charity schools all being known by the garb of the pupils.[34] The Red Sleeve and Green Sleeve schools came together in the 19th century when they merged with the Lancasterian School in Crown Street, established in 1811, three years after the setting up of the Royal Lancasterian Society, later known as the British and Foreign School Society. The girls had their Lancasterian school in Foundation Street, but in this case it was known as the Girls' School of Industry. Not far away was the Green Gown School, supported by the minister and congregation of Tacket Street Independent Chapel for the education of poor girls. The Baptists had a school in Stoke and the Wesleyans had theirs in Wykes Bishop Street, off Fore Hamlet.

A new British School was built in Turret Lane in 1848 to accommodate 230 boys, 173 girls and 125 infants. The relative figures of boys and girls is an indication of 19th-century attitudes. In the case of poor girls education was usually confined to teaching them such useful accomplishments as sewing. One establishment, the Ipswich District National Schools in St Matthew's Church Lane, 'respectfully informed' ladies 'that if they would send any plain work to the School, they would be materially contributing to the education of the Girls in one very important department, and that the Mistress would do her utmost to have every such Commission properly executed'.[35]

The National Schools were those connected with the National Society for the Education of the Poor in the Principles of the Established Church, formed in 1811. Children attending the Ipswich District National Schools set up in 1847 were not only required to attend church twice every Sunday throughout the year (including the holidays) but had to produce a certificate of baptism signed by a clergyman before they could be admitted to school.[36] Like the Grey Coat School, the one in St Matthew's Church Lane benefited from the devoted service of one man. In this case it was John Evans, who was headmaster from the opening of the school in 1847 until his death 40 years later. He was succeeded by his son Fred, who remained headmaster until 1919.

Another school that owed a very great deal to a single individual was the Ipswich Ragged School, which began operating in November 1849 in a cottage in St Clement's Church Lane thanks to the financial support of Richard Dykes Alexander. Anyone who was to teach 'a class of boys and girls who are prevented, either by their debased condition, by the worthlessness or criminality of their parents, or the tattered state of their garments, from receiving instruction at any previously existing school' had to be a very special person, and Joshua George Newman was just that. For 19 years he taught the most difficult of children, and achieved a great deal.[37] He was 30 when he came to Ipswich in 1851 to run a dormitory and training school supported by another set of subscribers. That project failed, but he stayed on as teacher of the Ragged School, teaching carpentry and woodwork as well as reading and writing. Photographs taken by R.D. Alexander show him superintending an apparently well-behaved class of boys chopping and bundling firewood; in fact the pupils were unruly, insubordinate and sometimes unmanageable.[38] With the help of his wife Deborah and a few volunteers Newman struggled to cope with large numbers of such youngsters. In 1859 he was said to have been coping single-handed with 135 children, 'and they receive the best instruction it is possible for one master to impart to so many'.

Following the inception in 1871 of the Ipswich School Board, formed under the provisions of the Forster Education Act of 1870, Newman was appointed the board's first school warden. His job as master of the Ragged School had gone as subscriptions to the Ragged School funds declined sharply, former subscribers believing falsely that the Forster Act had removed the need for such an establishment. The school building in Waterworks Street was offered to the school board and in 1872 became the board's first school, Waterworks Street Infants'. As was so often the case, after such devoted work for the least privileged children of the town Newman found himself on hard times. He was badly injured when thrown from a trap on Felixstowe Road, and as a result his appointment as school warden was terminated in 1877. The school board refused to vote him £10 out of its funds, but a subscription list was opened for him by some members of the board, doubtless those who had been supporters of the Ragged School. He died in 1881.

104   The Waterworks Street frontage of the Ipswich Ragged School, as extended after being taken over by the Ipswich School Board. The school was founded in 1849 to cater for children 'too poor, too ragged, too filthy, too ignorant, for ordinary instruction'.

The Ragged School building was handed back to its owners in 1873 and its educational work continued, though only as a Sunday school and in the evenings. New buildings for the Ragged School were erected in Bond Street at the beginning of the 20th century. Having opened its first, temporary, school in the old Ragged School premises, the school board embarked on an ambitious building programme. Schools for boys, girls and infants were built in Wherstead Road and Argyle Street and one for infants in Trinity Street in 1872; along with an existing girls' school in Trinity Street they provided accommodation for 2,063 children. By 1892 seven further schools had been added, bringing the total number of places available in the board schools to 4,598.[39]

Other schools, including the charity schools, the National and British schools and a number of parochial establishments, provided around 4,000 places in the 1890s. The time was coming when education would be available to all, but for some, especially girls, that education was to remain elementary in nature well into the 20th century. A pioneering development in improving the educational opportunities for girls came with the opening by the Girls' Public Day School Trust in the mid-1870s of the Ipswich High School for Girls. For some thirty years the school occupied the former Assembly Rooms in Northgate Street, moving to Westerfield Road in 1907.

Beer and Brewing

The old preoccupation with malting and brewing was as great in the 19th century as it had ever been; beer remained the principal drink of the working classes. Public houses

105 Old houses in St Mary Elms parish at the junction of Elm Street and Black Horse Lane in the mid-19th century, photographed by William Vick. Many of these timber-framed buildings survived into the 20th century, only to fall victim to slum clearance between the two world wars.

in Duke Street used to prepare for the rush of Ransomes' workers at dinnertime by lining up full glasses on the bar counters so that the foundrymen and others could quickly quench their thirst on the way home for their meal.

In 1844 there were no fewer than 18 maltsters and six brewers working in the town, and a decade later the number of brewers had more than doubled, though six of them appear to have been licensed victuallers with their own brewhouses rather than common brewers.[40] Pre-eminent among the common brewers, those who supplied the trade rather than merely brewing for consumption on the premises, was John Cobbold at Cliff Brewery. The half-dozen common brewers supplied more than 100 hotels, inns and taverns and about sixty beer houses in the town. Besides the well-remembered hostelries such as the *Coach and Horses, Cock and Pie, Crown and Anchor* and *Woolpack* there were forgotten houses like the *Chaise and Pair* in Woodbridge Road, the *Blue Bell* on the Cornhill and the *Ipswich Arms* in Lower Brook Street.

As the town grew, so did the number of licensed premises. In 1893 there were no fewer than 308 in the borough, and in spite of the temperance movement and the work of the Ipswich Moral Welfare League there were still 277 twenty years later, though some of them were mean little places. One of those in the Lower Wash (Lower Orwell Street), the *Blue Anchor*, had only a small bar and another small room normally accessible to the public, though at busy times customers were admitted to the family's single living room. A public house which does not appear in the directories was the *Sunk Light Inn*, an old vessel lying in a mud berth between the Cobbold brewery and Greenwich Farm around the middle of the 19th century. Large-scale maps of that period show that it was reached by a staging and a flight of steps. Perhaps it was an old light vessel; the Sunk lightship marks the entrance to the East Swin, some 12 nautical miles from Harwich.

Some of the Ipswich breweries were doubtless as small and ill-equipped as the taverns they supplied, but in 1856 Charles Cullingham & Co. opened a new 'steam brewery' on land that had once been gardens between Upper Brook Street and Tacket Street. Equipped with the very latest in brewing technology, the brewery had an adjunct in Upper Brook Street, the *Steam Brewery Inn*. The Cullingham brewery was bought by the three sons of the 1st Baron Tollemache of Helmingham in 1888; almost seventy years later the Tollemache and Cobbold breweries were to amalgamate. Four years after the aristocratic Tollemaches entered brewing the Cobbold family began the building of a new brewery that might also have been described as a 'steam brewery', for it had a steam engine produced by E.R. & F. Turner. The new brewery was designed by William Bradford, senior partner of a London firm of architects and consulting engineers, who a decade earlier had been responsible for the Unicorn Brewery in Foundation Street, built by Ipswich builders J.B. & F. Bennett for Catchpole & Co.

Besides being maltsters and brewers, the Cobbolds had commercial interests that spread into shipowning and banking. When the Blue Bank, founded in Tavern Street about 1786 by C.A. Crickett, J. Kerridge and William Truelove, failed in 1825 the Cobbolds put new capital into the business to save it from collapse. In 1839 the family also became involved in the Harwich bank founded by Charles Cox about 1775. Both John Cobbold and his son John Chevallier Cobbold became partners in the Blue Bank, and when John Cobbold died in 1860 his place in the partnership was taken by his grandson, John Patteson Cobbold.[41]

Not satisfied with all his other activities, including the chairmanship of the Eastern Union Railway Company throughout its life, J.C. Cobbold represented Ipswich in Parliament from 1847 to 1868. His public service to the town was recognised in 1875 when he was appointed High Steward, a most honourable position which he held until his death in 1882. One of J.C. Cobbold's sons, Felix Thornley Cobbold, entered Parliament in 1885 and was Mayor in 1896. He was instrumental in persuading the Corporation to construct the Fore Street Baths, opened in 1894, not only giving the land on which the swimming pool was built but providing £1,200 towards the building costs. Perhaps his greatest legacy to the town was Christchurch Mansion, which he presented in 1895 on condition that the Corporation bought the park.[42]

Water Supply and Drainage

The Cobbolds not only supplied good beer to the town but also provided a good many inhabitants with water from the springs of Holywells. In 1848 'Mr. Cobbold's water-heads, situated at the back of Holywells Gardens', supplied about 600 houses and were said to be second in importance among the town supplies to the Corporation springs in St Helen's, which supplied a large part of the town centre.[43] The Corporation's main supply was the springs in the Cauldwell Hall area which in the past had run down what is now known as Spring Road, through St Helen's and so into the Wash and to the Orwell. G.R. Clarke described these 'never-failing springs' in glowing terms, saying that the water was 'of so fine a quality as to excite the admiration of every person who tastes it':

106   One of the ponds at Holywells from which the Cobbolds supplied water to parts of the town. Holywells mansion, now demolished, can be seen in the background.

The various streams are collected into about a dozen different brick buildings, most of them arched over; from whence they are carried into two main pipes, one running on the left-hand side of Car-street, and another on the right-hand side of the same street. From these mains, quills, or smaller pipes, are laid on, branching off in all directions; and the water is carried to the intermediate parts of the town …[44]

When Henry Austin, who was consulting engineer to the Metropolitan Commissioner of Sewers, reported on the sanitary condition of Ipswich in 1848 he found the water supply sadly fragmented. Besides the Corporation springs and the Holywells water-heads there were seven smaller water undertakings each serving from 50 to 380 houses and a few public pumps. The various waterpipes were pierced with plugged holes through which water could be obtained to fight fires, but the amount of water that could be procured in this way was often too small to be of any real use. When fire broke out at the printing office of the *Ipswich Express* in the Buttermarket one bitterly cold night in January 1848 'the neighbouring plugs proved utterly useless, there not being pressure from the water-heads to produce a supply', but the situation was saved by W.C. Fonnereau opening the sluices of his ponds in Christchurch Park and sending a cascade of water down into Upper Brook Street, where a rough dam was thrown across the street to supply the fire engines.[45] Later the same year, when Ransons paper mill in St Clement's Back Street (now Waterworks Street) was destroyed by fire, putting 200 people out of work, much time was spent in obtaining water from the Wet Dock.

Though there was a relatively good supply of clean water to most parts of the town, there were few if any drains to clear away either storm water or sewage. Austin commented that the bad effects of the many cesspools, foul gutters and bad surface drains were as evident in Ipswich as in any town, but Ipswich had one advantage over many large towns, and this arose 'from the fact that the excrementitious matter is of sufficient value in the neighbourhood as manure to render it worth tolerably punctual removal'. The lack of proper drainage meant that much of the water supplied by the various water undertakers ran to waste through the streets. 'The foul matters which now abound in the Town for want of proper drainage are thus kept in a constant state of damp and decomposition,' Austin wrote, 'perpetually giving forth foul and poisonous emanations, and the site of the Town, and the foundations of the houses, are in many parts and in many seasons kept in a state of unwholesome damp and discomfort, from flood and soakage of the soil.'[46]

There was little improvement in the next quarter-century, to judge from the first report made to the town council by Dr. George Elliston after becoming the town's first Medical Officer of Health in 1874:

> The town contains a great many old and dilapidated dwellings, built with total disregard to the comfort and wants of the persons occupying them. . .the sanitary conditions of many of the courts and yards are in a very dirty and neglected state. The sewers are defective, and the drainage and water supply in a deplorable state. Typhoid Fever has been prevalent throughout the whole year, principal causes being the air poisoned by foul emanations from drains and sewers and pollution of the drinking water.

Diarrhoea was, as Dr. Elliston put it, 'always fatally prevalent in Ipswich every autumn', and when he made his report it had just killed 54 people, all but four of them children under five. Tuberculosis was the major cause of death, followed by heart disease and diarrhoea. Such were the conditions in some parts of the town that typhoid was also a killer disease, taking a toll of 17 lives in 1873–4.

Early in the same winter there was a typhoid epidemic in Whitton which began with four cases in Bedwell's Court, a group of ten houses not far from the Whitton Maypole. Eight of the houses were built back-to-back, with doors and windows only in the front of the house, and in those eight two-room houses lived 49 of the 61 residents. The well was found to be polluted, but as there was no other supply the residents continued to use it, and by 3 November the number of cases had reached eighteen. Dr. Elliston arranged for a water-cart to be made available each morning and the polluted well was sealed up, to remain so for three months. Eventually there were 25 cases at Bedwell's Court, including the head nurse, 'who was removed with another patient to the fever ward at the Workhouse', plus three at the Crown and two others. Five people died, including three members of one family.

The remedy was to be found in an improved supply of fresh water and in efficient drainage, but in the mid-19th century the town had no adequate sewerage system. In 1857 Peter Bruff, whom we have already met as a railway engineer, was commissioned by the Corporation to design a full-scale drainage system for the town, but there were as usual those who objected to money being spent even on so beneficial a scheme as that, and nothing was done. It was only in 1881–2 that the first effective step was taken towards providing the town with a satisfactory system of drainage with the construction

107   Upper and Lower Brook Street took their name from the brook that once flowed down them from the ponds in Christchurch Park. Heavy rain occasionally turns the clock back, as on this occasion at the beginning of the 20th century when water poured down the roadway to reach the Orwell.

of the main low-level sewer which ran through the heart of the town to outfall tanks on the bank of the Orwell some distance below the built-up area. On completion of the project, which cost £60,000, members of the Corporation and their guests were entertained to luncheon in a covered reservoir at the works. During the opening celebrations members of the Corporation and those connected with the building of the sewer, including Bruff, posed for their photograph with the mayor, Mr. A. Wrinch.[47]

The raw sewage was roughly screened by a revolving belt driven by an undershot waterwheel before being passed to settlement tanks. Even in normal conditions only a small proportion of the solids were removed before the treated sewage was discharged to the river; at times of heavy rainfall the works was apt to be overwhelmed and raw sewage found its way into the Orwell. The building of further sewers to serve other parts of the town at a total cost of £30,000 did nothing to ease the pressure on the already inadequate treatment works.

Housing in Ipswich

John Glyde tells us in his survey of the town that Ipswich had 263 streets, roads, lanes, courts and inhabited yards, of which 142 streets, roads and lanes were, as he put it, thickly inhabited. 'In some of these streets the settling of the water into the soil renders the houses quite damp,' he says.

In the upper part of St Margaret's, in many parts of St Matthew's, and in several other districts, dead wells abound. In St Matthew's parish alone nearly 300 houses, more than one-third of the entire number, have no other means of drainage, and 70 dwellings are without even this means of carrying off the waste …

The demoralizing practice of providing but one convenience for several houses is here seen in full force … The ventilation of the courts is bad, their situation often very confined, and the entrance in some instances narrow. Some of their houses are situated back to back. Above 500 of them have no back doors; and, in the major portion, the rooms are so small that, where they are occupied by families, they cannot fail of being crowded in the sleeping apartments.[48]

Glyde's measured prose does not, perhaps, give the full flavour, the full horror, of these awful housing areas, so far removed in condition if not in distance from the fine villas and terraces of Fonnereau Road, Berners Street and Henley Road. William Hunt wrote in 1864 of 'wretched plaster huts, such as only the descendants of the inhabitants of the squalid part of old towns would consent to live in; and in courts out of sight of the passer by are still worse tenements, such as are happily disappearing by degrees from the town.'[49]

The situation was undoubtedly exacerbated by the trebling of population between 1801 and 1851. Many of the new residents were country people attracted by the prospect of employment in the town's thriving industrial concerns. As the population grew the town expanded beyond the ancient ramparts and the medieval extramural suburbs. The new population 'spread itself out East and West, invading large gardens, pastures, and arable country; building suburban residences on the high roads; making colonies of cottages, in short straight streets intersecting each other, and becoming confusing by their number and their great similarity', William Hunt tells us.

Over the water too, past the dirty ancient suburb [by which he means 'Over Stoke', as it has been known to generations of Ipswich people] a small town of cottages has been built; while to the north, where until the last few years the town scarcely extended beyond the line of the old rampart, the wealthiest portion of the commercial population have taken possession almost to the brow of the hill, and built themselves residences which, if they do not rival in quaint oak carving, the dwellings which the merchant princes of Ipswich built for themselves in the lower part of the town in the Elizabethan days, more than equal them in dignity, in boldness of architecture, in spaciousness, and in their general adaptation to the comfort and enjoyment of the residents.[50]

However enthusiastic Hunt might have been about the comfort of the houses built by the wealthy, the terraces of little cottages put up by speculative builders for the working-class population in areas such as the Potteries had little to commend them. The Potteries, studied so effectively by Frank Grace,[51] took its name from the Rope Walk Pottery occupied in 1864 by George Schulen, 'manufacturer of Glazed Pipes and every description of Brown Earthenware'. It was in this area, in New Street, that Dr. Elliston found individual rooms in 'old and dilapidated houses' let out to families who

108   Cranfields' mills appear in the background of this William Vick view of St Peter's Dock, just below Stoke Bridge. Almost all the vessels to be seen are sailing craft; in the foreground are spritsail barges, with a big boomie barge alongside the mills and a three-masted barque on the other side of the dock at Flint Wharf.

lived, cooked, ate and slept in the one room, sometimes without any water supply. The Medical Officer of Health commented on the profits that might be made by a proprietor who paid £10 a year for a five-roomed house and let each room at up to four shillings and sixpence a week.[52]

Having heard how bad much of the housing was in the 19th century, it might seem surprising that the Ipswich and Suffolk Freehold Land Society, an organisation which came into being in 1849, the year of the California gold rush, was not at first primarily concerned with the provision of better housing.[53] The establishment of this society was a political matter. The Reform Act of 1832 had enfranchised the middle classes, but the artisans, as they were known to their Victorian contemporaries, did not obtain the vote until much later. The Chartist movement had failed, and only by acquiring a freehold worth at least 40 shillings (£2) a year could a man obtain the vote.

In the ordinary way this was beyond the reach of the working man, but it was realised that there were ways of making the 40-shilling suffrage available. R.D. Alexander, Quaker banker, philanthropist and early photographer, was one of those who realised the possibilities; he became first president of the Ipswich and Suffolk Freehold Land Society when it was formed with the object of improving the social position and promoting the moral elevation of the unenfranchised population, to quote the prospectus of the society, issued on 1 December 1849.[54] The idea was that working people should be encouraged to invest their small savings and that the society should use the accumulated money to buy large freehold estates, which would be divided into

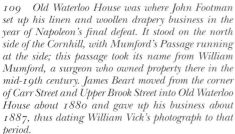

109 Old Waterloo House was where John Footman set up his linen and woollen drapery business in the year of Napoleon's final defeat. It stood on the north side of the Cornhill, with Mumford's Passage running at the side; this passage took its name from William Mumford, a surgeon who owned property there in the mid-19th century. James Beart moved from the corner of Carr Street and Upper Brook Street into Old Waterloo House about 1880 and gave up his business about 1887, thus dating William Vick's photograph to that period.

110 The same scene in 1979 with the rather ornate buildings by T.W. Cotman that replaced Old Waterloo House in 1890. Mumford's Passage has disappeared, but its place has been taken by Lloyd's Avenue, cut through Cotman's buildings in about 1930 to allow trolleybuses to approach the Cornhill directly from Tower Ramparts. The trolleybuses ceased running in 1963, but motor buses and other traffic continued to use Lloyd's Avenue until plans were put into effect to give pedestrians priority in the town centre.

plots large enough to confer on the owner the right of voting. These plots would be allotted to members at cost price.

Very shortly after the formation of the Freehold Land Society other more or less similar organisations were established in Ipswich, one of them being the Suffolk Improved Building and Investment Company and another the Ipswich Permanent Benefit Building Society. The latter might be said to have been born on 4 January 1850, at the home of William Hutchinson in Soane Street, but it was not until seven months later that a preliminary committee meeting was held at Alfred Cobbold's office in Tower Street; it had been thought wise to delay proceeding with the organisation 'in consequence of the delinquencies of Thomas Smeeton, the Secretary of two other Societies in this town'. Nevertheless, the Ipswich Permanent was formed, and celebrated its centenary in 1950.[55]

The Cauldwell Hall estate, on the eastern outskirts of Ipswich between Foxhall Road and Woodbridge Road, was the first property to be acquired by the Freehold Land Society. Under the original rules the society had no power to purchase land, and the Cauldwell Hall estate was in fact sold by John Edward Todd to John Footman, the draper, William Dillwyn Sims, partner in Ransomes and Sims, and William Fraser, a woollen draper, for the use of the society.[56] The 98¾ acres of the Cauldwell Hall estate cost the society £50 10s. an acre. Roads were laid out, and the land was divided into 282 allotments of from 45 to 61 rods, which were transferred to members for £23 each, this price including the cost of making the roads. The method of allotting plots was by ballot; two sets of numbered balls were used, one set relating to the numbered plots and the other to a numbered list of members.

A map drawn by Christopher Fleury, the society's surveyor, shows the layout of the plots; two copies in the archives of the society are marked with the allottees' names, and show that some people received as many as six or seven plots. Five people had six plots each, four people had five, 11 had four and 12 had three. It seems likely that these multiple owners were mainly speculators who built houses for renting. A copy of this map 'With names of Allottees written on Allotments for Mr Daniel' has the note

Names in Red Ink will pay up
Names in Black Ink will not pay up.

The fading of age has mixed the sheep with the goats. The failure of members of a national Land Society to continue their payments after they had received their allotment of land brought that organisation down, but the Ipswich and Suffolk Freehold Land Society somehow overcame that difficulty.

To begin with not everyone receiving a plot built a house on it. Some simply used their land as an allotment garden, though others did build small flint-walled dwellings on the back of the plots, with market gardens out in front. So busy was the scene in the early days that the area soon became known as 'the Diggings', a nickname that was changed before very long to California. The development is unlikely to have succeeded to any great extent in its original intention of enfranchising the working class. Many of those who contributed in the early days were relatively well-to-do people; some might have put in money in order to encourage the society in its aims, but most almost certainly saw investment in land on the outskirts of the town as an excellent long-term prospect.

A study of the Census returns over a number of decades illustrates the development of the Cauldwell Hall estate, which formed part of St Margaret's parish. In 1821 there were 3,214 residents in the parish, and by 1841 the population had increased to 4,539; in mid-century it was 5,892, and then in the next 20 years it soared to 9,615, largely as a result of the development at California. In the 1851 Census only 22 houses containing 100 people were listed under Cauldwell Hall, but ten years later there were 179 houses and 788 people. Of those 179 households, 68 had come to California from other areas of the town. By 1871 there were 228 houses and 1,060 people in the area, which was still developing apace, not only on the land acquired by the FLS. In time the entire area became built up, and it is today barely conceivable that in the beginning the idea of developing an estate so far from the centre of town was greeted with such derision.

Even in the 1870s when George Tomline built the railway line from Westerfield to Felixstowe the Corporation of Ipswich objected strongly to the placing of a station at Derby Road; the mayor and members of the Corporation told the Board of Trade inspector, Colonel Tyler, that such a station was so isolated as to be useless.

The Freehold Land Society seems to have made a small but useful profit on the sale of the Ipswich land, and it proceeded to purchase further areas in Bury St Edmunds, Stutton and Wickham Market. These were disposed of in the usual way as plots, but in 1866 the society decided to operate as a building society; that is, the society itself would build houses on its estates and sell them to members selected by ballot. The first houses to be built by the society were those in Palmerston Road and Lancaster Road, off St Helen's in Ipswich. These 'pretty and substantial six-room cottages' were sold for £145 each.

Brickmaking

The scale of town development naturally gave rise to a considerable demand for bricks, almost all supplied from works in and around the town itself or from brickyards in nearby villages. Bricks and tiles had been made in Ipswich for several centuries, and the trade received a boost as the town expanded.[37]

In 1771 there was a kiln in St Helen's parish occupied by a William Robinson, who advertised 'Pots for the Cure of Smokey Chimneys, adapted for 9 to 12 and 14-inch Funnels, as good as any in London; also fine Rubbing Bricks and black Cornice, red Pantiles and glazed ditto, and all sorts of Bricks and Tyles'. Rubbing bricks were soft fine-textured bricks which could be abraded to shape by the bricklayer for use over windows and in other positions where special shapes were required. Not far away Holy Trinity Church, built in 1835 to serve a part of St Clement's parish whose population was growing apace, gave its name to the Trinity Brickworks between Fore Hamlet and Back Hamlet. In 1874 John Morgan & Company was producing chimney pots and drainpipes 'for agricultural and sanitary purposes' as well as bricks in this yard, which was taken over in 1890 by Joseph Bird & Son, who had earlier been coal merchants at Stoke Bridge. The Trinity brickyard continued in use until about 1910, and during the First World War hangars were built in the pit for the construction by Ransomes of aircraft for the Royal Flying Corps.

Other brickyards operated on the other side of Bishops Hill where Myrtle Road was later laid out, on Hog Highland, Over Stoke, in the Cemetery Road area, and between Woodbridge Road and Spring Road, the last-named having found its memorial in the *Brickmakers Arms* public house in Spring Road. Two of the later and larger brickworks, the Valley Brickworks in Foxhall Road and the Dales Brickworks, were served by rail, the latter by a three-quarter-mile-long line which ran from the East Suffolk line near Westerfield station to the Grove Brickworks and on under the Henley Road to the bigger works. One parapet of the Henley Road bridge still exists. The Dales Brickworks was operated until 1901 by F. Rosher & Company, who also had lime works and a

111   The brickworks on Hog Highland at the beginning of the 20th century, with the kilns at the far end. One of the Great Eastern Railway steamers is nearing the end of its passage from Harwich, and across the river can be seen the Waterside Works of Ransomes & Rapier.

cement factory in Kent, and from that year by Bolton and Laughlin. The Grove Brickworks had ceased production by the turn of the century, but the Dales Brickworks remained in production until 1959, the last batch of 40,000 hand-made bricks being fired in that year. There were other brickyards to the north of the town at Broom Hill and Whitton.

Public Transport

As Ipswich grew far beyond the bounds of the old town there arose a need for public transport. When all the workers in the foundries and factories lived within a quarter-mile of their workplaces they could walk home for dinner, even pausing for a thirst-quencher on the way, but as the population grew and houses spread further out many found themselves unable to walk home and to return within the limits of their dinner hour.

The first attempt to provide public transport was a horse tramway scheme put forward in 1879. Like almost every other forward-looking proposal in Ipswich history this was opposed by some townsfolk, who managed to ensure that the section from Barrack Corner to Major's Corner was omitted from the plans as put into effect. Ipswich was to have a transport system which avoided the town's main streets.[58] The first line was laid from the railway station to Cornhill in the spring of 1880, but the contractor became bankrupt, holding up progress for a time. A single-deck tram was delivered

*112   A mid-19th-century view of the corner of the
Buttermarket and Queen Street. Towards the right are
the premises of Hutchinson, wig maker and ornamental
hair manufacturer.*

*113   A late 20th-century photograph of the same
corner. It is not only the buildings that have changed.*

during August, however, and the Mayor and Town Clerk rode on a trial trip, during
which the car was derailed, to the delight of the cabbies at the cab rank on Cornhill.
It was October before the tramway opened
to the public.

Another route, opened in March 1881,
diverged from the original one and ran
up Portman Road to Barrack Corner and
thence along Norwich Road to Brooks
Hall Road. The first promoters had been
from London, but during 1881 the Ipswich
Tramways Company was incorporated by
an Act of Parliament which authorised a
further route from Barrack Corner to
Cornhill, opened the following year. A
service from Major's Corner to Derby
Road Station began operating in 1883, the
two-horse double-deck cars having to be
assisted by a trace horse up the slope of St
John's Road. For a year this section of the
tramway was isolated from the rest of the

*114   The tiled wooden shed that once housed the horse
trams, seen about 1980 when the former tram depot in
Quadling Street was in use as a haulier's depot. The
rails can be seen running into the shed, although in
the entrance to the yard they had been concreted over.
The complex was cleared to make way for Cardinal
Park and its multiplex cinema.*

115   *Looking down on the dock area from the tower of Broughton Place in Belstead Road, a photograph dating from 1892. Although a smoke haze obscures the distance, many landmarks can be picked out. In the left foreground is the railway goods depot. The tower of St Peter's Church is prominent in the middle of the picture, and the white-painted weatherboard of the Eastern Union Mills stands out beside the river; part of this complex is the former Stoke tidemill, recognisable by its double-pitched roof. Immediately beyond the mills is the R. & W. Paul warehouse that was destroyed in a spectacular blaze in April 2000. Stoke Bridge is on the extreme right.*

system, but a link to Cornhill was ready in time for the Suffolk Show on Christchurch Park in the summer of 1884.

This might have seemed a victory for the tramway company over those who endeavoured to keep the trams out of the town centre, but in a rearguard action a tradesman with a horse and trap held up a tram in Carr Street for no less than 28 minutes.

In spite of problems over the tramway company's responsibility for repairing that section of roadway in which the lines were laid—the company's inability to pay the Corporation's repair bill in 1893 resulted in the tramcars being withdrawn for two weeks—the tramway operated satisfactorily until competition arrived in 1898 in the form of the Ipswich Omnibus Service. The introduction of the red horse-drawn 'Penny Omnibuses' was not the only problem looming for the horse trams; in 1897 the Corporation obtained authority to establish an electricity undertaking, and it was only a matter of time before it would seek authority to provide an electric tramway service. The Ipswich Corporation Tramways Act of 1900 gave the local authority that power.

XIII

The 20th Century

King Edward VII was proclaimed with all due ceremony on Cornhill on 21 January 1901 and the horse trams ceased running on 6 June 1903; the streets of Ipswich were to gain a new look in the Edwardian age. The roadworks involved in lifting the old horse tram rails and replacing them by new 3ft. 6in. gauge track for electric trams created quite a lot of problems, but the absence of the horse trams was compensated for by the operation of the horse buses.[1] Only five days after the withdrawal of the horse trams the whole stock of the old undertaking was sold at auction. The depot in Quadling Street became a haulier's depot, and remained so until it was demolished to make way for Cardinal Park; the tramcars found new uses as chicken coops and garden sheds.

Car sheds were built alongside the corporation's electricity generating station in Constantine Road. Steam for the Ipswich-built Reavell high-speed engines powering the generators was produced by a refuse destructor at the back of the site; power from waste is not as new as some would have us believe. The first trial trip took place late at night on 10 November 1903 and public services on the Whitton to Ipswich Station and Bourne Bridge route began on 23 November. Other routes were opened at intervals over the following six months, the lines eventually extending to more than ten miles. To make way for the trams a number of streets had to be widened.

Because the Board of Trade had set itself against allowing trams using the 3ft. 6in. gauge to be roofed, and because roofed double-deck trams would have been unable to pass under the railway bridges in Norwich Road and Wherstead Road, the Ipswich trams were open-topped. In wet weather the upper deck was shunned by passengers, who crowded into the lower saloon until they were packed like sardines in a lurching, jolting tin.

First engineer and manager of the tramway undertaking was Frank Ayton, who was an enthusiast for electric traction and saw the possibilities of battery-operated vehicles such as the lorries built by Ransomes, Sims & Jefferies as early as 1914. It was due to his influence that Ipswich became the first town to operate a municipal charging station for battery

116   Ipswich Corporation Tramways car no. 26 in its green and cream livery outside the Station Hotel *in Burrell Road. The trams were built by the Brush Electrical Engineering Co. Ltd., of Loughborough, and the motors and electrical equipment by the Westinghouse Company.*

199

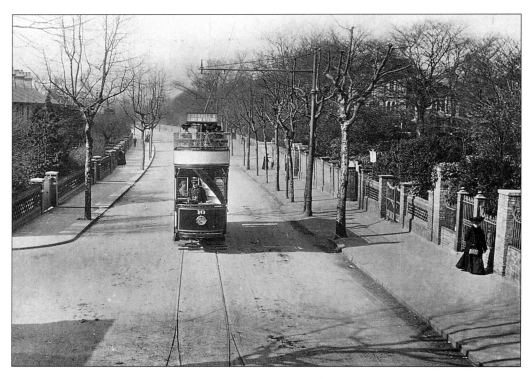

117   Tramcar no. 10 approaching the point in Norwich Road where the single 3ft. 6in. track splits into double track. It is on its way to Cornhill and thence to Derby Road Station. Three-fifths of the system was single track.

vehicles. In 1921 he left the corporation to join Ransomes, who were soon producing trolleybuses.[2] These vehicles, known at first as 'trackless trams', provided an economical replacement for the trams. Three trolleybuses were hired by the corporation from the Railless Company of Rochester in 1923, proving so successful that the following year Ransomes' first trolleybus was purchased. The takeover was rapid, and by 1926 the trams were being scrapped in Norwich Road as the first 30 'trolleys', 15 built by Ransomes and the rest by Garretts of Leiston, took over the various routes. Thenceforth the trolleybuses dominated the streets until 1963.

The first bus services in the rural areas served from Ipswich were introduced by the Great Eastern Railway between Ipswich Station and Shotley in 1905, while petrol-engined and petrol-electric buses were put on the road between Ipswich and nearby towns and villages in the summer of 1919 by Thomas Tilling, which soon became the Eastern Counties Road Car Company.

Nostalgia has clothed the Edwardian period in an aura of high living, but for many it was a period of struggle against poverty. In 1913 the *Evening Star* organised a competition open to the wives of labourers living in the town and earning less than £1 a week, with a prize of a sovereign for the best description of how to bring up a family on 'a quid a week'. 'We live very plainly, but we are all strong and healthy,' said the winner of the sovereign, a woman living in the California area of Ipswich. Plain living it certainly was, for the woman had eight children, the eldest 15 years old and the youngest as many months. Her husband gave her 18s. out of his £1 earnings, and the older children earned 6s. 9d. a week between them, of which they were allowed a shilling for pocket money. Her shopping list, containing no luxuries of any kind, plus the rent of 4s. 3d., came to just £1 3s. 8d., leaving a penny to be saved for the rainy day that was almost sure to come. That family fed well in spite of the low income, but another entrant told how she sometimes bought two pennorth of fat and lean pork: 'Father have that,' she said, 'mother only smell it.'

118 Trolleybus no. 13 soon after the introduction of the 'trackless trams'. One of the first 15 trolleybuses built for the Corporation by Ransomes Sims & Jefferies, no. 13 has solid-tyred wheels which were later replaced by pneumatic tyres.

However impoverished some of those who worked in Ipswich were, there were still many newcomers seeking their fortunes in the town's industries. The first Census of the new century showed that the population of Ipswich had grown to 66,630, and in the next decade it increased by another 7,000. The county borough (it had been raised to that status under the Local Government Act of 1888) was on the way to becoming a thriving modern county town and business centre. Engineering was the biggest employer of all, Ransomes, Sims & Jefferies alone having 3,000 workers. Another considerable employer was the business founded in 1790 as a wholesale tobacconist at Hyde Park Corner, close to where the West Gate had stood. Several generations of the Churchman family expanded the business, producing cigarettes in addition to the cigars and pipe tobacco that had been the staple product, until in 1898 the firm moved to a new factory at the junction of Princes Street and Portman Road. In days when cards were used to stiffen the cigarette packets Churchmans issued sets of cards with East Anglian subjects.

Coachbuilding had been a thriving trade in the 19th century when Edwin Quadling turned to building railway carriages as well as horse-drawn vehicles, and eight firms were still active in the town in the 1900s, turning their skills to the new motor cars. The largest of them, started by William Botwood in 1870, was by the turn of the century engaged in the export trade, producing special carriages for use in the colonies and even rickshaws.[3] There were also the flour mills of Cranfield Brothers, established in 1884, the oil mills of George Mason, who took over Handford Mill in 1873 and had more modern seed-crushing mills in the dock area, and the clothing factory of Phillips and Piper which employed some 600 people.

In Ranelagh Road, a 19th-century highway linking the railway station with Hadleigh Road, was the works of William Reavell & Co. Ltd., set up in 1898 to build high-speed totally enclosed steam engines of a design patented in 1894 by Reavell and W.H. Scott. From about 1908 the firm turned to the production of air-compressing machinery, for which it built up a great reputation. When the British Diesel Company was set up in 1912 the site chosen for the works in which the German-designed oil engines would be made was on the western outskirts of Ipswich, not very far from Reavells. Dr. Rudolf Diesel was on his way to the new works when he disappeared from the SS *Dresden*, one of the Great Eastern Railway steamers, as it made its way from Antwerp to Harwich on the night of 29-30 September 1913.

As the Diesel works went up on what was later to become the Hadleigh Road industrial estate, turmoil in the Balkans was pushing Europe towards war. As the crisis deepened on 3 August 1914 knots of people gathered outside newsagents' shops and outside the local newspaper office in Carr Street, eagerly reading the telegrams that were posted up in the windows regarding the situation in Europe. Crowds assembled towards nightfall, the biggest gathering of all being on the Cornhill, where a 'Stop the War' meeting was held by those who felt the European conflict was no business of Britain. It appears that not everyone there shared the views of the speakers. The outbreak of war found many Ipswich people at the seaside; it had become the custom for families to take the tram to Derby Road, from where the Great Eastern ran a shuttle service to Felixstowe Town, carrying passengers by the thousand each August Bank Holiday. The holiday crowds were thinned as reservists were called to the colours, and before the end of the year there was grief for many Ipswich families when the 2nd. Suffolks lost 720 men killed, wounded or missing at Le Cateau in a gallant stand that prevented the German troops from sweeping on towards Paris. In November King George V was in the Ipswich area visiting other East Anglian units as they prepared for action.

As the Orwell Works turned from ploughs and lawnmowers to munitions, 1,600 Ransomes employees joined the forces, their places being taken by women workers entering an engineering works for the first time. In the course of the war 130 of those men gave their lives; one who survived, Sgt. A.F. Saunders, won the V.C. The presence in the town of the Diesel works, taken over early in 1915 by Vickers, meant that Royal Navy submarines were often to be seen in the dock, where they were berthed during refits. Ten visited Ipswich in 1915, another 26 in 1916 and 18 the following year.

Ipswich was twice attacked by German Zeppelins, the first time on 30 April 1915. The Goldschmidt incendiary bombs dropped on that occasion started fires which kept the whole of the town's fire brigade busy, but they failed to spread terror among the inhabitants; residents in one street used 'domestic utensils' to deal with a bomb which fell in the roadway, according to a newspaper report. The second attack, on 31 March 1916, had more serious consequences, as one of the bombs dropped by L.15 fell at the back of the Customs House, killing a man who was standing outside the *Gun* public house at the bottom of the Lower Wash. The L.15 went on to attack London but, damaged both by AA fire and by the weapons of a British fighter, the airship descended into the Thames Estuary; the 14 survivors of her crew were picked up by the minesweeping trawler HMS *Olivine*.[4]

Some of the aircraft used on anti-Zeppelin patrols were built by Ransomes, Sims & Jefferies at premises erected in the brickearth pit of the Trinity Brickworks, which after the war was used as the firm's new lawnmower works. The White City, as this works became known, turned out large numbers of FE.2b fighters and also 400 Airco D.H.6 aircraft, known to pilots as the 'Widow Maker' because of their unsavoury reputation. Ransomes were also to have built the Vickers Vimy bomber, but this order was cancelled at the end of the war. Altogether 790 aeroplanes were built before production ceased.[5] According to a letter sent to Ransomes the first FE.2b built by the company was involved in the shooting down of the Zeppelin L.48, which crashed at Theberton on 17 June 1917.

As in the Dutch wars of the 17th century Ipswich found itself caring for large numbers of casualties, brought to the town this time by ambulance train. Between the outbreak of war and mid-1919 the East Suffolk and Ipswich Hospital received 7,777 casualties, the accommodation at the Anglesea Road hospital being supplemented by the use of Broadwater, a large house in Belstead Road, as a war hospital. In addition Ranelagh Road School was converted into a war hospital and Gippeswyk Hall into a measles hospital for soldiers. The matron of the Broadwater hospital, Miss Hall, was presented by the king with the Royal Red Cross in 1917 in recognition of her 'patient and splendid work', and later William Paul, the owner of Broadwater, was awarded the OBE for his work in organising the hospital.

Besides helping to transfer wounded men from the ambulance trains to hospital, members of the British Red Cross and St John Ambulance Brigade spent their time making up wound dressings and other medical necessities for use in France and other theatres of war. The Ipswich depot, established only two days after the declaration of war, sent out nearly two million articles in just over four years.[6]

Peace came at last, and great was the rejoicing in Ipswich. News of the signing of the Armistice reached Ransomes' Orwell Works by telephone at 9.30 a.m. on 11 November 1918, and the works closed at 11.30, the employees nevertheless being paid for the entire day. The company diary tells the story:

> The news was conveyed about the town by the sounding of all the buzzers. The employees flocked into the yard and there was a good deal of excitement and cheering. The town was soon covered with flags and a good deal of rejoicing took place in the vicinity of Cornhill.[7]

More than four years of war had proved costly not only in terms of human life but also in commercial terms. Ipswich industries that had thrived on exports to all parts of the world found their markets gone. Ransomes, which had had a depot in Odessa for many years, lost heavily as a result of the 1917 Russian Revolution; not only was that lucrative market closed but the firm received no payment for goods supplied before the Bolshevik takeover.

119   Members of the Ipswich and District branch of the National Association of Discharged Sailors and Soldiers are played to St Matthew's Church by a Boys' Brigade drum and fife band. Quite a crowd has gathered to watch as they wheel from St Matthew's Street into Mill Lane (now the upper end of Portman Road).

Men who returned after service in the armed forces, some of them broken in body and mind, did not find the 'Land fit for Heroes' that they had been promised. For many of them there was no work; in 1921 Ransomes had to close three departments and 1,500 men lost their jobs, the rest of the workforce being put on short time. The womenfolk who had taken over as conductors on the corporation trams and as workers in many factories and engineering works likewise found themselves cast aside.

120   Staff and patients at Broadwater War Hospital pose for the photographer.

The 1920s were a decade of hardship for many in Ipswich, conditions being made no easier by a succession of strikes which did further damage to companies already hit hard by difficult trading conditions. Matters came to a head with the 1926 General Strike, during which non-striking journalists at the *East Anglian Daily Times* produced daily emergency issues, printed on an old-fashioned flat-bed machine using type set by a jobbing printer. The vans bringing the type to the Carr Street offices had to have police protection.[8]

In spite of industrial unrest and poor trading prospects the port of Ipswich continued to progress. A new dock entrance had been provided in 1871, but with changing conditions it proved inadequate and in 1913 the Dock Commissioners received Parliamentary sanction for the construction of a new and larger lock which could take the steamers that were increasingly using the port. The outbreak of war prevented this proposal from going ahead, and increasing labour charges and cost of materials during the conflict precluded the implementation of that scheme when peace returned. Instead the Dock Commissioners decided to develop a new quay with deep-water berths on the east bank of the river below the dock. Construction of Cliff Quay began in 1923, the first section being completed in 1925, a second in 1929 and a third in 1938. Considerable changes were made within the dock during the same period, an old branch dock (formerly a tidemill pond) being filled in to provide space for timber storage and new quays being constructed, making possible an expansion of trade when better times arrived.[9]

With a legacy of seriously sub-standard houses and a continuing growth in population the Corporation was forced to consider the provision of council houses. It was the opening of the British Diesel Company works that prompted the first moves to provide council houses in 1912, when Mr. R.J. Jackson suggested that land on the Hadleigh Road belonging to the Corporation should be used for the building of 'workmen's dwellings'; each house was to have a bath, a proposal that raised controversy at the time.

With the outbreak of war nothing more was heard of the scheme for several years, but in 1918 the town council decided to built 1,400 houses on the Hadleigh Road and between Nacton Road and Felixstowe Road. Private builders played their part by developing other estates on the town's outskirts, and between 1921 and 1930 no fewer than 4,921 houses were built, 1,849 by the corporation and 3,072 by private enterprise.[10] A striking layout was adopted for the housing estate built on the former racecourse to the east of the town, long straight roads meeting at a focal point which served as the hub of a road forming three-quarters of a circle.

With the town developing rapidly to the east Lady de Saumarez, of Shrubland Hall, in 1924 gave land for a church to serve the new housing areas. The cost of building the church was paid by an Ipswich tailor, a Mr. Bantoft, in memory of his mother. Designed by H. Munro Cautley, St Augustine's Church with its central tower is medieval in concept but built in modern materials; it was consecrated in November, 1927. Despite the widening of many streets the town centre was becoming congested as traffic built up, and in the 1920s a by-pass was built from Woodbridge

121 *Detached houses being erected on the outskirts of the town, some of the 3,072 built by private developers between 1921 and 1930.*

122   Old houses in Stoke Street opposite St Mary Stoke Church seen on the eve of their clearance to make way for road improvements in 1933. The junction of Rectory Road is on the extreme right.

123   Bloomfield's Buildings in Stoke Street seen from the courtyard as they fall victim to slum clearance in April 1933. These were a little lower down the hill than the houses in the previous illustration.

Road to the London Road to carry through traffic on the A12 around the town. It was completed in 1929.

As new houses were built many of the town's older dwellings were cleared away, ridding the town of the worst and most insanitary buildings. 'Slum clearance' began in earnest in 1923 in the area of Black Horse Lane, Tanners Lane, Curriers Lane and Lady Lane, where 332 houses were demolished, and the clearance went ahead alongside the necessary provision of new houses. By 1938 the number of houses pulled down had reached 2,307, of which 946 were in the Rope Walk and Potteries area, where some of the worst and most crowded conditions were to be found.[11] The principle of slum clearance cannot be criticised, yet it is sad that considerable numbers of ancient timber-framed buildings disappeared along with the 18th- and 19th-century slums. Had they survived they would doubtless have been renovated and would today be 'prestige offices' or 'desirable period residences'. The building of the Racecourse Estate was followed by further development, both by the corporation and by private developers, to the east of the town. Altogether more than 4,000 council houses were built, nearly a quarter of them in the peak year of 1938 alone.

Ipswich Airport

Further along the Nacton Road was a stretch of land dipping down towards the Orwell that in the 1930s became the site of Ipswich Airport. The Ipswich Municipal Aerodrome, as it was at first known, was opened by the Prince of Wales, later King Edward VIII and then Duke of Windsor, during a crowded programme of visits and ceremonies on 26 June 1930. He flew from Northolt to Ipswich in his personal Westland Wapiti.

Earlier in the morning of that day Mr. A.L. Clouting, who was the first Labour Mayor of Ipswich, had flown in carrying the Air Ministry full licence for the aerodrome. The pilot of the Blackburn Bluebird which brought him from the old flying ground at

Hadleigh was Dr. Henry Paterson Sleigh, chairman of the Suffolk Aero Club, which was to manage the aerodrome on behalf of Ipswich Corporation.

The mayor, in his robes and cocked hat and wearing the mayoral chain, was waiting on the airfield, flanked by the two mace-bearers, when the Prince's machine circled the aerodrome before landing. There seems to have been a degree of informality about the Prince's arrival, to judge from the newspaper report the next day, and as he stripped off his flying gear in the clubhouse the prince congratulated Ipswich 'on its far-sighted policy of having an aerodrome, which every city and town in Great Britain will surely have in the not far distant future'.

All too soon he was whisked away for a visit to the Orwell Works of Ransomes, Sims & Jefferies, where he chatted with fitter Fred Southgate, who had been at work for 57 years and was one of Ransomes' oldest employees. In the course of his five-hour visit to the town the Prince fitted in a dozen engagements, including a visit to the Wolsey Pageant in Christchurch Park. While the Prince was hurrying from place to place in Ipswich, the crowds seem to have been enjoying the glorious weather at the aerodrome. They had their share of thrills, for there were two crashes during the day, neither of them resulting in injury to the pilots though one of the aircraft was wrecked, a Klemm flown by a Mr. Kinnaird, the Scottish agent for the company that built this type of aircraft. When the engine failed he had the choice of landing in a field where children were playing or in a tree, and he chose the tree; local newspaper readers were treated to a picture of the wrecked aeroplane perched in the branches.[12]

Within a month Ipswich had another royal visitor. Prince George, later to become King George VI on his brother's abdication, flew into the new aerodrome in one of a pair of RAF Wapitis on his way to name new lifeboats at Walton-on-Naze and Clacton. It was a fleeting visit, for after being greeted by the mayor the Prince boarded a Rolls Royce car for the journey into Essex. After the Prince's departure the mayor, Town Clerk Alex Moffat and others stood chatting to the two RAF pilots, one of whom commented on the convenience of the new aerodrome. He was quoted as saying 'If anyone cannot land here it's time he gave up flying.' Perhaps the remark said more about the inadequacy of some other aerodromes than about the virtues of the Ipswich field.

Great hopes were expressed at the time of the opening that airlines such as KLM and Lufthansa would operate services into Ipswich, but the hoped-for developments did not materialise. In the summer of 1935, however, Crilly Airways Ltd. advertised a Sundays-only service between Ipswich, Southend and Ramsgate using a de Havilland DH.84 Dragon. The return fare was £1 to Southend, 25 shillings to Ramsgate. The Suffolk Aero Club managed the airport for some years, and then in 1936 the management was taken over by the Whitney Straight Corporation, which set out to develop the airport's amenities. In 1938 the Under Secretary of State for Air, Captain Harold Balfour, opened new terminal buildings which were to be the first instalment of an ambitious scheme to provide a whole range of recreational facilities. The terminal buildings are now listed as of architectural or historic interest, but are disused and becoming dilapidated; in spite of their listed status Ipswich Borough Council has

124   Wells Street in St Helen's celebrates the Silver Jubilee of King George V and Queen Mary in 1935. This street of 'artisans' dwellings' was built about 1870 on the site of a sandpit, and was replaced by modern flats in the 1950s.

expressed a determination to see them demolished. During 1938 a daily service was operated by the Whitney Straight Corporation between Ipswich and an airfield at Clacton using a five-seat Short Scion for the 15-minute flight. With war looming Ipswich Airport took on a training role for men who wished to prepare themselves for aircrew duties.

The Second World War

Civil flying ceased immediately on the outbreak of war on 3 September 1939, Ipswich Airport being taken over by the Royal Air Force as a satellite base for RAF Wattisham, an Expansion Scheme station set up in the 1930s some miles north-west of Ipswich. One of the Wattisham squadrons, No. 110, moved its Bristol Blenheim IV aircraft to Ipswich, and it is said that the first air raid of the war was mounted from Wattisham and Ipswich Airport. Six aircraft from No. 110 Squadron from Ipswich and six from No. 107 Squadron from Wattisham attacked German warships in Schillig Roads; one of the Ipswich Blenheims failed to return, and so did four of those from Wattisham.[13] At a later stage of the war Ipswich changed from being a bomber station to having a fighter role, Supermarine Spitfires operating from the grass airfield.

As in the First World War the various industrial concerns in Ipswich were switched to armaments production. Furniture manufacturers Frederick Tibenham Ltd. made wooden airscrews for the Airspeed Oxford training aircraft, and Ransomes produced gun carriages and components for tanks while continuing to turn out ploughs and other agricultural implements that were essential to the drive to increase home food production. Again women were recruited to take the place of men conscripted into the forces, but this time the firm's work did not extend to aircraft.

As the British Expeditionary Force retreated before the German advance, Ipswich sailing barges were sent across the Channel to take part in the Dunkirk evacuation. Three of the five that went, all of them belonging to R.& W. Paul, were lost, the *Doris* sunk on the way over and the more modern *Barbara Jean* and *Aidie* abandoned on Dunkirk beach. Of the other two, the *Tollesbury* and the *Ena*, the former returned to Ramsgate with troops on board. The *Ena* was abandoned at anchor off Dunkirk, but was boarded by British soldiers who sailed her back across the Channel before accepting a tow into Ramsgate.

The barges continued trading, though to the normal perils of the sea were added the danger of enemy action and the regulations imposed by the naval authorities. Some barges bound to and from Ipswich were lost by enemy action, even sailing vessels falling victim to mines laid by aircraft in the narrow channels off the Essex coast. Larger craft also fell victim to air attack and mining. The colliers *Cormount* and *Skum*, the latter a Norwegian vessel, were bombed off Harwich when bound for Ipswich, and another Norwegian collier, the *Skaggerak*, was blown in two when she detonated two mines laid by an aircraft in the Orwell off Shotley as she sailed upriver. Eighteen men, including the Ipswich pilot, died in the *Skaggerak*; there were only five survivors.[14]

A partial antidote to the magnetic mine was found in 'wiping' ships with a powerful electric current to counter the vessels' magnetism. Ships visiting Ipswich were 'wiped' in Buttermans Bay by the degaussing vessel HMS *Torchbearer*, formerly the sailing barge *Bluebell* belonging to Erwarton farmer Sydney Wrinch. No submarines came into the dock for refit, the Diesel works having closed down in 1929 when Vickers-Petters transferred production to Petters' original works in Yeovil, but nevertheless the port became busy with a host of naval craft. For a time after the outbreak of war the North Sea packets operated by the London & North Eastern Railway ended their voyages from continental ports at Ipswich, since their normal berths at Parkeston Quay had been requisitioned by the Admiralty.[15]

In July 1940 Ipswich's Cliff Quay became a base for armed patrol trawlers, an offshoot from HMS *Badger* at Parkeston Quay. In September 1940 HMS *Bunting*, a steam yacht built in 1896 and taken up by the Navy earlier in the year, arrived at Ipswich as base ship, her name being officially adopted by the Ipswich base. This vessel was soon to change names with HMS *Freelance*, a twin-screw motor yacht which took over as base ship towards the end of the year.[16] The paddle steamer *Emperor of India*, well known on the south coast as one of Cozens' excursion steamers operating out of Weymouth, arrived at Cliff Quay as accommodation ship in 1943 and was renamed *Bunting* in 1944. Cliff Quay served as a base for 20 auxiliary patrol trawlers and 11 motor launches operating in the northern half of the Harwich sub-command, and later in the war had a role in supporting the tank landing craft from HMS *Woolverstone*, the combined operations base at Woolverstone Hall.

When in 1944 it became necessary to mislead the enemy over Allied intentions concerning the invasion of Europe, Woolverstone Park had its part to play in the deception plan; when the real landing craft departed in the approach to D-Day dummy landing craft of wood and canvas on a skeleton of scaffold tubes, kept afloat on oil drums, were moored in the Orwell to give the impression to enemy reconnaissance pilots that a large force was being held back for an attack on the Pas de Calais.[17] As Allied forces advanced through occupied Europe plans were made for an airborne operation code-named Market Garden to secure certain bridges over the Rhine. Many people then living in Ipswich still remember the sight of troop-carrying gliders and their towing aircraft passing over the town on 17 September 1944 on their way to the Arnhem landings. Among those airborne troops was at least one man who looked down and picked out his Ipswich home as his glider approached the coast.

Air Raids

The Spanish Civil War had shown all too clearly how vulnerable the civilian population was to air attack, and preparations to provide shelters and to recruit Air Raid Precautions volunteers were being made even before the Munich Crisis of 1938. In Ipswich a grandiose scheme was hatched for an underground car park in Tower Ramparts that should double as an air-raid shelter for 800 people, and for similar shelters in other parts of the town. In the event less extravagant plans were put into effect, though as late as 1942 Ipswich MP Mr. Richard Stokes was still agitating for the construction of a deep shelter under Alexandra Park. Still surviving are the shelter at Clifford Road School, turned by the school into a 1939–45 museum, and that at the rear of the Priory Heath trolleybus depot, now used as a store by the Ipswich Transport Museum.

An ARP wardens' organisation was set up in March 1938 and training began, the town being divided into 13 groups, designated A to M, and 186 sectors. An effort was made to find enough wardens to cover the town, but in the town centre and on some of the new estates there was a serious lack of interest; in one area containing 6,000 people only nine came forward. When war began 867 wardens had been enrolled, and by the end of the year there were 1,000. The air-raid sirens wailed out their warning for the first time on 4 September, just a day after the outbreak of war, and 700 wardens reported for duty. It was the first of 1,165 alerts, to which must be added four occasions on which the 'crash alarm' was sounded without an alert having been sounded.[18] The 'crash alarm' or 'cuckoo', which indicated that an attack was imminent, was set off by observers posted on factory roofs and in similar places when they spotted enemy aircraft approaching the town.

The town came under direct attack from enemy aircraft more than fifty times in the course of five years of war. The first serious incident occurred on the night of 21 June 1940 when a bomb scored a direct hit on a house in Dale Hall Lane, killing three people. Not all the bombs that were dropped in subsequent raids exploded, it being left to the Royal Engineers to defuse and remove a large unexploded bomb from Christchurch Park. Less successful was a Royal Navy team that was called to deal with a parachute mine that fell in the Cemetery Road area; it proved impossible to disarm this huge weapon, and when it was detonated enormous damage was done to houses in the area whose occupants had, fortunately, already been evacuated; 62 of the houses were destroyed. Eight bombs dropped on the dock area on 8 July 1940 all failed to explode. Two hit R. & W. Paul's building and penetrated right to the ground floor; another was found under the choir stalls of St Mary-at-the-Quay Church.[19]

One raider that overflew Ipswich in August 1940 was shot down by a British fighter; it crashed in Gippeswyk Park after the crew of four had escaped by parachute. They descended on to the roof of Cocksedge's works, where they were kept at bay by local women residents in the street below brandishing kitchen knives. In October and November 1940 raiders dropped on Ipswich the first 'butterfly' anti-personnel bombs to fall in Britain. These small bombs had a steel casing that unfolded after they had been released from the large container dropped from the aircraft; the casing, which gave the bomb its familiar name, acted as a parachute and also operated the arming device. A policeman was killed and two soldiers were seriously hurt when one of the bombs exploded.[20] One of the worst incidents occurred on 25 August 1942, when a bomb scored a direct hit on an Anderson shelter at the corner of Nacton Road and Lindbergh Road, killing 14 people. The very next day three people died when an incendiary bomb container fell on another Anderson shelter in Avondale Road.[21]

After the invasion of Europe eastern England came under attack by V1 flying bombs, some of them launched by Heinkel He111 bombers operating over the North Sea out of sight of the coast. Only two fell in Ipswich, one in Maryon Road and the other in Halton Crescent, six people being killed in these incidents. Another 'buzz-bomb' destroyed Chelmondiston parish church. Probably the last raid on Britain by a manned aircraft occurred on 4 March 1945, when two bombs were dropped on a house in Seymour Road, killing nine people and severely injuring six more.[22] In all, the air raids had destroyed 255 houses in Ipswich and had seriously damaged another 774, providing the Corporation with something of a housing shortage.

In May Ipswich, with the rest of Britain, celebrated Victory in Europe, and then in August came VJ Day, when the surrender of Japan was hailed with more relief than jubilation. Men and women began to return to the town from war service, and none were given a greater welcome than those who had been prisoners of the Japanese; their sufferings had in many cases been horrendous.

Post-War Planning

Towards the end of the war the town council began discussing its future plans, and in particular proposals for building a new civic centre that would replace the Victorian Town Hall and the 15 other buildings housing the different departments of town administration. The Town Hall of 1867, with the police station housed in the basement, had long been seen as inadequate. When the borough produced its development plan

125   St Mary Elms Church, in a photograph taken in 1980 from almost the same position as William Vick's on page 186. The old houses have all been cleared away, and the character of the area has entirely changed; the police station and Civic Centre are to the photographer's left.

in 1951 a site south of St Matthew's Street and Westgate Street, largely occupied at that time by narrow streets of small terrace houses, was earmarked for a new civic centre with police station and law courts.[23]

Though thoughts might turn towards a new home for the town's administration, the immediate post-war problem was to provide homes both for those who had lost theirs to bombing and for those returning home from the war. Among the first houses erected when housebuilding resumed were 'prefabs', sectional bungalows constructed in factories that had been producing aircraft and similar war material. Although the town was allocated 400 prefabricated bungalows only 142 were in fact erected, as it was found that dwellings could be built by traditional forms of construction as quickly as the government could supply 'prefabs'. Those bungalows were intended merely to overcome the immediate shortage and were said to have a planned life of about ten years; fifty years after their erection some 'prefabs' were still in existence in north Ipswich.

With more than 3,000 people waiting for rented homes in 1949 the corporation was faced with the need for a concerted housebuilding drive. Development of the Chantry housing estate began in 1951, the corporation concentrating mainly on building houses for family occupation there and on other available sites around the town. Towards 1960 there was a trend towards the building of blocks of single-bedroom flats for the accommodation of younger people who had not yet started a family.[24] Once the immediate post-war shortage of houses was on the way to being resolved the corporation turned again to slum clearance in 1954. By 1967 some 1,600 houses had been demolished, to be replaced by new houses and flats, and later a great many older houses were given new life by providing bathrooms, indoor toilets and hot water systems with the aid of local authority grants.[25]

By the time detailed plans for the new civic centre were being drawn up the possibility of town expansion was having to be taken into account, and provision had to be made for the expansion of services which this would entail. Construction of a spiral underground car park began in October 1964 and erection of the police headquarters and courts commenced in April 1965. At the same time the western section of a new dual carriageway named Civic Drive and

126 The changing scene in the 1980s: the main streets have been cleared of most traffic for much of the day, and walkers have more or less regained the freedom that they had before the advent of the motor car. This view from Tavern Street into Carr Street shows the Carr Street shopping precinct or Eastgate Centre.

Franciscan Way was under construction.[26] This entirely new road cut a swathe through the old street pattern; it was originally intended that it would sweep onwards across Turret Lane and Lower Brook Street, but in the event it deposited its traffic in the narrow St Nicholas Street and proceeded no further. Later plans were altered and the eastern end of the road became merely a car park.

On 3 February 1965 Richard Crossman, Minister of Housing and Local Government in Harold Wilson's government, told the House of Commons of plans to provide additional housing for Londoners by expanding Ipswich and two other towns. It was proposed that about 70,000 people should be absorbed by 1981, followed by 'natural growth' thereafter, necessitating the building of 1,500 houses a year for 12 years in addition to the houses being built for the town's own needs. There would have to be matching growth in shopping, educational, social and recreational facilities and a major redevelopment of the town centre. Substantial funding would be provided through a development corporation appointed and financed by the government, the borough's boundaries being pushed out to the south and west to absorb Wherstead, Belstead, Copdock, Burstall, Sproughton and Bramford.

Three years later, almost to the day, a draft order was issued designating the borough and the additional land to the south and west of the town an area for development; a

127   Looking the other way across White Horse Corner, the mock-Tudor shop on the junction has become a building society office. Just beyond is Croydon's the jewellers whose façade was sufficiently well designed to convince many visitors that it was genuine.

total population of 250,000 was envisaged at that time. A report on a survey carried out by planning consultants Graeme Shankland and Oliver Cox, of Shankland, Cox and Associates, contained a proposal that additional expansion areas at Needham Market, Stowmarket and Haughley should provide for an eventual population of 400,000 in the 'development band', including Ipswich. There was much speculation about what lay in the future for Ipswich, with talk of a new road network that was to include a flyover crossing Cornhill and massive rebuilding of the town centre, but in June 1969 the Minister of Housing and Local Government announced that he had decided not to go ahead with expansion after all. Instead Ipswich was to be allowed to expand at its own rate without further government interference.

The unfortunate Greyfriars development, whose drab concrete walls gave it the appearance of a piece of Hitler's Atlantic Wall transplanted to the side of the new Franciscan Way, was made virtually redundant by the Minister's backward slide. Not even the transfer of the provision market to its bowels could save what had become a white elephant, and it mouldered on until taken over by Willis, Faber & Dumas, the insurance brokers who had built a revolutionary block of glass-walled offices on the corner of Princes Street and Franciscan Way. That office block was to become the town's most modern listed building, listed not for historic but for architectural interest.

It should, perhaps, be left to future generations to assess the effect on the town of the rejection of those plans for virtually doubling the population in so short a time. Many Ipswichians regard it as a narrow escape, judging from the experience of some of the New Towns set up in the same period and of East Anglian towns that did experience 'London overspill'. Ipswich lost its county borough status with local government reorganisation in 1974 but was successful in its petition for the restoration of borough status, retaining its old arms. While some new boroughs were given much wider jurisdiction Ipswich retained its old boundaries, being considered large enough to be a district unto itself.

The phenomenal growth of the port of Felixstowe from the 1950s eventually resulted in its becoming Britain's largest and busiest container port, with a startling increase in the number of heavy goods vehicles passing along the old Ipswich by-pass. The fact that this had since its construction attracted residential development meant that many Ipswich residents now suffered severely from traffic disturbance, quite apart from the inadequacy of the road to carry such a volume of lorry traffic. Not until the late 1970s did the government wake up to the need for better access to the blossoming port. Construction of a proper by-pass incorporating a bridge across the Orwell between Wherstead and Nacton between 1978 and 1982 belatedly gave better access to Felixstowe and a degree of relief for the people of Ipswich. Completion of the Orwell Bridge in 1982 was celebrated by a mass walk across it the day before its opening to traffic; one man drove a cow across the bridge.

128   Inside the Carr Street precinct the lack of bustle is indicative of a failure to attract customers to the shops which the change of name to Eastgate Centre did not entirely remedy.

The eyes of Britain focused briefly on Ipswich in 1978 when Ipswich Town Football Club, which had in 1962 beaten Aston Villa to win the First Division championship at their first attempt, humbled Arsenal in a Wembley Cup Final and returned to Portman Road with the F.A. Cup. In 1981 the club followed up their F.A. Cup success by winning the UEFA Cup, putting Ipswich firmly on the European football map.

Once a centre for the farming community of Suffolk, Ipswich has lost its market town status with the closure of the livestock market. The firm of Ransomes & Rapier that had built the first railway in China and the sluices for the Aswan Dam on the Nile was closed down after being acquired by Robert Maxwell; Ransomes, Sims & Jefferies sold off its agricultural implements division and became simply manufacturers of grass machinery, eventually being taken over by an American company; and the Cliff Brewery, closed down in 1989 after being acquired by the Brent Walker leisure group, was only saved by a management buyout which resulted in its reopening as a kind of working museum the following year.

If the town's industrial base has been severely reduced, the town has gained the insurance businesses of Guardian Royal Exchange (now Axa) in Civic Drive and Willis, Faber & Dumas (now Willis Corroon). The transfer of the Post Office Research Establishment (now BT Research Establishment) from Dollis Hill to the former RAF station at Martlesham Heath in the 1960s brought a centre of new technology to the Ipswich area, but by and large it has not attracted firms dealing in the new technology to the extent that might have been expected. The new village of Martlesham Heath, built on the former airfield that was once the home of the RAF Aeroplane and Armament

129   Where the Saxons once lived and worked, on the site of the provision market of 1812 and the later Royal Mail sorting office, construction of the Buttermarket shopping centre begins in 1990.

Research Establishment, has provided a dormitory for Ipswich, as have other lesser developments outside the borough. There are some who see the absorption of such outlying communities as a way of raising the population, and the council tax income, to a more sustainable level. The closure of Ipswich Airport by a borough council that declared the land was needed for housing has not assisted in the commercial development of the town and its hinterland. Hopes that it might be replaced by a commercial airport on the former US Air Force base at Bentwaters or elsewhere have been proved false.

With the beginning of a new century and a new millennium the borough council campaigned for Ipswich to become a city, but the same councillors that travelled to London to present the town's case followed up by making a decision to run down the town's museum service in order to save money. Having opened one of the earliest provincial public museums in 1847, Ipswich seems intent on squandering its historical heritage to save a few thousand pounds a year. Yet there are also people who suggest that the future prosperity of the town lies with tourism.

References

Abbreviations:
  CPR Calendar of Patent Rolls
  HMC Historical Manuscript Commission 9th Report (1883)
  IATN *Ispwich Archaeological Trust News*
  PSIA *Proceedings of the Suffolk Institute of Archaeology and History*
  SROI Suffolk Record Office, Ipswich
  VCH *Victoria County History of Suffolk*

I Romans and Britons

1. cf. Ian Stead, CA126, CA135, and *Celtic Art*, British Museum, 1985; J.W. Brailsford in *PSIA* XXXI, 1968, pp.158-9; J.E. Brailsford and J.E. Stapely, 'The Ipswich Torcs', in *Proceedings of the Prehistoric Society*, 38, 1972, pp.219-34.
2. *PSIA* XXXVII, 1992, pp.384-6; *IATN* 33. The Foxhall houses are described and illustrated in E. Martin, 'Suffolk in the Iron Age', in J. Davies and T. Williamson (eds.), *Land of the Iceni: The Iron Age in Northern East Anglia*, UEA Norwich (1999).
3. *PSIA* XXXVIX, 1998, p.234.
4. *PSIA* XXXIV, p.295, and *PSIA* XXXV, p.234.
5. *PSIA* XXXVII, 1990, p.160; *IATN* 28 & 48.
6. *PSIA* XXI.
7. *PSIA* XXII, 1935, pp.14-19.
8. *PSIA* XXXVII, 1992, pp.387-8; *IATN* 34.
9. *PSIA* XXXVII, 1992, p.385; *IATN* 33 & 34.
10. *PSIA* XXXVIII, 1996, p.476; *IATN* 43.
11. There was no known bridge in this area until the construction of the Orwell Bridge in the 1980s, but this name has been used for many years.
12. J.E. Taylor in *PSIA* VI, p.341.

II The Saxon Town

1. Charles Green, 'East Anglian Coast-line Levels Since Roman Times', in *Antiquity* XXXV (1961), pp.21-8.
2. Norman Scarfe, *The Suffolk Landscape* (1972), p.101.
3. Christopher Scull, 'A cemetery of the 7th and 8th centuries at St Stephen's Lane/Butter Market, Ipswich'.
4. Norman Scarfe, *op. cit.*, p.101.
5. Norman Scarfe, *Suffolk in the Middle Ages* (1986), p.43.
6. Norman Scarfe, *The Suffolk Landscape* (1972), p.122.
7. Keith Wade, 'The urbanisation of East Anglia: the Ipswich Perspective', in *Flatlands and Wetlands: Current Themes in East Anglian Archaeology*, EAA 50.
8. Scull, *op. cit.*
9. Wade, *op. cit.*
10. *PSIA* VI, p.341.
11. *Theodred's Will*, published in *English Historical Documents*, vol.1, reveals his involvement in East Anglia, including ownership of a house in Ipswich.
12. Cyril Hart, *The Danelaw* (1992).
13. E.O. Blake (ed.), *Liber Eliensis* (1962), pp.111-13.

14. Wade, *op. cit.*
15. John Newman in M. Anderton (ed.), *Anglo-Saxon Trading Centres* (1999).
16. Dr. Steven Plunkett, pers. com.
17. J.C. Sadler, *A History of the Ipswich Mint and Its Saxon and Norman Moneyers* (1976).
18. Wade, *op. cit.*
19. *IATN* 6.
20. Wade, *op. cit.*

III   The Norman and Medieval Town

1. R. Allen Brown, *The Normans and the Norman Conquest* (1985), p.4.
2. F.M. Stenton, *Anglo-Saxon England*, Oxford, 3rd edn. (1971), quoted in R. Allen Brown.
3. Quoted in R. Allen Brown, p.170.
4. David Dymond and Peter Northeast, *A History of Suffolk* (1985), p.32.
5. See H.C. Darby, *The Domesday Geography of Eastern England* (1971), p.190.
6. Copinger MSS I, pp.313-17.
7. Domesday 25.1 and 25.52 give us Aelfric of Clare, son of Withgar and father of another Withgar, being predecessor of Richard, son of Count Gilbert as lord of Clare and of the holding of St Peter's Church in Ipswich.
8. G.R. Clarke, *The History and Description of the Town and Borough of Ipswich* (1830), p.183, calls him R. Bedile, and adds that Brokes was held in 1282 by the de Bois family. He says that Brokes Hall is in St Matthew's parish and the hamlet so called takes in part of this and parts of the parishes of Bramford, Whitton, Thurleston and Westerfield.
9. *Manors of Suffolk* II, 238 (Badley).
10. Testa de Nevill (1807), p.296.
11. SROI HD226/1.
12. SROI HD226/1, pp.9 ff.
13. Darby, pp.93-4.
14. Norman Scarfe, *The Suffolk Landscape*, p.162.
15. For a discussion of the use of timber in castle building, see Robert Higham and Philip Barker, *Timber Castles*, London (1992).
16. Norman Scarfe, *Suffolk in the Middle Ages* (1986), p.64.
17. Keith Wade, 'Anglo-Saxon and Medieval Ipswich', in David Dymond and Edward Martin, *An Historical Atlas of Suffolk* (1988); pers. comm. from Keith Wade.
18. Sir Travers Twiss, *The Black Book of the Admiralty*, Appendix, Part II, vol. II, London (1873), pp.xi-xii.
19. G.R. Clarke and other sources give the date of the charter as 1199, but this appears to be an error. John was crowned on 27 May, Ascension Day, 1199, and alone of all monarchs of this period dated his regnal year from his coronation; as Ascension Day is a movable feast and the regnal year was determined as beginning on Ascension Day rather than on 27 May the end of the first year of his reign fell on 17 May 1200. It has been stated that the date of the charter is 25 May in the first year of John's reign, but in fact there is no such date as the regnal year began only on 27 May; it might be that one of the royal clerks was confused by the tying of the regnal year to a movable feast and expected the first year to go on until 27 May, but this we shall never know. G.H. Martin in *The Early Court Rolls of the Borough of Ipswich* states unequivocally that 'the charter was sealed on the 25th of May 1200'.
20. [R. Canning], *The Principal Charters Which have been Granted to the Corporation of Ipswich in Suffolk Translated* (1754).
21. Nathaniell Bacon, *The Annalls of Ipswiche*, ed. W.H. Richardson, Ipswich (1884), p.6.
22. G.H. Martin, *The Early Court Rolls of the Borough of Ipswich*, University College of Leicester (1954), pp.8-10; Bacon, *Annalls*, pp.6-7.
23. HMC, Ninth Report (1883), p.240.
24. Martin, *op. cit.*, p.9.
25. Bacon, *op. cit.*, p.18.

26. Martin, *op. cit.*, p.7.

27. S. Alsford, 'Thomas le Rente: A medieval town ruler', *PSIA* XXXV (1982), pp.105-15.

28. Keith Wade in *Waterfront Archaeology in Britain and Northern Europe*, CBA Research Report no.41 (1981), p.130.

29. This is rendered in Latin figures, ixm iiic. Does it in fact mean 9003 hundredweight?

30. HMC, pp.257-8.

31. G. Hutchinson, *Medieval Ships and Shipping*, Leicester University Press (1994), p.23.

32. Hundred Rolls, 3 Richard II, quoted in Carlyon Hughes, *The History of Harwich Harbour* (1939).

IV   The Later Medieval Port and Town

1. Nathaniell Bacon, *The Annalls of Ipswiche*, p.64.

2. Calendar of Patent Rolls, 12 Edward III, pt.II, 16.

3. Bacon, *op. cit.*, pp.80-1.

4. *The Principal Charters* (1754).

5. HMC, p.258.

6. *Ibid.*, p.259.

7. *Ibid.*, p.259.

8. E.F. Jacob, *The Fifteenth Century 1399–1485* (1961), p.493.

9. Roger Virgo, 'The death of William de la Pole, Duke of Suffolk', in *East Anglian Society and the Political Community of Late Medieval England* (1997), p.248.

10. *Ibid.*, p.249.

11. *Ibid.*, p.251.

12. HMC, p.213.

13. Bacon, *op. cit.*, p.141.

14. *Ibid.*, p.467.

15. HMC, p.258.

16. G.H. Martin, 'Shipments of wool from Ipswich to Calais, 1399–1402', in *The Journal of Transport History*, vol. II (1956), pp.177-81.

17. HMC, p.235.

18. John Kirby, *The Suffolk Traveller* (1764), p.43.

19. John Wodderspoon, *Memorials of the Ancient Town of Ipswich* (1850), p.333.

20. Miss K.J. Galbraith, 'Early Sculpture at St. Nicholas Church, Ipswich', *PSIA* XXXI (1968), p.172; the date is confirmed as the first quarter of the 12th century by Dr. S.J. Plunkett—personal comment.

21. H.P. Drummond, Suffolk Archaeological Association, Original Papers III (November 1848).

22. Pers. com. Dr. John Blatchly.

23. CPR 1334–8, p.476.

24. Pat. R. 11 Ed. III, pt.2, m.17 (copy). CPR 1334–8, p.476.

25. H.A. Cronne, *The Reign of Stephen*, p.268, quoting *Regesta Regum Anglo Normannorum 1066–1154*, vol.3, p.416.

26. C. Harper-Bill, *Charters of Dodnash Priory* (1998).

27. Corder, *History of Christchurch*, p.6.

28. Corder prints a version of this and refers to Dugdale, *Monasticon*; Tanner, Not. Mon.; Davy MSS at Brit. Mus. Add. MSS 19,093 pp.281-315.

29. 5 Edward III in CCR, vol. IV, Edward III, p.215.

30. Two Rentals of the Priory of the Holy Trinity, transcribed by W.P. Hunt, Ipswich (1847).

31. Richard clearly had problems in securing this holding, as 100 acres and a mill were claimed by the king's manor of Bramford—Domesday Book 25.52.

32. Wodderspoon, *op. cit.*, pp.245-54.

33. HMC, p.225.

34. Lilian Redstone, *Ipswich Through the Ages* (1948), p.77; details are in Percevale's Great Domesday Book, book 3; cf. HMC, p.245.

35. There is a detailed description in *IATN* 7 (1984); *PSIA* XXXIV (1977). See also *IATN* nos. 11, 12, 13, 16, 44, 46, and a compilation of articles and illustrations on 'The Blackfriars, Ipswich' by Dr. John Blatchly.
36. V.B. Redstone in *PSIA* X, p.189.
37. Lilian Redstone, *Ipswich Through the Ages*, p.78.
38. *IATN*, 23-7.
39. Keith Wade, *The Origins of Ipswich*.
40. Bacon, *op. cit.*, p.73.
41. *Ibid.*, p.124.
42. *Ibid.*, p.11.
43. *Ibid.*, p.70.
44. HMC., pp.226-7.
45. Dr. Calvin Wells, who pioneered the study of archaeological pathology, gave a demonstration of his reconstruction at a meeting of the Norfolk Research Committee at the Castle Museum, Norwich, with Miss Barbara Green taking the part of the victim.
46. Bacon, *op. cit.*, p.124.
47. *Ibid.*, p.221.
48. *Ibid.*, p.221.
49. *Ibid.*, p.130.
50. *Ibid.*, p.96.
51. *The Black Book of the Admiralty*, vol. II, p.187.
52. E.O. Blake (ed.), *Liber Eliensis*, Camden Soc. (1962), pp.112-13.
53. SROI HD226/1.
54. Bacon, *op. cit.*, p.62.
55. SROI S Ipsw 333,32 23968.
56. HMC, p.231.
57. *Ibid.*, p.246.
58. Bacon, *op. cit.*, pp.162, 164.
59. *Ibid.*, p.134.
60. *Ibid.*, p.149.
61. *Ibid.*, p.42.
62. *Ibid.*, pp.294-5.

V The Tudor Town

1. J.D. Mackie, *The Earlier Tudors 1485–1558*, pp.108-11.
2. *Ibid.*, p.462-3.
3. *VCH Suffolk*, pp.257-9.
4. Nathaniel Bacon, *The Annals of Ipswiche*, p.105.
5. Bacon, *op. cit.*, p.253.
6. Bacon, *op. cit.*, p.307.
7. HMC, p.256.
8. *VCH*, p.258.
9. SP Dom Elizabeth, cxiv, 32, quoted in *VCH*, p.258.
10. L & P Henry VIII, xiv (1), 874; *VCH*, p.259.
11. Bacon, *op. cit.*, p.97; R.A. Pelham, *Fulling Mills, A Study in the Application of Water Power to the Woollen Industry*, Society for the Protection of Ancient Buildings (1958).
12. *Ibid.*, p.289.
13. *Ibid.*, p.336.
14. *VCH*, p.261.
15. Brewer, *The Reign of Henry VIII*, vol.II, p.261.
16. T.S. Willan, *Studies in Elizabethan Foreign Trade* (1959), p.74.
17. SP Dom Elizabeth, ccix, 102; *VCH*, p.261.

18. HMC, p.255.
19. Bacon, *op. cit.*, p.365.
20. *Ibid.*, p.366.
21. *Ibid.*, p.395.
22. Muriel Clegg, 'Roof wanderings in Ipswich', *Suffolk Review* vol.IV (1974), pp.136-8; *Ipswich Journal*, 16 May 1840.
23. CPR, 16 Elizabeth, part XIV, 375.
24. *Ibid.*
25. *The Ipswich Probate Inventories 1583–1631*, ed. Michael Reed, pp.82-5.
26. J.D. Mackie, *op. cit.*, pp.286-8.
27. G.R. Clarke, *The History & Description of the Town and Borough of Ipswich*, p.239.
28. Charles Ferguson, *Naked to Mine Enemies*, p.15; Vincent Redstone, 'Social Condition of England during the Wars of the Roses', *Transactions of the Royal Historical Society*, vol. XVI (1902), appendix, pp.199, 200.
29. Quoted in I.E. Gray and W.E. Potter, *Ipswich School 1400–1950*, p.13.
30. Mackie, *op. cit.*, p.288.
31. S.J. Gunn and P.G. Lindley, *Cardinal Wolsey: Church, state and art* (1991), p.157.
32. *Ibid.*.
33. J. Newman, 'Cardinal Wolsey's collegiate foundations', in Gunn and Lindley, *op. cit.*, pp.113-5.
34. *Ibid.*, p.107.
35. Clarke, *op. cit.*, p.251, gives a translation of the Latin inscription in which he describes Longland incorrectly as Bishop of Lincoln.
36. Clarke, *op. cit.*, pp.28-32.
37. Roger Bowers, 'The cultivation and promotion of music in the household and orbit of Thomas Wolsey', in Gunn and Lindley, p.198.
38. Clarke, *op. cit.*, p.30.
39. Bowers, *op. cit.*, p.199.
40. L & P, IV (iii) 5159.
41. D. MacCulloch, *Suffolk and the Tudors: Politics and Religion in an English County 1500–1600* (1986).
42. Clarke, *op. cit.*, p.178.
43. MacCulloch, *op. cit.*
44. The term Protestant is derived from the 'Protestation' made by some Lutheran-sympathising princes at the Imperial Diet of Speyer in 1529 against decisions taken by the Roman Catholic majority.
45. Foxe's Book of Martyrs, p.446.
46. Tony Copsey, *Book Distribution and Printing in Suffolk, 1534–1850* (1994), p.x.
47. *Ibid.*, p.91.
48. *Ibid.*, pp.x-xi.
49. Foxe, pp.776 and 927; Nina Layard, *Seventeen Suffolk Martyrs*, pp.67-79.
50. Foxe, p.962; Layard, *op. cit.*, pp.83-8.
51. Foxe, p.967; Layard, *op. cit.*, pp.92-8.
52. S. Smith, *The Madonna of Ipswich* (1980).
53. Diarmaid MacCulloch and John Blatchly, 'Recent discoveries at St. Stephen's Church, Ipswich: The Wimbill Chancel and the Rush-Alvard Chapel', *PSIA* XXXVI, pp.101-14.
54. HMC, p.260.
55. Bacon, *op. cit.*, p.277.
56. 13 Elizabeth I Cap 24, An Acte for Paving of the Towne of Ipswiche, 1570.
57. [R. Canning], *An Account of the Gifts and Legacies*, W. Craighton, Ipswich (1747).
58. Bacon, *op. cit.*, p.180.
59. Coke is said to have first been made from coal in 1640.
60. Clarke, *op. cit.*, p.300.
61. John Webb, *Great Tooley of Ipswich*, Suffolk Records Society (1962).

62. Bacon, *op. cit.*, p.197.
63. Bacon, *op. cit.*, pp.197-8.
64. Marcel Backhouse, 'Arrival in Britain 1550–1570', in *European Settlers in Britain 1550–1720* (1995).
65. Jo Campling, 'Ipswich out of England, or Antwerp in England', *Suffolk Review*, vol. 4, no. 4 (1975/6), pp.170-2.
66. J. Wheeler, *A treatise of commerce*, p.20.
67. T.S. Willan, *Studies in Elizabethan Foreign Trade* (1959), p.62.
68. Bacon, *op. cit.*, pp.346-7.
69. Peter Kent, *Fortifications of East Anglia* (1988), p.100.
70. Bacon, *op. cit.*, p.353.
71. Bacon, *op. cit.*, p.355.
72. W.G. Hoskins, *The Listener*, 13 June 1957.
73. George Bodley Scott, *The Old Neptune Inn* (1970).
74. Bacon, *op. cit.*, p.109.
75. Bacon, *op. cit.*, p.145.
76. SROI, S Ipsw 333.32 23968.
77. Bacon, *op. cit.*, p.244.
78. Bacon, *op. cit.*, p.196.
79. Bacon, *op. cit.*, p.302.
80. John Webb, *The Town Finances of Elizabethan Ipswich*, Suffolk Records Society (1996), p.70.

VI   Stuart and Commonwealth Ipswich

1. Hugh Moffat, 'Shipbuilding at Ipswich', *The Norfolk Sailor* no.8 (1964), p.33.
2. SROI, C/4/3/1/3.
3. Nathaniel Bacon, *Annals of Ipswiche*, p.424.
4. SROI, C/2/2/2/1.
5. John Blatchly, *The Town Library of Ipswich*, pp.9-13.
6. Bacon, *op. cit.*, p.479.
7. Quoted in R.W. Ketton-Cremer, *Norfolk in the Civil War* (1985), pp.53-4.
8. Ketton-Cremer, *op. cit.*, p.57.
9. John Aubrey, *Brief Lives* (1982 edn.), p.81.
10. A religious movement that took its name from the Dutch theologian Jacobus Arminius, who challenged the Calvinist doctrine of predestination. This group within the Church of England sought to revive Catholic ceremony and ritual, to which the Puritans were fiercely opposed.
11. Bacon, *op. cit.*, p.509*n.*
12. Ketton-Cremer, *op. cit.*, p.61.
13. Clarendon, *The History of the Rebellion and Civil Wars in England*, Vol.I, p.82.
14. Ketton-Cremer, *op. cit.*, pp.66-7.
15. Alfred Kingston, *East Anglia and the Great Civil War* (1897), p.26.
16. Ketton-Cremer, *op. cit.*, p.64.
17. *Ibid.*, p.69.
18. J. Gardiner and N. Wenborn (ed.), *The History Today Companion to British History*.
19. State Papers Dom. Ser. vol.cclx. no.17, quoted in Bacon, p.523.
20. Leonard Weaver, *The Harwich Story* (1975), pp.30-3.
21. Charles Edward Banks, *The Winthrop Fleet of 1630* (1930). John Winthrop himself did not sail from Ipswich but joined the fleet elsewhere, leading to the suggestion that the fleet did not in fact begin its voyage from the Orwell. It is unfortunate that the port books for this period are missing from among those in the Public Record Office; one suspects they might have crossed the Atlantic in the wake of the settlers in the 19th or 20th century.
22. Bacon, *op. cit.*, p.523*n.*
23. Charles Edward Banks, *The Planters of the Commonwealth* (1930).

24. Bacon, *op. cit.*, p.522.
25. Thomas Carlyle, *Past and Present*.
26. Bacon, *op. cit.*, p.530.
27. *Ibid.*, p.533. 'Crowdbarrow' is a dialect word for a wheelbarrow, from the Dutch *kruijen*, to push.
28. *Ibid.*, pp.534-5. The difference between ward and watch seems to be that during the day sentries were posted at various fixed points; at night the watch was peripatetic, moving around the streets in the manner of a policeman on his beat.
29. *Ibid.*, p.529.
30. *Ibid.*, p.531.
31. Clive Holmes, *The Eastern Association in the English Civil War* (1974), p.124.
32. Bacon, *op. cit.*, p.532.
33. Sterling Westhorp, 'Memoir of Nathaniell Bacon', in Bacon (1884), p.v.
34. *Ibid.*, pp.ii-iii.
35. *Ibid.*, p.v.
36. Frank Hussey, *Suffolk Invasion* (1983); A.G.E. Jones, 'The Sick and Wounded in Ipswich during the First Dutch War', *The Suffolk Review*, vol. I no.1 (1956), pp.1-7.
37. G.R. Clarke, *The History of Ipswich* (1830), p.240.
38. *The Diary of Samuel Pepys*, ed. Robert Latham and William Matthews (1970), vol.I, p.113.
39. G.C. Moore Smith, *The Family of Withypoll* (1936), p.91.
40. G.N. Clark, *The Later Stuarts 1660–1714* (1944 edition), pp.18-19.
41. *Ibid.*, p.21.
42. Lilian Redstone, *Ipswich Through the Ages*, p.94.
43. A.G.E. Jones, 'The Sick and Wounded in Ipswich during the Second Dutch War', in *The Suffolk Review*, vol.1 (1956), pp.26-31.
44. *The Diary of Samuel Pepys*, vol.VI, p.217.
45. Captain George Cocke, a Baltic merchant and navy contractor, was Treasurer of the Commission for Sick and Wounded Seamen.
46. *The Diary of Samuel Pepys*, vol.X, p.69.
47. Frank Hussey, *Suffolk Invasion*, p.39.
48. *The Diary of Samuel Pepys*, vol.VIII, pp.316-17.
49. Hussey, *op. cit.*, pp.117-19.
50. G.C. Moore Smith, *op. cit.*, p.91.
51. Clarke, *op. cit.*, p.52.
52. Bacon, *op. cit.*, p.457.
53. *Ibid.*, p.427.
54. *Ibid.*, p.436.
55. *Ibid.*, p.440.
56. *Ibid.*, pp.457-8.
57. *Ibid.*, p.472.
58. *Ibid.*, p.478.
59. *Ibid.*, p.497.
60. There is a Maidensgrave at the southern end of Woodbridge; could this be the site of the pest houses?
61. Clarke, *op. cit.*, p.50.
62. D.F. van Zwanenberg, *The Last Epidemic of Plague in England? Suffolk 1906-1918*.

VII   Celebrating the Glorious Revolution

1. William Laird Clowes, *The Royal Navy*, pp.323-4.
2. G.R. Clarke, *The History of Ipswich* (1830), p.64; J.W. Fortescue, *A History of the British Army*, vol.I (2nd edn., 1910), p.336; HMC, series 75 Downshire I (1), p.317; HMC, series 71 Finch, II, p.495.
3. *Ibid.*, p.68.
4. Clarke, *op. cit.*, pp.321-2.

5. K.G. Pert and Barbara Cotgrove, *Reflections on an old Meeting House* (1976)
6. *Ibid.*, p.7.
7. *Ibid.*, p.3.
8. T.J. Hosken, *History of Congregationalism, and memorials of the churches of our order in Suffolk* (1920), pp.92-5.
9. Clarke, *op. cit.*, p.275.
10. *The Illustrated Journeys of Celia Fiennes 1685–c.1712*, edited by Christopher Morris (1982).
11. SROI EL1/9/1/1, p.13.
12. *Ipswich Journal*, 29 January 1743.
13. Daniel Defoe, *Tour Through the Whole Island of Great Britain* (1724–6).
14. Ralph Davis, *The Rise of the English Shipping Industry* (1962), p.119.
15. My attention was directed to this document by Tony Cox, of the College Gateway Bookshop, Ipswich.
16. *House of Commons Journals*, quoted by Davis, *op. cit.*, p.92.
17. SROI, FB98/912/1.
18. Dr. Pat Murrell, personal comm.
19. SROI, FB95/93/1.
20. SROI, FB95/93/46.
21. SROI, FB95/93/101.
22. SROI, FB95/93/51.
23. Henry Fielding, *Proposals for making an effectual provision for the Poor* (1753).
24. SROI, FB95/93/30.
25. SROI, FB95/95/53.
26. John Aubrey, *Brief Lives*, pp.224-7.
27. Municipal Corporations of England and Wales: Appendix to the First Report of the Commissioners (1835), p.2298.
28. Clarke, *op. cit.*, p.172.
29. Glyde, *Illustrations of Old Ipswich* (1889), p.71; J.E. Taylor, *In and About Ancient Ipswich* (1888), p.88.
30. Glyde, *op. cit.*, p.69.
31. *Ipswich Journal*, 5 July 1740.
32. Clarke, *op. cit.*, p.170.
33. Muriel Clegg, *Streets and Street Names in Ipswich* (1984), p.5.
34. Nathaniell Bacon, *Annalls of Ipswiche*, p.486.

VIII   The Georgian Town

1. John Wodderspoon, *Memorials of the Ancient Town of Ipswich* (1850), p.218.
2. 'The Salt Trade of Ipswich, 1718–31,' in *The Suffolk Review*, The Bulletin of the Suffolk Local History Council, no.7 (1955).
3. *Ipswich Journal*, 8 January 1742–3.
4. John E. Barnard, *Building Britain's Wooden Walls: The Barnard Dynasty, c.1697–1851* (1997).
5. *Ipswich Journal*, 4 July 1740.
6. Hugh Moffat, 'Vessels shown in John Cleveley's paintings of Ipswich', *Suffolk Review*, vol.II, no.7 (1964), pp.240-1.
7. Barnard, *op. cit.*, p.35.
8. Hugh Moffat, 'Shipbuilding at Ipswich', *The Norfolk Sailor*, no.8 (1964), pp.33-40.
9. Barnard, *op. cit.*, pp.37-44.
10. David Lyon, *The Sailing Navy List* (1993), p.140.
11. A contemporary account of the event is in G.R. Clarke, *The History & Description of the Town and Borough of Ipswich*, pp.307-8.
12. *Ipswich Journal*, 10 March 1753.
13. *Ibid.*, 25 April 1767.

14. R.W. Malster, 'By steam and horse', in *The Norfolk Sailor* No.7 (1963), p.32.
15. John Kirby, *The Suffolk Traveller*, 2nd edn. (1764), p.14.
16. SROI, C/2/8/5, Headboroughs' Book.
17. Clarke, *op. cit.*, pp.171-2.
18. *Ipswich Journal*, 31 July 1813; C. Brown, B. Haward and R. Kindred, *Dictionary of Architects of Suffolk Buildings 1800–1914*.
19. Municipal Corporations of England and Wales: Appendix to the First Report of the Commissioners (1835), p.2298.
20. Clarke, *op. cit.*, p.172.
21. John Glyde, *Illustrations of Old Ipswich* (1889), p.71; J.E. Taylor, *In and About Ancient Ipswich* (1888), p.88.
22. *Ipswich Journal*, 1 November 1777.
23. 33 George III, An Act for Paving, Lighting, Cleansing and otherwise Improving the Town of Ipswich.
24. J.E. Taylor, *In and About Ancient Ipswich* (1888), p.118.
25. Muriel Clegg, *The Way We Went: Streets in nineteenth century Ipswich* (1989), pp.7-9.
26. East Anglian Miscellany, Part I, Jan–Mar. 1926, p.2.
27. Clarke, *op. cit.*, p.192.
28. *Ibid.*, pp.123-4.
29. *Ibid.*, p.128.
30. *Ibid.*, p.320.
31. D.F. van Zwanenberg, 'Medical Episodes in the History of a River', *Modern Geriatrics*, October 1974, pp.416-24.
32. *Ipswich Journal*, 13 March 1813.
33. Clarke, *op. cit.*, p.218.
34. *Ibid.*, p.192.
35. Elizabeth Grice, *Rogues and Vagabonds, or The Actors' Road to Respectability* (1977).
36. *Ipswich Journal*, 14 December 1754.
37. Philip Orwell, 'Ipswich Races', *East Anglian Magazine*, Vol. 6 (1947), pp.386-90.
38. *Bury & Norwich Post*, 1 July 1795.
39. Francois de La Rochefoucauld, *A Frenchman's Year in Suffolk, 1784*, ed. Norman Scarfe (1988), p.45.
40. *Ipswich Journal*, 15 October 1785.
41. La Rochefoucauld, *op. cit.*, pp.42-4.
42. *Ipswich Journal*, 2 March 1744–5.
43. *Suffolk Chronicle*, 4 April 1818.
44. *Ibid.*, 11 July 1818.
45. *Ipswich Journal*, 21 January 1821.
46. *Ibid.*, 15 January 1825.
47. *Ibid.*, 24 November 1827.
48. White's Suffolk (1844), p.82.
49. Report of Committee on the Poor and the Workhouse, Ipswich, 1822, printed by John Bransby (1822), p.7.
50. SROI, FB95/96/6.
51. SROI, C/4/3/1.
52. SROI, FB95/99/53.
53. SROI, FB95/99/28.
54. SROI, FB95/99/40 and 41.
55. Report of Committee on the Poor and the Workhouses, Ipswich (1822).
56. *Ibid.*, p.4.
57. *Ibid.*, p.6.
58. [R. Canning], *An Account of the Gifts and Legacies That have been given and bequeathed to Charitable Uses in the Town of Ipswich*, printed by W. Craighton, Ipswich (1747), pp.178-80.

59. White's Suffolk (1844), p.82.
60. *Gifts and Legacies*, p.180.
61. White's Suffolk (1844), p.82.
62. *Gifts and Legacies*, 2nd edn. (1819), pp.223-4.
63. *Ibid.*, p.227.
64. *Ipswich Journal*, 1 November 1777.
65. *Ibid.*, 23 May 1778 and 7 November 1778.
66. *Ibid.*, 17 January 1756.
67. *Ibid.*, 2 May 1767.
68. *Ibid.*, 15 December 1744.
69. *Ibid.*, 8 July 1773.
70. *Ibid.*, 5 March 1742–3.
71. J.R. Smith, *The Speckled Monster* (1987), p.34.
72. *Ibid.*, p.68.
73. *Ibid.*, p.80.
74. Clarke, *op. cit.*, p.108.
75. *Ibid.*, p.138.
76. *Ipswich Journal*, 21 January 1721.
77. Tony Copsey, *Book Distribution and Printing in Suffolk 1534–1850* (1994).
78. *Ibid.*, pp.40-1.
79. John Blatchly, *Eighty Ipswich Portraits* (1980).
80. Kirby, *op. cit.*, p.52.
81. *Ipswich Journal*, 16 March 1782.
82. Robert Malster, *250 Years of Brewing in Ipswich* (1996).
83. *Ipswich Journal*, 22 January 1742–3. My thanks to Dr. Pat Murrell for drawing my attention to this reference.
84. Clarke, *op. cit.*, p.348.
85. Harold Lingwood, SROI, HA213/1287/1.
86. *Ibid.*

IX   'Ill-regulated republic'

1. Clive Homes, *The Eastern Association in the English Civil War*, pp.1-4; cf. chapter six above.
2. Municipal Corporations of England and Wales: Appendix to the First Report of the Commissioners as ordered by the House of Commons to be presented 30 March 1835.
3. Redstone, *Ipswich Through the Ages*, p.63.
4. Clarke, *The History & Description of the town and Borough of Ipswich*, p.65.
5. Dr. Pat Murrell, 'Suffolk: The political behaviour of the county and its Parliamentary boroughs from the Exclusion Crisis to the Accession of the House of Hanover', D.Phil. thesis, University of Newcastle-upon-Tyne, 1982.
6. Clarke, *op. cit.*, p.80.
7. Canning (1749), preface, pp.iii-iv.
8. John Blatchly, *The Town Library of Ipswich*, pp.50-3.
9. Clarke, *op. cit.*, pp.72-6.
10. Municipal Corporations of England and Wales, p.2296.
11. *Ibid.*, p.2297.
12. *Ibid.*, p.2298.
13. *Ibid.*, p.2305.
14. *Ibid.*, p.2340.
15. John Blatchly, *Eighty Ipswich Portraits* (1980).

X   The Beginnings of Modern Industry

1. Bennet Woodcroft, *Alphabetical Index of Patentees of Inventions* (1854; new edn, 1969).

2. *Ipswich Journal*, 9 September 1786.
3. *Ipswich Journal*, 21 March 1789.
4. This building became the Women's Meeting when a larger meeting house was built of brick in 1798; the timber frame survived until 1996, when the site was cleared.
5. Harold Preston, *Early East Anglian Banks and Bankers* (1994).
6. SROI EL1/1/3/4.
7. Edward Paget-Tomlinson, *The Illustrated History of Canal and River Navigations* (1993).
8. SROI EL1/7/3/1.
9. 30 Geo. III Cap. LVII.
10. SROI EL1/1/9/1/1, p.62.
11. *Ibid.*, p.72.
12. *Ibid.*, p.78.
13. Bennet Woodcroft, *op. cit.*
14. D.R. Grace and D.C. Phillips, *Ransomes of Ipswich: A History of the Firm and Guide to its Records* (1975), p.2.
15. SROI C/2/9/1/2/4/4, reports by William Cubitt to bailiffs and magistrates regarding Stoke Bridge.
16. *Ransomes' 'Royal' Records: A Century and a Half in the Service of Agriculture*, Ransomes, Sims & Jefferies Ltd. (1939), p.45.
17. SROI EL1/7/12/3-6.
18. SROI S Ips 387.
19. *Ipswich Journal*, 30 January 1836.
20. 1 Victoria, Cap. LXXIV.
21. SROI EL1/1/9/1/2.
22. *Ipswich Journal*, November 1836.
23. SROI EL1/1/9/1/1, p.67.
24. SROI EL1/5/8,9.
25. G.R. Clarke, *The History and Description of the Town and Borough of Ipswich* (1830), p.297.
26. SROI EL1/5/5.
27. SROI EL1/5/5.
28. SROI EL1/5/2.
29. *Ipswich Journal*, 26 June 1839.
30. *Ipswich Mercury*, 8 October 1839.
31. *Ipswich Journal*, 29 February 1840.
32. *Ipswich Journal*, 7 March 1840.
33. SROI EL1/11/22.
34. SROI EL1/1/4/2.
35. *Ipswich Mercury*, 15 September 1840.
36. *Ipswich Mercury*, 18 January 1842; *Ipswich Journal*, 22 January 1842.

XI   Ships and Railway Engines

1. John Leather, 'The Shipbuilding Bayleys', *The Mariner's Mirror*, vol.51, pp.131-45.
2. *Ibid.*, p.132.
3. R.H. Gower, *Original observations regarding the inability of ships to perform their duty with promptitude and safety, with suggestions for their improvement, as practised on board the Transit, an experimental vessel, invented, built, and commanded by the author* (1833).
4. H. Benham, *Once Upon a Tide*, London (1955).
5. *Colchester Gazette*, 18 November 1820.
6. Leather, *op. cit.*, p.136.
7. Jean Sutton, *Lords of the East* (1981), p.168.
8. *Ipswich Express*, 6 July 1847.
9. *Ipswich Journal*, 1 January 1842.

10. *Mercantile Navy List* (1899).
11. Roger Finch, *A Cross in the Topsail* (1979), p.111.
12. Christine Clark, *The British Malting Industry since 1830* (1998), p.54.
13. *Ipswich Express*, 12 January 1847.
14. *Ibid.*, 2 February 1847.
15. Robert Malster, *Ipswich, town on the Orwell* (1978), pp.31-3.
16. Hugh Moffat, *East Anglia's First Railways* (1987), pp.5-6.
17. *Ipswich Journal*, 6 January 1844.
18. Moffat, *op. cit.*, pp.26-7.
19. *Ipswich Journal*, 8 May 1846.
20. *Ibid.*, November 1846.
21. For a full account of the Eastern Union Railway and its associated lines see Hugh Moffat's book, which is the source for most of this abbreviated account.
22. *Ransomes' 'Royal' Records*, p.47.
23. *Ibid.*, pp.47, 50.
24. W.J. Hughes, *A Century of Traction Engines* (1959).
25. *Ibid.*
26. *Illustrated London News*, 13 January 1849.
27. Anthony Beaumont, *Ransomes Steam Engines* (1972), pp.22-3.
28. Bennet Woodcroft, *op. cit.*, p.372.
29. Institute of Agricultural History, TR RAN AC7/9.
30. Michael Lane, *The Story of the Steam Plough Works* (1980), p.7.
31. *Ibid.*, p.14.
32. *Ibid.*, p.70.
33. *Ibid.*, p.29.
34. William White, *History, Gazetteer and Directory of Suffolk* (1855), p.68.
35. Mary Mills, *Greenwich Marsh: The 300 Years before the Dome* (1999).
36. E.R. & F. Turner's Catalogue No. 82.1, July 1882.
37. *Flour and Provender Milling Machinery*, E.R. & F. Turner Ltd. [1937]; this lists offices in Ipswich, London, Manchester and Dublin and overseas agents in Australia, New Zealand, South and East Africa, India, and ten other countries around the world.
38. *Mr. Edward Packard* (1900), reprint from *Ipswich Journal*.
39. Tony Copsey, *Book Distribution and Printing in Suffolk, 1534–1850* (1994).
40. Walter White, *Eastern England from the Thames to the Humber* (1865), p.154.
41. Kenneth Leighton, 'Ipswich and the China Project', *Transport Matters*, Ipswich & District Historical Transport Society, no.161, 1993, pp.7-10.
42. The Woosung tramway was 2ft. 6in. gauge, the Southwold Railway was 3ft., and the rails for the Suffolk line were supplied by the Tredegar Iron Co.; the fact that they were brought to Southwold by sea might have encouraged the erroneous belief that they had come from China. Ransomes and Rapier supplied the signalling and switchgear for the Southwold Railway, but the engines for that line were built by Sharp, Stewart & Co. Ltd., of Manchester. See A.R. Taylor and E.S. Tonks, *The Southwold Railway* (1979).
43. R. Stanley Ellis, *Eighty Years of Enterprise 1869–1949*, W.S. Cowell for Ransomes & Rapier, 1950. The information in this book regarding the Southwold Railway is erroneous.

XII   The Victorian Town

1. See chapter 10.
2. W. Hunt, *Descriptive Handbook of Ipswich* (1864), p.21.
3. J. Glyde, *Illustrations of Old Ipswich* (1889), p.31.
4. *Ibid.*, pp.35-6.
5. Muriel Clegg, *Streets and Street Names in Ipswich* (1984), p.25.
6. J. Blatchly, 'Thomas Seckford's Great Place: a lost Ipswich town house', in C. Rawcliffe, R. Virgoe

and R. Wilson, *Counties and Communities: Essays on East Anglian History* (1996), pp.203-12.

7. R. Markham, *A Rhino in the High Street* (1990).
8. Clegg, *op. cit.*, p.25.
9. Hunt, *op. cit.*, p.12; the road layout is well shown by Edward White's map of 1867.
10. Clegg, *op. cit.*, p.24.
11. Anon., *The Ipswich Gas Light Company: A Hundred Years of Public Service* (1921), pp.3-4.
12. *Ibid.*, pp.26-7.
13. 1 and 2 George IV, An Act for Lighting with Gas the Town and Borough of Ipswich in the County of Suffolk.
14. *The Ipswich Gas Light Company*, p.11.
15. C. Brown, B. Haward and R. Kindred, *Dictionary of Suffolk Architects 1800–1914*, p.98.
16. Pawsey & Hayes' Guide to Ipswich, edition for Ancient Order of Foresters High Court (1892), pp.xxv-xxvii.
17. Glyde, *op. cit.*, p.180.
18. *Ibid.*, p.70.
19. Herbert Walker, *The Ipswich Institute 1824–1924* (1924), pp.1-2.
20. *Ibid.*, pp.5-6.
21. Pawsey & Hayes, p.78.
22. Glyde, *op. cit.*, p.71.
23. *Ibid.*, p.62.
24. *Ibid.*, pp.76–80.
25. Robert Malster, *Ipswich, town on the Orwell* (1978), pp.31-3.
26. I.E. Gray and W.E. Potter, *Ipswich School 1400–1950*, p.3.
27. *Ibid.*, p.84
28. A. Flowerdew, *Poems on Moral and Religious Subjects to which are prefixed Introductory Remarks on A Course of Female Education*, 3rd. edition (1811), pp. iii-x, quoted in M. Clegg, 'Private Enterprise in Education', *Suffolk Review*, vol.5 (1981), pp.69-77.
29. J. Glyde, jun., *The Moral, Social and Religious Condition of Ipswich in the Middle of the Nineteenth Century* (1850), p.144.
30. *Ibid.*, p.145.
31. *Gifts and Legacies* (1747), pp.62-73; *White's Directory* (1844), pp.77-8.
32. Valerie Youngman, 'The Ipswich Grey-Coat and Blue-Coat Schools', *Suffolk Review*, vol.5 (1981), p.53-67.
33. *Gifts and Legacies* (1747), p.172.
34. Glyde, *op. cit.*, p.116.
35. Ipswich District National Schools in the Parish of St Matthew, First Report, 1848.
36. *Ibid.*
37. Ruth Serjeant, 'Joshua George Newman and the Ipswich Ragged School', *Suffolk Review*, vol.5 (1981), pp.79-89.
38. Glyde, *op. cit.*, p.126.
39. Kelly, 1879 and 1892.
40. William White, *History, Gazetteer and Directory of Suffolk* (1844, 1855).
41. Harold Preston, *Early East Anglian Banks and Bankers* (1994).
42. Robert Malster, *250 Years of Brewing in Ipswich* (1996).
43. Henry Austin: Report on the present sanitary condition of the Town of Ipswich (1848).
44. G.R. Clarke, *The History & Description of the Town and Borough of Ipswich* (1830), p.316.
45. *Ipswich Mercury*, 1 February 1848.
46. Henry Austin (1848).
47. Robert Malster, *Ipswich, town on the Orwell* (1978), pp.72-4.
48. John Glyde, jun., *The Moral, Social and Religious Condition of Ipswich in the Middle of the Nineteenth Century* (1850), p.35-6.
49. W. Hunt, *Descriptive Handbook of Ipswich* (1864).
50. *Ibid.*, pp.4-5.

51. Frank Grace, *The Late Victorian Town* (1992).

52. Dr. G. Elliston, Annual Report of the Medical Officer of Health (1874).

53. *Jubilee of the Ipswich & Suffolk Freehold Land Society*, Ipswich (1899); unpublished paper by Hilary Platts.

54. *Ibid.*, p.9.

55. *One Hundred Years of Service 1850-1950: A brief History of the Ipswich Permanent Benefit Building Society Originally established in 1850 and Incorporated in 1896 under the Companies Acts*, Ipswich (1950), p.11.

56. The Ipswich Building Society, as the Freehold Land Society is now known, retains a most important archive, and thanks are due to the directors of the society and to Mrs. Margaret Hancock, their librarian, for the opportunity to study early records, on which this account is based.

57. Robert Malster, 'Suffolk Brickmaking', in *The Suffolk Review*, vol. 5 (1983), pp.173-186.

58. R. Markham, *Public Transport in Ipswich 1880–1970* (1970).

XIII   The Twentieth Century

1. R. Markham, *Public Transport in Ipswich*, 1880–1970.

2. *Ibid.*

3. J.F. Bridges, *Early Country Motoring*, p.55.

4. *East Anglian Daily Times 1874–1974*, pp.25-6.

5. C. & M. Weaver, *Ransomes: A Bicentennial Celebration, 1789–1989*, p.60.

6. *Ipswich in the Great War 1914–1918. Programme of Unveiling of the Christchurch Park War Memorial* (1924); Jill Freestone, 'A parish at war', *Suffolk Review*, no.17 (1991).

7. Weaver, *op. cit.*, p.62.

8. *East Anglian Daily Times 1874–1974*, p.9.

9. R. Malster and R. Jones, *A Victorian Vision* (1992), pp.72-5.

10. *Ipswich Information*, nos. 15, 18, 19, 20.

11. *Ipswich Information*, no.22.

12. *East Anglian Daily Times*, 27 June 1930.

13. Some authorities have cast doubt on the use of Ipswich for launching this raid, but see correspondence in *East Anglian Daily Times*, 5, 7, and 28 February and 11 March 1969.

14. J.P. Foynes, *The Battle of the East Coast (1939–1945)*, p.214.

15. Richard Smith, pers. com.

16. Foynes, *op. cit., passim*; J.J. Colledge, *Ships of the Royal Navy: An historical index*, vol.2; *Lloyd's Register of Yachts*, 1939, and supplement (1949).

17. Peter Tooley, *Operation Quicksilver* (1988).

18. *The Warble Victory Souvenir* (1945), p.5.

19. *Ibid.*, p.19.

20. *Ibid.*, p.340.

21. *Ibid.*, p.340.

22. *Ibid.*, p.7.

23. *Ipswich Information*, no.5.

24. *Ibid.*, no.23.

25. *Ibid.*, nos.24, 25.

26. *Ibid.*, nos.5, 9.

Bibliography

Allen, D., *Ipswich Borough Archives 1255–1835: A Catalogue*, Suffolk Records Society, 2000

A Hundred Years of Public Service, Ipswich Gas Light Company, Ipswich 1921

Bacon, N., *The Annalls of Ipswiche, The Lawes Customes and Government of the Same* (Richardson, W.H., ed.), Ipswich, 1884

Bennett, C., *Christchurch Mansion & Park, Ipswich*, Ipswich Borough Council, 1989

Bevis, T.A., *The Ipswich Bellfounders*, n.d.

Bishop, P., *The History of Ipswich: 1500 Years of Triumph & Disaster*, Unicorn Press, London, 1995

Blatchly, J., *Eighty Ipswich Portraits: Samuel Read's Early Victorian Sketchbook*, Ipswich, 1980

Blatchly, J., *The Town Library of Ipswich Provided for the Use of the Town Preachers in 1599: A History and Catalogue*, Boydell Press, 1989

[Canning, R.], *An Account of the Gifts and Legacies that Have been given and bequeathed to Charitable Uses in the Town of Ipswich*, Ipswich 1747; 2nd edn., Ipswich, 1819

[Canning, R.], *The Principal Charters Which have been Granted to the Corporation of Ipswich in Suffolk Translated*, London, 1754

Clarke, G.R., *The History & Description of the Town and Borough of Ipswich*, Ipswich, 1830

Clegg, M., *Streets and Street Names in Ipswich*, Salient Press, Ipswich, 1984

Clegg, M., *The Way We Went*, Salient Press, Ipswich 1989

Copsey, T., *Book Distribution and Printing in Suffolk 1534–1850*, Ipswich, 1994

Cross, R.L., *Ipswich Corporation Civic Regalia*, Ipswich Corporation, Ipswich, n.d.

Cross, R.L., *Ipswich Markets and Fairs*, Ipswich Corporation, Ipswich, 1965

Cross, R.L., *Justice in Ipswich, 1200–1968*, Ipswich Corporation, Ipswich, 1968

Cross, R.L., *The Living Past – A Victorian Heritage*, Ipswich Borough Council, Ipswich, 1975

Everitt, A. (ed.), *Suffolk and the Great Rebellion 1640–1660*, Suffolk Records Society, 1960

Feldman, H.A., *The Ancient House*, Ipswich Borough Council, Ipswich, n.d.

Freeman, J.I., *The Postmaster of Ipswich: William Stevenson Fitch, Antiquary and Thief*, The Book Collector, London, 1997

Glyde, J.G., *The Moral, Social and Religious Condition of Ipswich in the Middle of the Nineteenth Century*, Ipswich, 1850

Glyde, J., *Illustrations of Old Ipswich*, Ipswich, 1889

Grace, D.R. and Phillips, D.C., *Ransomes of Ipswich: A History of the Firm and Guide to its Records*, University of Reading Institute of Agricultural History, Reading, 1975

Grace, F., *The Late Victorian Town*, British Association for Local History, Chichester, 1992

Gray, I.E. and Potter, W.E., *Ipswich School 1400–1950*, Ipswich, 1950

Gunn, S.J. and Lindley, P.G. (eds.), *Cardinal Wolsey: Church, state and art*, Cambridge University Press, 1991

Hanson, E.H., *An Historical Essay of the Ipswich Institute 1925–1987 with a reprint of 'The Ipswich Institute 1824–1924 by Herbert Walker'*, The Committee of the Ipswich Institute, 1989

Hunt, W., *Descriptive Handbook of Ipswich*, Ipswich, 1864

Ipswich, The Industrial Capital of East Anglia, Ipswich Industrial Development Association, 1932; reprinted as *Souvenir of the Royal Show*, 1934

Jubilee of the Ipswich & Suffolk Freehold Land Society 1849–1899, East Anglian Daily Times, Ipswich 1899

Kirby, J., *The Suffolk Traveller*, 1st edn. Ipswich, 1735; 2nd edn. with alterations and additions by several hands, Ipswich, 1764

Lewis, R.S., *Eighty Years of Enterprise: Being the initimate story of the Waterside Works of Ransomes & Rapier Limited*, W.S. Cowell, Ipswich, 1950

Malster, R. and Jones, R., *A Victorian Vision: The Ipswich Wet Dock Story*, Ipswich Port Authority, Ipswich, 1992

Malster, R., *Ipswich, town on the Orwell*, Terence Dalton, Lavenham, 1978

Malster, R., *Ipswich, A Pictorial History*, Phillimore, Chichester, 1991

Malster, R., *250 Years of Brewing in Ipswich: The story of Tollemache and Cobbold's Cliff Brewery, 1746–1996*, Malthouse Press Suffolk for Tollemache and Cobbold Brewery Ltd., Ipswich, 1996

Markham, R., *Public Transport in Ipswich, 1880–1970*, Ipswich Information Office, 1971

Markham, R., *100 Years of Public Transport in Ipswich: A Pictorial Survey*, Ipswich Borough Council, Ipswich, 1980

Martin, G.H. (ed.), *The Ipswich Recognizance Rolls 1294–1327: A Calendar*, Suffolk Records Society, 1973

Morrison, R.K.McD. (ed.), *History of Engineering in Ipswich*, Ipswich Engineering Society, Ipswich, 1974

One Hundred Years of Service 1850–1950: A brief History of the Ipswich Permanent Benefit Building Society Originally established in 1850 and Incorporated, in 1896, under the Companies Acts, W.S. Cowell, Ipswich, 1950

Plunkett, S.D., *Guardians of the Gipping: Anglo-Saxon Treasures from Hadleigh Road, Ipswich*, Ipswich Borough Council, Ipswich, 1994

Redstone, L., *Ipswich Through the Ages*, East Anglian Magazine, Ipswich, 1948

Redstone, V.B., *The Ancient House or Sparrow House, Ipswich*, W.B. Harrison, Ipswich, 1912

Reed, M. (ed.), *The Ipswich Probate Inventories 1583–1631*, Suffolk Records Society, 1981

Report of the Summer Meeting of the Royal Archaeological Institute at Ipswich, 1951, reprinted from the *Archaeological Journal* vol. CVIII, London, 1952

Smith, G.C. Moore, *The Family of Withypoll, With special reference to their Manor of Christchurch, Ipswich*, Walthamstow Antiquarian Society, 1936

Taylor, J.E., *In and About Ancient Ipswich*, Norwich, 1888

Trades Union Congress, Ipswich, 1909, Souvenir issued by the Ipswich and District Trades and Labour Council, Ipswich, 1909

Weaver, C. & M., *Ransomes: A Bicentennial Celebration*, Ipswich, 1989

Webb, J., *Great Tooley of Ipswich*, Suffolk Records Society, 1962

Webb, J. (ed.), *Poor Relief in Elizabethan Ipswich*, Suffolk Records Society, 1966

Webb, J. (ed.), *The Town Finances of Elizabethan Ipswich*, Suffolk Records Society, 1996

Wodderspoon, J., *Memorials of the Ancient Town of Ipswich*, Ipswich, 1850

Index

Ipswich in the 18th century: a section from the prospect of the town by Samuel and Nathaniel Buck, 1741.